GED® TEST

Reasoning Through Language Arts Prep 2015

KAPLAN
PUBLISHING
New York

ACKNOWLEDGEMENTS

Special thanks to the team that made this book possible:
Arthur Ahn, Mikhail Alexeeff, Gina Allison, Kim Bowers, Erik Bowman, Julie Choi, Margaret Crane, Alisha Crowley, Lola Dart, Boris Dvorkin, Paula Fleming, Tom Flesher, Joanna Graham, Allison Harm, Gar Hong, Kevin Jacobson, Wyatt Kent, Jennifer Land, Heather Maigur, Terrence McGovern, Eli Meyer, Kathy Osmus, Anthony Parr, Rachel Pearsall, Neha Rao, Rachel Reina, Teresa Rupp, Scott Safir, Glen Stohr, Alexandra Strelka, Lee Weiss, and many others who have shaped this book over the years.

Published by Kaplan Publishing, a division of Kaplan, Inc.
395 Hudson Street
New York, NY 10014

Printed in the United States of America

10 9 8 7 6 5 4 3 2 1

ISBN: 978-1-62523-235-9

Kaplan Publishing books are available at special quantity discounts to use for sales promotions, employee premiums, or educational purposes. For more information or to purchase books, please call the Simon & Schuster special sales department at 866-506-1949.

CONTENTS

Kaplan's GED® Test Book and Online Center v

GED® Test Overview viii

GED® Computer-Based Testing x

Pretest 1

Pretest Answers and Explanations 19

Kaplan GED® Reasoning Through Language Arts Test Study Planners 22

About The Reasoning Through Language Arts Test 25

Interpreting Nonfiction and Informational Text

Lesson 1: Main Ideas and Details 30

Lesson 2: Restatement and Summary 32

Lesson 3: Application of Ideas 34

Lesson 4: Cause and Effect 36

Lesson 5: Compare and Contrast 38

Lesson 6: Conclusions and Generalizations 40

Lesson 7: Word Choice 44

Lesson 8: Writer's Tone and Point of View 46

Lesson 9: Text Structure 48

Interpreting Nonfiction and Informational Text Practice Questions 50

Analyzing Nonfiction and Informational Text

Lesson 1: Purpose of Text 54

Lesson 2: Effectiveness of Argument 56

Lesson 3: Validity of Arguments 58

Lesson 4: Text Related by Theme or Topic 60

Lesson 5: Texts with Opposing Arguments 62

Lesson 6: Texts with Related Graphic Information 64

Analyzing Nonfiction and Informational Text Practice Questions 66

Interpreting Fiction

Lesson 1: Plot Elements 70

Lesson 2: Inferences 72

Lesson 3: Character 74

Lesson 4: Theme 76

Lesson 5: Style and Point of View 78

Lesson 6: Figurative Language 80

Interpreting Fiction Practice Questions 82

Writing Effective Sentences

Lesson 1: Simple Sentences 86

Lesson 2: Compound and Complex Sentences 88

Lesson 3: Run-Ons and Comma Splices 92

Lesson 4: Subordinate Ideas 94

Lesson 5: Modify Ideas 96

Lesson 6: Parallel Structure 98

Writing Effective Sentences Practice Questions 100

Connecting Ideas

Lesson 1: Organize Ideas into Paragraphs 104

Lesson 2: Use Logical Order and Relevant Ideas 108

Lesson 3: Relate Sentences and Paragraphs 110

Connecting Ideas Practice Questions 112

Writing About Text

Lesson 1: Unpack the Writing Prompt 116

Lesson 2: Identify a Writer's Arguments and Assumptions 118

Lesson 3: Develop a Thesis Statement 120

Lesson 4: Collect Supporting Evidence 122

Lesson 5: Plan Your Response 124

Lesson 6: Draft Your Response 128
Lesson 7: Revise and Edit Your Response 134
Writing About Text Practice 138

Polishing Your Writing
Lesson 1: Strengthen Sentences 142
Lesson 2: Improve Organization 144
Lesson 3: Word choice 146
Polishing Your Writing Practice Questions 148

Using Grammar Correctly
Lesson 1: Noun and Pronoun Agreement 152
Lesson 2: Verb Forms and Tenses 156
Lesson 3: Subject-Verb Agreement 160
Using Grammar Correctly Practice Questions 164

Using Writing Mechanics
Lesson 1: Comma Use 168
Lesson 2: Capitalization 172
Lesson 3: Possessives and Contractions 174
Lesson 4: Homonyms 176
Using Writing Mechanics Practice Questions 178

Practice Questions Answers and Explanations 182

Practice Test 199

Practice Test Answers and Explanations 221

Practice Test Evaluation Charts 224

GED® Reasoning Through Language Arts Test Resources
Extended Response Evaluation Guide 225

Index 226

KAPLAN'S GED® TEST BOOK AND ONLINE CENTER

Congratulations on your decision to pursue high school equivalency, and thank you for choosing Kaplan for your GED® test preparation.

You've made the right choice in acquiring this book—you're now armed with a GED® Reasoning Through Language Arts test preparation program that is the result of years of researching the GED® tests and teaching thousands of students the skills they need to succeed. You have what you need to pass the GED® Reasoning Through Language Arts test and score higher; the next step is to make the commitment to your study plan.

The next section will tell you everything you need to know to take advantage of your book and your Online Center.

Your Book

This book contains a complete study program, including the following:

- Detailed instruction covering the essential concepts for Reasoning Through Language Arts
- Time-tested and effective methods and strategies for every question type
- A Pretest designed to help you diagnose your strengths and weaknesses
- Hundreds of practice questions, followed by answer explanations
- A timed, full-length Reasoning Through Language Arts Practice Test

Your Online Center

Your Kaplan Online Center gives you access to additional instruction and practice materials to reinforce key concepts and sharpen your GED® test skills. The following list summarizes the resources available to you:

- An additional full-length Reasoning Through Language Arts Practice Test, so that you can practice the computer-based question formats used on the actual test
- Analysis of your performance on your Practice Test, including detailed answer explanations for the computer-based practice test
- Video lessons featuring Kaplan's top instructors

GETTING STARTED

Studying for the GED® test can be daunting, and with so many resources available to you, it may not be clear where to begin. Don't worry; we'll break it down one step at a time, just as we will with the GED® test questions that you will soon be on your way to mastering.

GETTING STARTED

1. Take the diagnostic Pretest.
2. Create a study plan.
3. Register your Online Center.
4. Learn and practice using both this book and your Online Center.
5. Work through the Practice Tests to gauge your progress.

STEP 1: TAKE THE DIAGNOSTIC PRETEST

It's essential to take the diagnostic Pretest before you begin to study. Doing so will give you the initial feedback and diagnostic information that you will need to achieve your maximum score. Place enough importance on completing the Pretest—turn off your cell phone, give the tests your full attention, and learn from your performance.

Once you have finished your Pretest, check your answers starting on page 19. Mark the questions that you got correct and **carefully read the answer explanations** of those that you got wrong.

When you have finished the Pretest, make a list of the questions that you got correct and use that list to fill out the Kaplan GED® Test Study Planner on page 22. Use the results to target your weak areas.

Another option is for you to go online and enter your answers so that the Kaplan Online Center can generate your results. Note which sections and which question types you need to target.

Review the detailed answer explanations in the book to better understand your performance. Look for patterns in the questions you answered correctly and incorrectly. Were you stronger in some areas than in others? This analysis will help you target your study time to specific concepts.

STEP 2: CREATE A STUDY PLAN

Use what you've learned from your initial Pretest to identify areas for closer study and practice. Take time to familiarize yourself with the key components of your book and Online Center. Think about how many hours you can consistently devote to GED® test study.

Schedule time for study, practice, and review. It works best for many people to block out short, frequent periods of study time throughout the week. Check in with yourself frequently to make sure you're not falling behind your plan or forgetting about any of your resources.

Step 3: Register Your Online Center

Register your Online Center using these simple steps:

1. Go to **kaptest.com/booksonline**.
2. Follow the on-screen instructions for GED®. Please have your book available.

Access to the Online Center is limited to the original owner of this book and is nontransferable. Kaplan is not responsible for providing access to the Online Center to customers who purchase or borrow used copies of this book. Access to the Online Center expires one year after you register.

Step 4: Learn and Practice

Your book and Online Center come with many opportunities to develop and practice the skills you'll need on Test Day. Depending on how much time you have to study, you can do this work methodically, covering every unit and lesson, or you can focus your study on those content areas that are most challenging to you. You will inevitably need more work in some areas than in others, but the more thoroughly you prepare, the better your score will be.

Initially, your practice should focus on mastering the needed skills and not on timing. Add timing to your practice as you become familiar with skills and methods.

Step 5: Work Through the Practice Tests

As you move through your GED® studies, take advantage of both the full-length Reasoning Through Language Arts Practice Test available in this book and also the one in your Online Center.

Review your Practice Test results thoroughly to make sure you are addressing the areas that are most important to your score. Allot time to review the detailed explanations so that you can learn from your mistakes and review the relevant chapters in the book for additional study.

If you find that you would like access to more of Kaplan's instructional content or practice material, look into our other subject books, our comprehensive GED® preparation books, or our On Demand course option available at **kaptest.com/GED.**

Thanks for choosing Kaplan. We wish you the best of luck on your journey to completing your high school equivalency and taking a vital step toward college and career readiness.

GED® TEST OVERVIEW

The GED® test is a widely used examination that demonstrates high school equivalency as well as college and career readiness. It includes the reading, writing, thinking, and problem-solving skills needed for postsecondary educational programs and for the world of work. This means that your high school equivalency diploma is not an end in itself—it is the springboard to more education, to better-paying jobs, and to more rewarding career paths.

Take Four Subtests in Four Content Areas

Reasoning Through Language Arts—2.5 hours (one 10-minute break)

- Roughly 50–55 questions
- Includes 1 extended written response to reading passages—up to 45 minutes

Mathematical Reasoning—1 hour, 55 minutes

- Roughly 40–45 questions
- First section—5 questions, no calculator allowed
- Second section—calculator allowed (Texas Instruments TI-30XS MultiView™ calculator)

Social Studies—1.5 hours

- Roughly 30–35 questions
- Includes 1 extended written response to passages and/or graphics—up to 25 minutes

Science—1.5 hours

- Roughly 30–35 questions
- Includes 2 short-answer written responses to passages and/or graphics—up to 10 minutes each

You can read detailed information about the test in the *About the Test* section.

Respond to Seven Computer-Based Question Formats

To test a range of skills, the GED® test uses a variety of computer-based question formats. You will see examples of each type of question in *GED® Computer-Based Testing* and in the *About the Test* section. When you take the test, you will use these question formats:

- **Multiple-choice**—click to choose from four choices (A through D).
- **Fill-in-the-blank**—type a word, a phrase, or numbers in a box.
- **Drag-and-drop**—move words, numbers, or objects across the computer screen.
- **Drop-down**—select from menus embedded in text on the computer screen.
- **Hot spot**—click on graphics on the computer.
- **Short-answer**—write a paragraph or two of explanation in response to passages or graphics or a combination of the two.
- **Extended response**—compose a well-developed and supported response to passages or graphics or a combination of the two.

Read and Write Throughout the Test

You will read and interpret passages and word problems on all four tests. In addition, three out of four subtests (*Reasoning Through Language Arts, Social Studies,* and *Science*) require that you read a passage or two and compose a response about what you have read.

The type of writing that you will use is called *evidence-based writing*, which means that you need to cite specific evidence from the readings in your response. This is a key characteristic of the type of writing that is required in workplaces and in educational programs. This book contains special lessons and practice activities to help you write effectively on all three of the subtests.

Perform Math Skills Throughout the Test

In addition to the questions on the *Mathematical Reasoning Test*, math items also appear on the *Science Test* and the *Social Studies Test.*

On all three of these tests, you may use either a hand-held or an on-screen version of the Texas Instruments TI-30XS MultiView™ calculator to use with math items. If you wish to use a hand-held version of the calculator, you may need to take one with you on test day. **You are strongly encouraged to purchase a hand-held version of this calculator to use if you are going to study for any of those three GED® Tests**. You can buy this calculator at stores that carry office and school supplies and through online vendors. Kaplan's GED® Test prep books for the *Mathematical Reasoning Test, Science Test,* and *Social Studies Test* explain how to use this calculator.

Use the GED Testing Service® MyGED™ Internet Portal

MyGED™ is a personalized online program that will be your entry point to all test activities, including scheduling testing and retesting (if necessary), viewing score reports, ordering transcripts and your diploma, and investigating your next steps in making the transition to college or to a career.

Take the Test: Understand Your Score

Each GED® Test is scored on a scale from 100 to 200. There are three possible scores that you can receive on the GED® Test:

- **Not Passing**—lower than 150 on any of the four tests. You can reschedule up to two times a year to retake any or all of the tests.
- **GED® Passing Score**—at or higher than the minimum score (150 per test) needed to demonstrate high school equivalency–level skills and knowledge. Points on one test do not carry over to the others; that is, if you score 200 on one and 100 on another, that is not equivalent to scoring 150 on both. You need to score 150 on each of the four tests.
- **GED® Score with Honors**—at or higher than the minimum needed (170 per test) to demonstrate career and college readiness

Your score is determined by the number of points you earn on each test, but questions vary in point value. Therefore, there is no fixed number of questions you need to get correct on each test in order to pass or pass with honors.

GED® COMPUTER-BASED TESTING

The GED® Test is delivered on a computer. That means that you will need to familiarize yourself with basic computer skills and computer-based question formats in order to succeed on the test.

NOTE: *The GED® Test on computer is only offered at official Pearson Vue Testing Centers. Any Internet-based test that claims to be the GED® Test is not the actual test. At the MyGED™ portal, you can access study resources, take a practice test, or schedule your test. You cannot take the real GED® test online.*

To become familiar with the computer-based functions, you should review the GED® Test Tutorial available through the GED® Testing Services website. Before you take the actual test, you can practice computer-based testing functions with the Practice Test available in Kaplan's Online Center and with the GED® Testing Service's GED Ready™ Test.

Computer-Based Testing Functions and Tools

The GED® Test uses many computer **functions,** some of which you may already know. It also offers specific **tools** that you will utilize in different test areas.

Use the **mouse** to

Tab through the pages of a reading passage

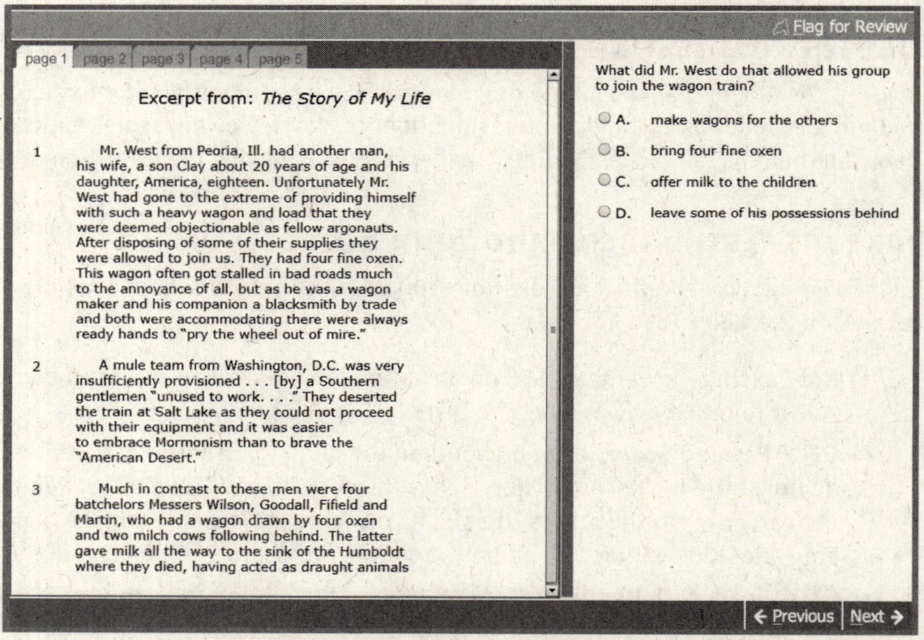

Scroll up and down a page when a scroll bar appears

Click on Previous and Next navigation buttons to move forward or backward

Use the **mouse** to (continued)

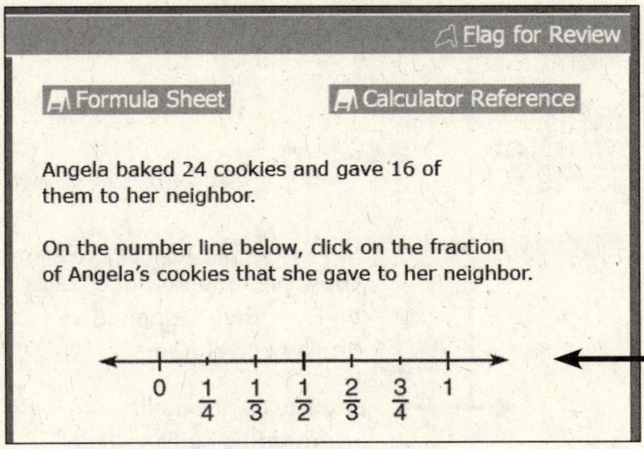

Click on an answer choice, a "Select" menu, or a point on a graphic

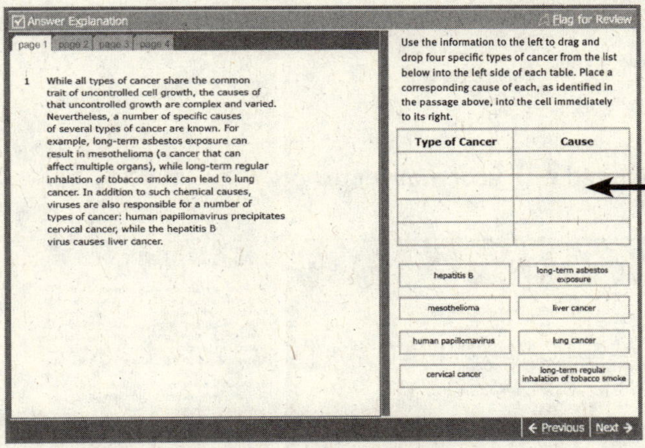

Drag and drop text, numbers, or images into a shape on the computer screen

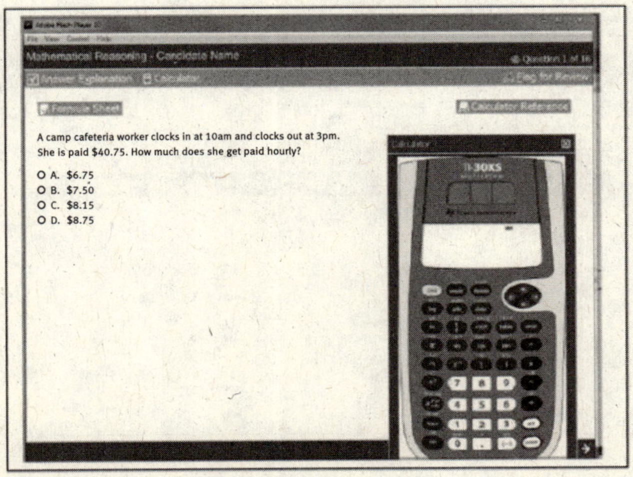

Click to open, move, and close information windows and math resources—such as the calculator, formula sheet, or symbol toolbar

Use **word processing skills** to

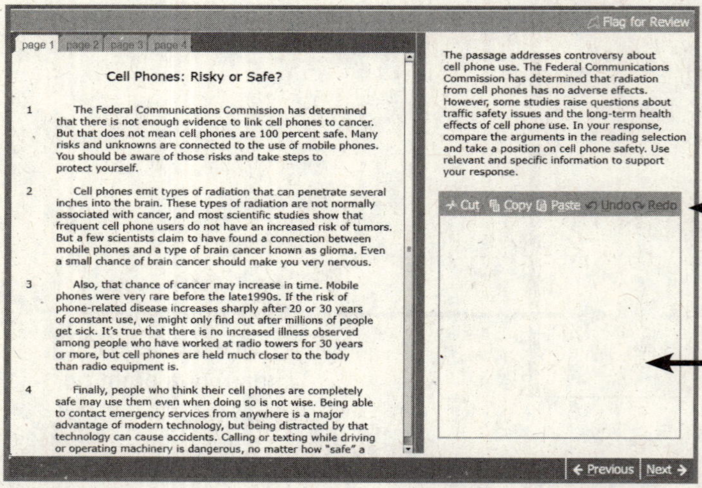

Click with the mouse to **cut, copy, paste, undo,** and **redo** on Extended-Response and Short-Answer items

Enter text with basic keyboarding skills in text boxes (shown here) and fill-in-the-blank questions

Use **the online highlighter,** operated with your mouse, to

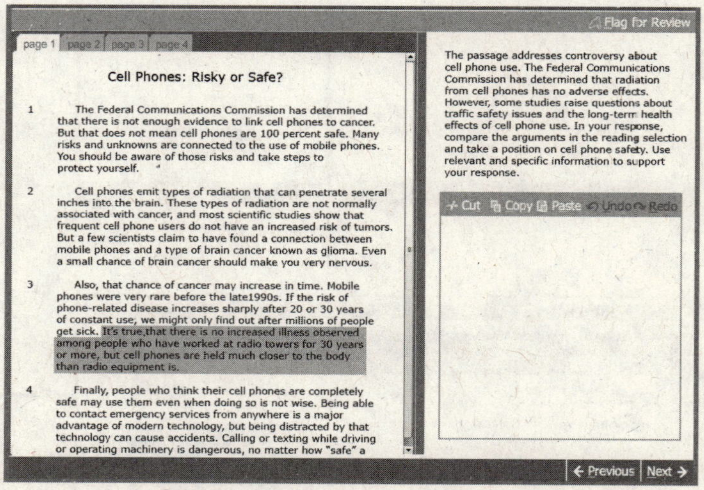

Highlight specific information that you will use as evidence in writing your Extended Responses and Short Answers.

Use the offline, **erasable wipe-off board**, which will be provided at the testing center, to

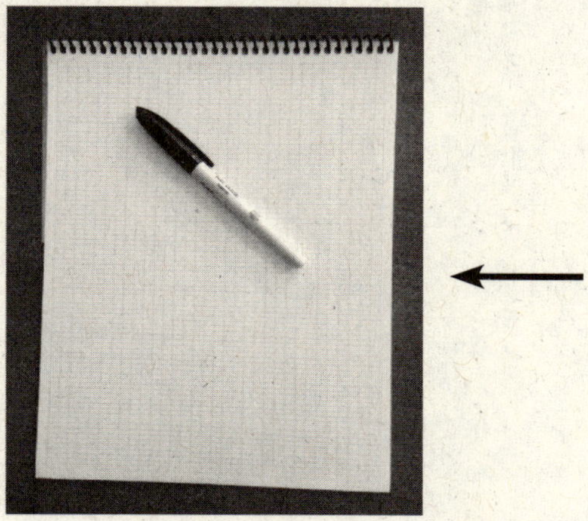

Plan your Extended Response (*Reasoning Through Language Arts* and *Social Studies Tests*) and Short Answers (*Science Test*) before you begin writing

Use three **onscreen test-tracking tools** at the top of the computer screen to

- **See how much time you have left**: ***Time Remaining*** shows how much time is left to complete each test.
- **Monitor your progress** through each test by viewing the ***Question Line***. You can check how far you have progressed and how many more questions you need to answer. Budget your time carefully to allow for these writing tasks:
    - 45 minutes for the Extended Response at the end of the first section of the *Reasoning Through Language Arts Test*
    - 25 minutes for the Extended Response at the end of the *Social Studies Test*
    - 10 minutes for each of the Short Answer questions that are interspersed with other questions in the *Science Test*
- **Click** on the ***Flag for Review*** if you are unsure of an answer. (You should never skip a question.) If you click on it, the flag will display in yellow and will be marked on the Review Screen.

At the end of each test, if you have time left, you can use the **Review Screen** to go back and review questions that you marked.

Pretest

The purpose of this pretest is to help you decide what you need to study to pass the actual GED® Reasoning Through Language Arts Test. You will use the pretest along with the explanations and the study planner that follows to determine what course of study works best for you.

This pretest is specially designed to make your study as efficient as possible. If you want to see what the actual GED® Reasoning Through Language Arts Test looks like, look at the *Practice Test* beginning on page 199.

1. **Take** the pretest:

   - **Reasoning Through Language Arts, pages 2–17**
     - Part I: Reading—20 Questions
     - Part II: Writing and Language Skills—18 Questions
     - Part III: Extended Response

   Most of the questions are in multiple-choice format. There is one extended response activity in the pretest.

   - For the **multiple-choice questions,** you may fill in the circles next to the correct answers in this book, or you can write your answers on a separate piece of paper.
   - You can write the **extended response** on a computer or, if one is not available, on a sheet of paper.

     NOTE: Writing your responses on a computer is preferable because you will be composing your responses on a computer when you take the GED® test. However, if you do not have a computer available when you take these pretests, write your responses on paper so that you can evaluate your writing samples.

2. **Check** your answers with the *Pretest Answers and Explanations* that begin on page 19.
3. **Fill in** the *Pretest Study Planner* on page 22. These charts will allow you to target your problem areas so that you can study in the most efficient manner.
4. **Use the study planner** on pages 22-23 to map out your work. Once you have completed your study, take the *Practice Test* on pages 199-219.

Part I: Reading

Directions: You may fill in the circles next to the correct answers or write your answers on a separate piece of paper.

Questions 1 through 5 refer to the following passage about introverts.

Excerpted from "Don't Call Introverted Children 'Shy'"

1 Imagine a 2-year-old who greets you with a huge smile, offering a toy. Now here's another child who regards you gravely and hides behind his parent's leg. How do you feel about these two children? If you're like most people, you think of the first child as social and the second as reserved or . . . "shy." . . . But this misses what's really going on with standoffish kids. Many were born with a careful, sensitive temperament that predisposes them to look before they leap. And this can pay off handsomely as they grow, in the form of strong academics, enhanced creativity, and even a unique brand of leadership and empathy.

2 One way to see this temperament more clearly is to consider how these children react to stimuli. When these children are at 4 months, if you pop a balloon over their heads, they holler and pump their arms more than other babies do. At age 2, they proceed carefully when they see a . . . toy robot for the first time. When they're school age, they play matching games with more deliberation than their peers. . . . Notice that none of these things—popping balloons, toy robots, matching games—has anything to do with people. In other words, these kids are not antisocial. They're simply sensitive to their environments. . . . [Children with this type of temperament are highly likely to grow up to be introverted, but s]hyness and introversion are not the same thing. Shy people fear negative judgment, while introverts simply prefer less stimulation. . . .

3 Children with an alert, sensitive temperament also pay close attention to social cues and moral principles. By age 6, they cheat and break rules less than other kids do—even when they believe they won't be caught. At 7, they're more likely than their peers to be described by parents and caregivers as empathetic or conscientious. As adults, introverted leaders have even been found to deliver better outcomes than extroverts when managing employees, according to a recent study by management professor Adam Grant of the Wharton School of the University of Pennsylvania, because they encourage others' ideas instead of trying to put their own stamp on things. And they're less likely to take dangerous risks. . . .

4 But we wouldn't want to live in a world composed entirely of cautious introverts. . . . The two types [introverts and extroverts] need each other. Many successful ventures are the result of effective partnerships between introverts and extroverts. The famously charismatic Steve Jobs teamed up with powerhouse introverts at crucial points in his career at Apple, cofounding the company with the shy Steve Wozniak and bequeathing it to its current CEO, the quiet Tim Cook. . . .

5 The ideal scenario is when those two toddlers—the one who hands you the toy with the smile and the other who checks you out so carefully—grow up to run the world together.

1. Which one of the following best expresses the main idea of the passage?

 - A. Companies should include both introverted and extroverted workers on teams.
 - B. There are advantages to being sensitive and introverted.
 - C. Children who are sensitive are more deliberate when playing a game.
 - D. Introverts simply prefer less stimulation than others do.

2. According to the passage, children with sensitive temperaments are more likely to be which of the following?

 - A. empathetic
 - B. risk-taking
 - C. antisocial
 - D. noisy

3. According to the passage, the partnership between Steve Jobs and Steve Wozniak is an example of which of the following?

 - A. the negative consequences of a mixture of different personality types in the workplace
 - B. a successful collaboration between two introverts
 - C. a successful collaboration between an introvert and an extrovert
 - D. a combination of people who should "run the world"

4. Which one of the following is the best summary of the second paragraph?

 - A. Some children respond more dramatically than others to unfamiliar or startling events.
 - B. Observing how children respond to stimuli is the best way to study different kinds of social behavior.
 - C. Children who are perceived as "shy" are actually more sensitive than other children to stimuli in their environments.
 - D. If sensitivity in a child is not corrected by around age 2, that child will grow up to be an oversensitive adult.

5. Based on the passage, which one of the following activities would an introvert most likely prefer?

 - A. enjoying a quiet dinner with a handful of friends
 - B. going alone to a club to enjoy loud dance music
 - C. accompanying one friend to a crowded street festival
 - D. participating solo in a sport called "extreme ice-slope surfing"

Questions 6 through 10 refer to the following information about forklifts and the related diagram.

Excerpt from "Forklift Safety Guide"

1 Driving a forklift differs from driving a car. In a car or truck, the front wheels steer the vehicle. A forklift has the steering wheels in the rear. The rear end of the forklift swings in a circle around the front wheels, which support most of the load. The operator must check that there is room for the rear end to swing when making turns. This clearance can be maintained in your workplace by permanently marking aisles with painted lines or arranging storage racks in a way that creates obvious aisles for travel. However, these marked aisles will only be effective if you keep them clear of stored materials.

2 A forklift is not as responsive as a car when the steering wheel is turned. Rear-wheel steering makes it difficult to stop a forklift quickly or swerve and still maintain control. It is important, then, not to drive a forklift fast or around corners quickly.

3 Driving with the load downhill can result in loss of the load and control of the forklift. If you drive a forklift on an incline, you must keep the load on the uphill side. Otherwise, you may have no weight on the wheels that steer, and you can lose control! The load could also fall off or cause the forklift to tip.

4 Often a large forklift load obstructs the driver's view in one direction. It may be necessary to travel long distances with the load to the rear (in reverse for most forklifts). Use extra caution when traveling in reverse.

Adapted with permission from the State of Washington, Department of Labor and Industries.

6. According to the passage, which one of the following is an effect of rear-wheel steering on a forklift?
   - A. The front wheels carry most of the load.
   - B. The driver may have some difficulty in controlling the forklift.
   - C. There is a danger that the forklift will tip over.
   - D. The forklift driver may have little visibility.

7. Which one of the following identifies a pair of things or ideas between which the author draws a contrast?
   - A. driving a forklift and driving a car
   - B. the turning radius of a forklift and the turning radius of a car
   - C. a warehouse with clearly marked aisles and a highway with clearly marked lanes
   - D. driving a forklift in reverse and walking backward

8. Together, the passage and the graphic support which one of the following conclusions?
   - A. A forklift should never carry a load taller than the forklift itself.
   - B. A forklift should travel backward only when traveling downhill.
   - C. A forklift cannot drive uphill unless it is carrying a load.
   - D. A forklift that is traveling downhill with a heavy load should travel backward.

9. Which of the following best describes the author's purpose?
   - A. to inform drivers of cars about the differences between driving a car and driving a forklift
   - B. to warn the general public about the dangers of forklifts
   - C. to explain safe practices to forklift drivers
   - D. to describe the difference between skilled and unskilled forklift drivers

10. Which of the following best describes the organization of the passage?
   - A. The author lists potential dangers inherent in forklift driving and explains how to avoid them.
   - B. The author states that forklift driving is dangerous and gives examples of forklift accidents to support that idea.
   - C. The author lists the features of forklifts and describes their benefits.
   - D. The author explains the pros and cons of forklift driving to present a balanced picture of the value of forklifts.

Questions 11 through 15 refer to the following selections about genetically modified organism (GMO) foods.

World Food Prize Goes to Three Biotech Scientists

1 The World Food Prize Foundation took the bold step of awarding this year's prize to three pioneers of plant biotechnology whose work brought the world genetically modified crops.

2 Van Montagu and Chilton independently developed the technology in the 1980s to stably transfer foreign genes into plants, a discovery that set up a race to develop tools to genetically engineer plants. It allowed other scientists to incorporate genetic traits that allow plants to better withstand drought and extreme heat and to fight off pests and disease. Fraley was the first to successfully transfer immunity to specific bacteria into a plant. Fraley genetically engineered the first herbicide-resistant soybean in 1996.

3 Genetically enhanced crops are grown on more than 420 million acres in nearly 30 countries by over 17 million farmers worldwide, the foundation said. More than 90 percent of the users are small, resource-poor farmers in developing countries.

4 Many U.S. farmers credited genetic modifications in corn with saving last year's crop from all but total devastation, as half of the nation endured the worst drought in 60 years. Modern corn plants are more stable and can withstand a wider variety of climate conditions because of genetically improved leaves, roots, and reproductive capability.

5 Fraley said biotechnology will enable the farming industry to meet the needs of a growing global population. "We know we need from a demand perspective to double food production around the world in the next 30 years," he said.

Adapted from David Pitt, "World Food Prize goes to 3 biotech scientists," Associated Press, June 19, 2013

Dangers of GMO Foods

1 The rise in autoimmune diseases, infertility, gastrointestinal problems, and chronic diseases may be associated with the introduction of GMO (genetically modified organism) foods. In a position paper by the American Academy of Environmental Medicine, the authors ask all physicians to consider the role of GMO foods in the nation's health crisis and advise their patients to avoid all GMO foods whenever possible. The Academy also recommends a moratorium on GMO seeds and calls for immediate independent safety testing and the labeling of all food items containing genetically modified products.

2 As the reliance on GMO seeds expands worldwide, concerns about food supply and safety continue to escalate. Genetically engineered seeds are identical in structure, and if a problem affects one particular crop, a major crop failure can result. For example, following the recent failure of three GMO corn crops in three South African provinces, the Africa Centre for Biosecurity has called for an investigation and immediate ban of all GMO food. Corn is a primary source of food for southern African nations.

3 Most GMO seeds are genetically engineered to be herbicide tolerant and resistant to insect infestation and disease. Environmentalists worry that the characteristics of GMO crops may encourage farmers to increase their use of herbicides and pesticides, which will raise human consumption of dangerous toxins. GMO crops also manufacture their own pesticides, which puts further poisons into humans and soil and may cause unforeseen changes in the environment.

Adapted from Susan Brassard, "Dangers of GMO Foods," Livestrong.com, September 2, 2010

11. The author of Passage 1 most likely notes that the majority of GMO crops are cultivated by "small, resource-poor farmers in developing countries" in order to

- A. highlight how GMO foods can be harmful to struggling farmers.
- B. suggest that GMO foods can be beneficial to struggling farmers.
- C. illustrate how GMO foods can be more expensive for consumers.
- D. explain why GMO crops often fail.

12. Passage 2 is primarily concerned with

- A. the uses and misuses of GMO foods
- B. the origin and development of GMO foods
- C. the unexpected benefits of GMO foods
- D. the safety and reliability of GMO foods

13. What can be inferred from the first paragraph of Passage 2?

- A. American physicians, as a group, are completely unaware of the potential dangers of GMOs.
- B. The labels of some foods containing GMO ingredients do not indicate that the products contain genetically modified components.
- C. GMO foods have been proven to cause certain chronic conditions.
- D. Independent safety testing has been completed for most GMO foods.

14. The two passages primarily disagree about whether or not

- A. GMO foods can help support a growing world population
- B. GMO foods are better able to withstand drought and insect infestation than natural foods
- C. GMO foods are largely a positive development for global food production
- D. scientists who study GMO foods are worthy of recognition

15. Passage 2 cites the example of a major crop failure in South Africa to illustrate the dangers of planting with GMO seeds. Which paragraph in Passage 1 offers a counterexample that weakens this position?

- A. paragraph 1
- B. paragraph 2
- C. paragraph 4
- D. paragraph 5

Questions 16 through 20 refer to the following.

Excerpted from *Black Beauty*

1 The first place that I can well remember was a large, pleasant meadow with a pond of clear water in it. Some shady trees leaned over it, and rushes and water lilies grew at the deep end. Over the hedge on one side we looked into a plowed field, and on the other we looked over a gate at our master's house, which stood by the roadside. . .

2 One day, when there was a good deal of kicking, my mother whinnied to me to come to her, and then she said:

3 "I wish you to pay attention to what I am going to say to you. The colts who live here are very good colts, but they are cart-horse colts, and of course they have not learned manners. You have been well-bred and well-born; your father has a great name in these parts, and your grandfather won the cup two years at the Newmarket races; your grandmother had the sweetest temper of any horse I ever knew, and I think you have never seen me kick or bite. I hope you will grow up gentle and good, and never learn bad ways; do your work with a good will, lift your feet up well when you trot, and never bite or kick even in play."

4 I have never forgotten my mother's advice; I knew she was a wise old horse, and our master thought a great deal of her. Her name was Duchess, but he often called her Pet.

5 Our master was a good, kind man. He gave us good food, good lodging, and kind words; he spoke as kindly to us as he did to his little children. We were all fond of him, and my mother loved him very much. When she saw him at the gate she would neigh with joy, and trot up to him. . . . All the horses would come to him, but I think we were his favorites. My mother always took him to the town on a market day in a light gig.

6 There was a plowboy, Dick, who sometimes came into our field to pluck blackberries from the hedge. When he had eaten all he wanted, he would have what he called fun with the colts, throwing stones and sticks at them to make them gallop. We did not much mind him, for we could gallop off, but sometimes a stone would hit and hurt us.

7 One day he was at this game, and did not know that the master was in the next field, but he was there, watching what was going on; over the hedge he jumped in a snap, and catching Dick by the arm, he gave him such a box on the ear as made him roar with the pain and surprise. As soon as we saw the master, we trotted up nearer to see what went on.

16. Who is the narrator in this passage?
- A. a servant
- B. a hired plowboy
- C. a young horse
- D. a child

17. What is the setting of the story?
- A. a town
- B. a racetrack
- C. a forest
- D. a farm

18. The narrator's account of his youth can best be described as
- A. melancholy
- B. contented
- C. regretful
- D. humorous

19. The narrator would most likely describe the master in the story as
- A. affectionate and protective
- B. arrogant and abusive
- C. playful and light-hearted
- D. bold and aggressive

20. The mother's speech in paragraph 3 most likely serves to
- A. correct the narrator for playing too roughly
- B. assure the narrator he will grow up to win races like his grandfather
- C. reprimand the narrator for insulting the master
- D. accuse the narrator of stealing blackberries

Answers and explanations start on page 19.

PART II: WRITING AND LANGUAGE SKILLS

Directions: You may fill in the circles next to the correct answers or write your answers on a separate piece of paper. Some of the questions in this section mimic the GED test's drop-down menu question format. Wherever the word "Select" appears, choose the option that best completes the passage.

Questions 1 through 6 refer to the following paragraphs.

To: Parents and Guardians
From: Sonia Vasquez, School Nurse

(1) A student in [Select...] diagnosed with strep throat. (2) Strep throat is a highly contagious disease and a common illness in children. (3) Unlike most sore throats, which are caused by viruses, strep throat is caused by bacteria and is treatable with antibiotics. (4) The time between exposure to the disease and the appearance of symptoms is usually one to three days. (5) To safeguard your child's health, please take the following precautions. (6) Watch your child for strep [Select...] sore throat, fever, swollen glands, and headache. (8) If your child [Select...]. (9) If a throat culture is positive, treatment can be started. (10) It is extremely important to take all the prescribed medicine until it is gone.

(11) Children should get immediate treatment for several reasons. (12) For one, treatment reduces spread of the disease. (13) [Select...] prevent rheumatic fever. (14) Treatment also prevents other rare but possibly dangerous complications.

(15) [Select...] medicine for 24 hours, he or she may return to school. (16) Please call us with any questions or concerns you have.

1. A student in [Select...] diagnosed with strep throat.

   - ○ A. you're child's class has been
   - ○ B. your child's class have been
   - ○ C. your children's class has been,
   - ○ D. your child's class has been

2. Watch your child for strep [Select...] sore throat, fever, swollen glands, and headache.

   - ○ A. symptoms. Such as
   - ○ B. symptoms, the best known are
   - ○ C. symptoms, such as
   - ○ D. symptoms examples are

3. If your child [Select...].

- A. develops any of these symptoms, take them to the doctor
- B. develops any of these symptoms, take him or her to the doctor
- C. will develop any of these symptoms, take him or her to the doctor
- D. developed any of these symptoms, take them to the doctor

4. Which revision would improve the effectiveness of the passage?

Begin a new paragraph with

- A. sentence 3
- B. sentence 4
- C. sentence 5
- D. sentence 6

5. [Select...] prevent rheumatic fever.

- A. In addition, antibiotics may
- B. In addition antibiotics may
- C. Additionally antibiotics, may
- D. When taking antibiotics, may

6. [Select...] medicine for 24 hours, he or she may return to school.

- A. After the fever is gone and your child has taken
- B. Your child must have no fever and having taken
- C. Your child, once having no fever and having taken
- D. The fever must be gone and once your child is taking

Questions 7 through 12 refer to the following paragraphs.

Compulsive Gambling

(A)

Most of us can [Select...] with little damage to our finances. In contrast, compulsive gamblers cannot stop even when their behavior [Select...] to ruin their lives.

(B)

Gambling frequently occupies the thoughts of compulsive gamblers. For instance, they may be reliving past gambling experiences or coming up with schemes to get more money for gambling. Although they may have tried several times to stop gambling, their efforts met with failure. When trying to stop gambling, they feel irritable and restless. They need to gamble with more and more money in order to enjoy [Select...] money increases their desire to gamble. They may even [Select...] to get the funds to continue their habit. Many of them have lost jobs, important relationships, or career opportunities because of their involvement with gambling.

(C)

Compulsive gambling is like any other addiction. As gamblers lose control over gambling, they lose control over their lives as well. They may become anxious and [Select...] may fail to live up to their obligations, causing others to stop trusting them.

7. Most of us can [Select...] with little damage to our finances.

- A. bet on a football game, or buy a lottery ticket
- B. make bets on football games, or lottery tickets
- C. bet on a football game or buy a lottery ticket
- D. place bets on football games, or on lottery tickets

8. In contrast, compulsive gamblers cannot stop even when their behavior [Select...] to ruin their lives.

- A. had threatened
- B. will threaten
- C. threatens
- D. having threatened

9. Which sentence would be most effective if inserted at the beginning of paragraph B?

- A. Compulsive gamblers have a lot of problems.
- B. Some people engage in compulsive gambling.
- C. Gamblers escape from negative emotions.
- D. Compulsive gamblers display a number of consistent traits.

10. They need to gamble with more and more money in order to enjoy [Select...] money increases their desire to gamble.

- A. it. Losing
- B. it but losing
- C. it, losing
- D. it and losing

11. They may even [Select...] to get the funds to continue their habit.

- A. commit fraud, forgery, or theft
- B. commit fraud forgery or theft,
- C. commit fraud or forgery or theft
- D. commit fraud forgery or theft,

12. They may become anxious and [Select...] may fail to live up to their obligations, causing others to stop trusting them.

- A. depressed, or they
- B. depressed, they
- C. depressed. And they
- D. depressed and they

Questions 13 through 18 refer to the following paragraphs.

Choosing a Pet

(A)

(1) [Select...] just because they see an adorable puppy or kitten. (2) Unhappily, these poor creatures are likely to end up at animal shelters [Select...]. (3) To avoid this outcome, choose your pet wisely. (4) Remember that your pet will become a member of your family and a daily responsibility.

(B)

(5) [Select...] when selecting a pet. (6) First of all, do you have the time to care for a pet? (7) While some pets require little care, puppies and kittens need to [Select...]. (8) If the animal needs exercise, is your home large enough? (9) Would you enjoy taking your pet outdoors for exercise? (10) Do you think people should get a lot of exercise? (11) Can you afford the costs of food, vaccinations, and health checkups? (12) Does your building allow pets? (13) Finally, if you must leave home for a few days, can you find someone to care for your pet?

(C)

(14) Once you choose a pet that is appropriate for your lifestyle, bring the animal to a veterinarian for examination. (15) You should be able to return the pet [Select...].

13. [Select...] just because they see an adorable puppy or kitten.

- A. Being impulsive, people often make buys at Pet Stores
- B. People often make impulse buys at pet stores
- C. Often, people buy on impulse at Pet Stores
- D. It often happens that people buy on impulse at pet stores

14. Unhappily, these poor creatures are likely to end up at animal shelters [Select...].

- A. when the owner find out he can't care for the animals
- B. the owners having discovered they can't take care of the animals
- C. their owners finding out that he can't care for the animals
- D. when the owners find they can't care for the animals

15. Select... when selecting a pet.

- A. There are several factors to consider
- B. There is several factors to consider
- C. There being several factors to consider
- D. There are several factors considering

16. While some pets require little care, puppies and kittens need to Select... .

- A. be housebroken and to train them
- B. housebreaking and training
- C. be housebroken and trained
- D. be housebroken and training

17. Which revision should be made to the placement of sentence 10?

- A. move sentence 10 to the beginning of paragraph B
- B. move sentence 10 to follow sentence 6
- C. move sentence 10 to the beginning of paragraph C
- D. remove sentence 10

18. You should be able to return the pet Select... .

- A. if the animal was unhealthy
- B. if the animal were going to be unhealthy
- C. if the animal will be unhealthy
- D. if the animal is unhealthy

Answers and explanations start on page 20.

PART III: EXTENDED RESPONSE

Directions: Read both the selection and the writing prompt and answer the questions that follow.

Questions 1–10 are based on the process of writing a response to a reading selection.
NOTE: Do not start writing your response until you are asked to do so at question 9.

Identity Theft

Identity theft happens when someone steals your personal information and uses it without your permission. It's a serious crime that can wreak havoc on your finances, credit history, and reputation — and can take time, money, and patience to resolve. If identity thieves have your personal information, they can drain your bank account, run up charges on your credit cards, open new utility accounts, or get medical treatment on your health insurance.

How do identity thieves get your personal financial information? They might go through trash cans and dumpsters, stealing bills and documents that have sensitive information. Or an identity thief might misuse the name of a legitimate business, and call or send emails that trick you into revealing personal information. Finally, an identity thief might steal your wallet, purse, backpack, or mail, and remove your credit cards, driver's license, passport, health insurance card, and other items that contain personal information.

There are three important ways in which you can protect yourself from identity thieves. First, keep your financial papers secure. Lock your financial documents and records in a safe place at home, and lock your wallet or purse in a safe place at work. When you go out, take only the identification, credit and debit cards you need, and leave your Social Security card at home. Shred receipts, credit offers, credit applications, insurance forms, physician statements, checks, bank statements, expired charge cards, and similar documents when you don't need them any longer. Take outgoing mail to post office collection boxes or the post office, and promptly remove mail that arrives in your mailbox. If you won't be home for several days, request a vacation hold on your mail. When you order new checks, don't have them mailed to your home, unless you have a secure mailbox with a lock.

Second, make sure you know who is getting your personal or financial information. Don't give out personal information on the phone, through the mail, or over the Internet unless you've initiated the contact or know who you're dealing with. If a company that claims to have an account with you sends email asking for personal information, don't click on links in the email. Instead, type the company name into your web browser, go to their site, and contact them through customer service. Ask whether the company really sent a request.

Finally, take steps to protect your online information as well. A "lock" icon on the status bar of your Internet browser means your information will be safe when it's transmitted. Look for the lock before you send personal or financial information online. Use strong passwords with your laptop, credit, bank, and other accounts. Install anti-virus software, anti-spyware software, and a firewall, and set your preference to update these protections often. Don't open files, click on links, or download programs sent by strangers.

Adapted from the Federal Trade Commission's website: www.consumer.ftc.gov.

Writing Prompt

The passage above outlines specific ways in which identity thieves go about stealing financial information from others. Read the passage closely.

Write a response to this passage that analyzes the mistakes that can make people vulnerable to identity theft. Use relevant and specific information from the reading selection to support your response.

Unpack the Writing Prompt

1. What is the topic of the writing prompt?

2. What does the prompt ask you to do?

3. What does the prompt tell you that you need to include in the response?

4. Are you being asked to give your opinion or to explain something?

Develop Your Argument, Thesis Statement, and Evidence

5. What is the writer's main point about the topic?

6. What will be your main point in response to the writing prompt?

7. What are three pieces of evidence from the text that you will use to support your point?

Plan, Draft, Revise, and Edit Your Response

8. On a piece of paper, make a plan for your response.
9. On a computer or on a piece of paper, write a response to the prompt that includes an introduction, a body, and a conclusion.
10. On the computer or on the paper, make revisions to improve your response and edit to correct errors in grammar, usage, spelling, capitalization, and punctuation.

The *Extended Response Evaluation Guide* starts on page 21.

STOP

Congratulations! You have completed the GED® Reasoning Through Language Arts Pretest.

Reminder: your next step is to check your answers with the Pretest Answers and Explanations and fill in the study planner that follows those explanations.

PRETEST ANSWERS AND EXPLANATIONS

Part I: Reading, page 2

1. **B. There are advantages to being sensitive and introverted.** The main idea of a passage is the idea that is most important to the author. The author wrote this passage to convey the idea that being introverted can be beneficial. Choices (C) and (D) both contain ideas the author expresses, but neither of those are the main idea of the entire passage. Choice (A) might be a reasonable inference based on the fourth paragraph, but it is not the author's main point.
2. **A. empathetic** The third passage states that children with sensitive temperaments "are more likely than their peers to be described by parents and caregivers as empathetic or conscientious." Choice (B) is contradicted by the author's statements that sensitive children tend to grow up to be introverts, and that introverts are less likely than others "to take dangerous risks." The author says explicitly that sensitive children "are not antisocial," so choice (C) is incorrect. Choice (D) is not supported by the passage.
3. **C. a successful collaboration between an introvert and an extrovert** The author mentions the partnership between Jobs and Wozniak in order to support her point that "[m]any successful ventures are the result of effective partnerships between introverts and extroverts."
4. **C. Children who are perceived as "shy" are actually more sensitive than other children to stimuli in their environments.** The author's purpose in the second paragraph is to help her readers understand the temperaments of the so-called "shy" children introduced in the first paragraph.
5. **A. enjoying a quiet dinner with a handful of friends** The author explains that introverts are not antisocial, so an introvert will not necessarily prefer to be alone. However, introverts are more sensitive to stimuli in their environment, so an introvert would not be likely to prefer (B) loud dance music or (C) a crowded street festival. Moreover, the author says that introverts are "less likely to take dangerous risks," and you can infer that (D) "ice slope surfing" is a dangerous sport.
6. **B. The driver may have some difficulty in controlling the forklift.** Paragraphs one and two discuss rear-wheel steering in forklifts. According to the second paragraph, rear-wheel steering is the reason why forklifts are not as responsive as cars and can be difficult to control.
7. **A. driving a forklift and driving a car** The first and second paragraphs discuss the differences between driving a car and driving a forklift.
8. **D. A forklift that is traveling downhill with a heavy load should travel backward.** The third paragraph explains that, when driving a forklift with a load on an incline, "you must keep the load on the uphill side." The graphic reinforces this by showing a forklift with the load on the uphill side. The arrow above the graphic points in two directions, and this suggests that the forklift should keep its load on the uphill side and travel backwards when going downhill.
9. **C. to explain safe practices to forklift drivers** The author is primarily concerned with helping drivers of forklifts understand and use safe practices. The author's primary focus is on safety, not on convincing people that forklifts are dangerous, as choice (B) suggests, or describing different kinds of forklift drivers, as choice (D) suggests. The differences between driving a car and driving a forklift, mentioned in choice (A), are discussed in the passage. However, the author's purpose in discussing those differences is to help forklift drivers understand how to operate forklifts safely.
10. **A. The author lists potential dangers inherent in forklift driving and explains how to avoid them.** Each paragraph discusses a different potential danger of forklift driving: first paragraph: the forklift's wide swing when turning; second paragraph: the difficulty of controlling a forklift; third paragraph: the dangers of driving on an incline with the load facing downhill; fourth paragraph: large loads that obstruct the driver's view. Each paragraph also discusses how best to deal with those dangers.
11. **B. suggest that GMO foods can be beneficial to struggling farmers.** This detail supports the overall purpose of the passage—to highlight the benefits of GMO foods for world food production. The fact that "small, resource-poor farmers" would choose to produce GMO crops implies that these are more reliable and potentially more lucrative than natural crops.
12. **D. the safety and reliability of GMO foods** Passage 2 primarily discusses how GMO foods can pose a threat to human health and how GMO crops can be especially susceptible to massive failures.
13. **B. The labels of some foods containing GMO ingredients do not indicate that the products contain genetically-modified components.** The last sentence of the first paragraph states that the American Academy of Environmental Medicine called for "the labeling of all food items containing genetically-modified products." Therefore, at least some GMO foods do not yet have this labeling.
14. **C. GMO foods are largely a positive development for global food production** The authors of the two passages disagree primarily about whether

GMO foods are beneficial or dangerous.

15. **C. Paragraph 4** In Passage 1, paragraph 4 details how GMO corn crops survived a devastating drought that natural corn crops would not have been able to withstand. This addresses the issue of reliability raised by the example of the South African corn in Passage 2.

16. **C. a young horse** The context clues in the passage indicate that the speaker is actually a horse. In paragraph 2, we learn that the speaker's mother "whinnied," and in paragraph 4, she is specifically referred to as a horse. In paragraph 5, the speaker mentions that he and his mother are the master's favorites among all of the horses.

17. **D. a farm** The description of the setting in paragraph 1 indicates that the story takes place in a rural location. In paragraph 6, the speaker's reference to an event that occurred in his "field" also supports this setting.

18. **B. contented** The overall tone of the speaker's account is positive. The passage describes the pleasant setting of his childhood, the respect he had for his mother, and the kind treatment he received from his master. Even the one negative memory, the occasional teasing by the plowboy, serves to show how the speaker was cared for by his master.

19. **A. affectionate and protective** Paragraph 5 describes the master's gentle way of treating his horses. Paragraph 7 recounts how the master punished the young boy who was harming the horses.

20. **A. correct the speaker for playing too roughly** The mother's speech is introduced in paragraph 2 after the phrase "when there was a good deal of kicking." Toward he end of the speech in paragraph 3, the mother implores the speaker to "grow up gentle and good" and "never to bite or kick even in play."

Part II: Writing and Language Skills, page 10

1. **D. your child's class has been** The third-person singular subject student requires the verb form <u>has</u>.

2. **C. symptoms, such as** Choice (C) correctly joins the list of symptoms to the main clause. Choice (A) creates a sentence fragment. Choices (B) and (D) create two independent clauses without joining them with conjunctions.

3. **B. develops any of these symptoms, take him or her to the doctor** The verb should be in the present tense because the action is occurring in the present. Moreover, the present tense is consistent with the majority of verbs in the passage. Also, because "child" is singular, the plural pronoun "them" is incorrect.

4. **C. sentence 5** Sentences 1–4 explain basic facts about strep throat. Sentences 5–10 explain what parents should do if their child has strep throat.

5. **A. In addition, antibiotics may** Generally, an introductory phrase is followed by a comma.

6. **A. After the fever is gone and your child has taken** Combining the detail about taking medicine and the detail about the fever into an introductory subordinate clause results in a smooth, effective sentence.

7. **C. bet on a football game or buy a lottery ticket** No comma is needed between two verbs in a compound predicate (*<u>bet</u> on a football game or <u>buy</u> a lottery ticket*).

8. **C. threatens** The action is always true, so the present tense is correct. Moreover, the present tense is consistent with the majority of verbs in the passage.

9. **D. Compulsive gamblers display a number of consistent traits.** This is the only topic sentence that sums up the main point and is neither too specific nor too general.

10. **A. it. Losing** Choice (A), which forms two complete sentences, is the only choice given that avoids errors. Choice (B) joins two independent clauses but omits the necessary comma. Choice (C) creates a comma splice. Choice (D) is incorrect because a comma must precede *and* in a compound sentence.

11. **A. commit fraud, forgery, or theft** Commas are required between items in a series.

12. **A. depressed, or they** A comma should precede a coordinating conjunction that joins independent clauses.

13. **B. People often make impulse buys at pet stores** This term *pet stores* should not be capitalized, because it is not the name of a store; it is just a type of store. That eliminates choices (A) and (C). Choice (D) is needlessly wordy.

14. **D. when the owners find they can't care for them** The antecedent *owners* is plural, so *they* is the correct pronoun to use. Choice (B) is incorrect because of its awkward construction.

15. **A. There are several factors to consider** The verb agrees with the subject, "several factors," which is plural. Choice (D) is incorrect because it suggests that the factors are doing the considering.

16. **C. be housebroken and trained** Only choice (C) has both verbs in parallel structure and creates a correct sentence.

17. **D. remove sentence 10** The sentence about exercise and people is not relevant to pets, the topic of the article.

18. **D. if the animal is unhealthy** The statement is always true, so the present tense is correct. Moreover, the present tense is consistent with the majority of verbs in the passage.

Part III: Extended Response, page 16

Your responses to questions 1 through 5 may vary but should be similar to the following:

1. identity theft
2. explain how people can become vulnerable to identity theft
3. specific information from the reading selection
4. to explain something
5. There are several things you can do to protect yourself from identity theft.

Your responses to questions 6 and 7 may vary. Sample responses are below.

6. People might become vulnerable to identity theft if they are careless about papers, information access, or online activities.
7. (1) Identity thieves might go through a person's garbage looking for financial papers. (2) You shouldn't have checks sent to your mailbox unless your mailbox locks. (3) You should update your anti-spyware software to protect yourself from identity theft.
8. **Planning Checklist** Check off each task that you performed. Give yourself a score of 0–3 based on how many checks you made.

   _______ I wrote a central idea (thesis statement) for my response.

   _______ I made a plan for what I wrote.

   _______ In my plan, I related each point to a piece of evidence or information in the text.

9. **Drafting Checklist** Check off each task that you performed. Give yourself a score of 0–5 based on how many checks you made.

   _______ I wrote an introduction to my response based on my central idea (thesis statement).

   _______ I developed several paragraphs responding to the prompt.

   _______ In my response, I cited specific evidence from the text to support my central idea.

   _______ In my response, I provided additional relevant information based on my own knowledge and perspectives.

   _______ I wrote a conclusion that summarized my position or restated my central idea in a different way.

10. **Revising and Editing Checklist** Give yourself a score of 0–6 based on how many checks you made.

   _______ My piece was well organized, or I improved its organization so that one idea relates to another.

   _______ I made sure that my sentences were complete, clear, and correct.

   _______ Each of my paragraphs has a central idea and supporting evidence from the text.

   _______ My piece has a clear beginning, middle, and ending.

   _______ I corrected subject-verb agreement, pronoun agreement, and verb tense errors.

   _______ I have corrected punctuation, capitalization, and spelling.

Kaplan Reasoning Through Language Arts Test Study Planner

Take the Pretest, starting on page 1. Check your answers in the Pretest Answers and Explanations. Use the results to fill in the charts below so that you can target the areas that need the most work.

Part I: Reading, 20 questions

Circle the *Question Numbers* that you answered correctly in the second column. Write the *Number Correct* in the third column. Compare your "number correct" to the "mastery" number in the fourth column. If you do not have time to review all of the *Reading* sections, target your study to the *Content Areas* in which you did not score at the mastery level.

Content Area	Question Numbers	Number Correct	Mastery/Total
Interpreting Nonfiction and Informational Text Pages 30–53	1, 2, 3, 4, 5, 6, 7, 12, 13		**7 out of 9**
Analyzing Nonfiction and Informational Text Pages 54–69	8, 9, 10, 11, 14, 15		**4 out of 6**
Interpreting Fiction Pages 70–85	16, 17, 18, 19, 20		**3 out of 5**

Part II: Writing and Language Skills, 18 questions

Circle the *Question Numbers* that you answered correctly in the second column. Write the *Number Correct* in the third column. Compare your "number correct" to the "mastery" number in the fourth column. If you do not have time to review all of the *Writing and Language* sections, target your study to the *Content Areas* in which you did not score at the mastery level.

Content Area	Question Numbers	Number Correct	Mastery/Total
Writing Effective Sentences and **Connecting Ideas** Pages 86–103 and 104–115	2, 6, 9, 10, 12, 17		**4 out of 6**
Polishing Your Writing Pages 142–151	4, 16		**1 out of 2**
Using Grammar Correctly Pages 152–167	1, 3, 8, 14, 15, 18		**4 out of 6**
Using Writing Mechanics Pages 168–181	5, 7, 11, 13		**3 out of 4**

Part III: Extended Response

Circle the *Question Numbers* that you answered correctly in the second column. Write the *Number Correct* in the third column. Compare your "number correct" to the "mastery" number in the fourth column and target your study to the *Content Areas* in which you did not score at the mastery level.

Content Area	Question Numbers	Number Correct	Mastery/Total
Unpack the Writing Prompt Pages 116–117	1, 2, 3, 4		**3 out of 4**
Identify a Writer's Arguments and Assumptions, Develop a Thesis Statement, and Collect Supporting Evidence Pages 118–123	5, 6, 7		**2 out of 3**
Plan Your Response Pages 124–127	8	My score is _____ based on the Planning Checklist, page 21.	**2 out of 3**
Draft Your Response Pages 128–133	9	My score is ______ based on the Drafting Checklist, page 21.	**4 out of 5**
Revise and Edit Your Response Pages 134–137	10	My score is ______ based on the Revising and Editing Checklist, page 21.	**4 out of 6**

About the Reasoning Through Language Arts Test

The GED® *Reasoning Through Language Arts Test* (RLA) evaluates your reading and writing skills: You will have 2½ hours for about 46 questions that require you to

- answer questions based on single passages <u>and</u> on passages that are paired together (reading and thinking skills);
- review written text and select words and phrases so that the final product is written correctly (language skills); and
- compose an extended response to a writing prompt based on reading one or two passages or a passage accompanied by a graphic (writing skills).

The first section of the test includes reading and language questions and concludes with about 45 minutes for the Extended Response. You will have a 10-minute break before the second section, which includes reading and language questions only.

You will need a minimum score of 150 to pass the RLA Test, which is one of the four tests you will need to pass in order to earn a high school equivalency diploma.

Reading Content Areas

You will answer questions based on a wide range of types of reading materials. Seventy-five percent of the questions are based on **informational texts**, which include workplace- and community-based documents, **general nonfiction**, and **nonfiction related to general interest social studies and science** topics. Twenty-five percent of the questions are based on **fiction** selections.

Language Content Areas

The language skills model real-life editing to ensure correct **sentence structure**, **agreement** (subject-verb and pronoun-antecedent), **capitalization, punctuation**, **homonyms,** and **possessives**. The questions also assess appropriate **word choice** and **elimination of informal usage** to fit the purpose of the writing task.

Extended Response

The Extended Response requires reading text materials and responding to a writing prompt (assignment) by **developing an argument and supporting your ideas with evidence** from the text.

Computer-Based RLA Test Question Formats

You will work with several different question formats on the RLA Test. Many of the questions will be in the familiar multiple-choice format, but you will need to be acquainted with the other formats as well.

Multiple-choice questions have four options (A through D). You will **click** on the best answer.

> In this passage, William tells Jordan about his life experiences and plans for the future. What do his stories indicate about his past?
>
> ○ A. He has already seen too much.
> ○ B. He has never been certain of his place in the world.
> ○ C. He wishes he had made different decisions in the past.
> ○ D. He is proud of his accomplishments and hopes to help others.

Fill-in-the-blank questions will require you to **type** a word, phrase, or number in a box that appears on the screen.

> Which phrase from paragraph 2 describes how an employee should fill out the shipping authorization form? Type your answer in the box below.
>
> [   ]

Drop-down questions give you the opportunity to **click** the word "Select" and choose the option that correctly completes the sentence. (This format is only used to assess language skills.)

GED® TEST TIP

Test each one of the drop-down options in the context of the sentence before you make your final choice. Do not select an option that "seems" right until you have tested all of the choices and have a clear idea about why it is correct.

> Technical Corporation strives to provide excellent service. We have a history of providing outstanding technical and customer support and always aim to give 100%. When customers express concerns or complaints, we respond immediately to show that we value [Select... ▾] feedback.

The words that appear in a drop-down menu when you **click** on "Select" are

his
her
its
their

You would choose **their** because the sentence should read: *When customers express concerns or complaints, we respond immediately to show that we value* <u>*their*</u> *feedback.*

Some of the questions in this book are designed to mimic this drop-down menu format. When you see the word "Select" in a question in this book, choose the option that best completes the sentence.

Drag-and-Drop items require you to **click** on a word or short phrase and to **drag** and **drop** it to a specified location on the computer screen.

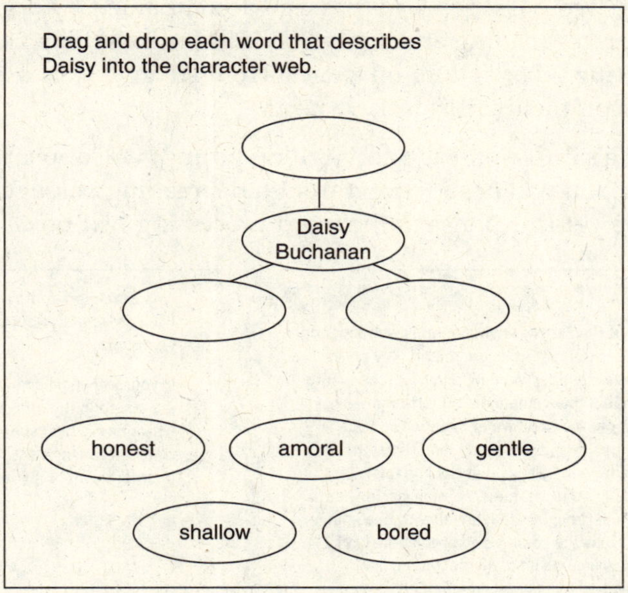

An ***Extended-Response*** item requires you to **type** in a **text box** in response to a **prompt** (writing assignment) based on one or more short passages, a graphic, or a combination.

You will have 45 minutes to read the materials and to plan, write, and revise your response.

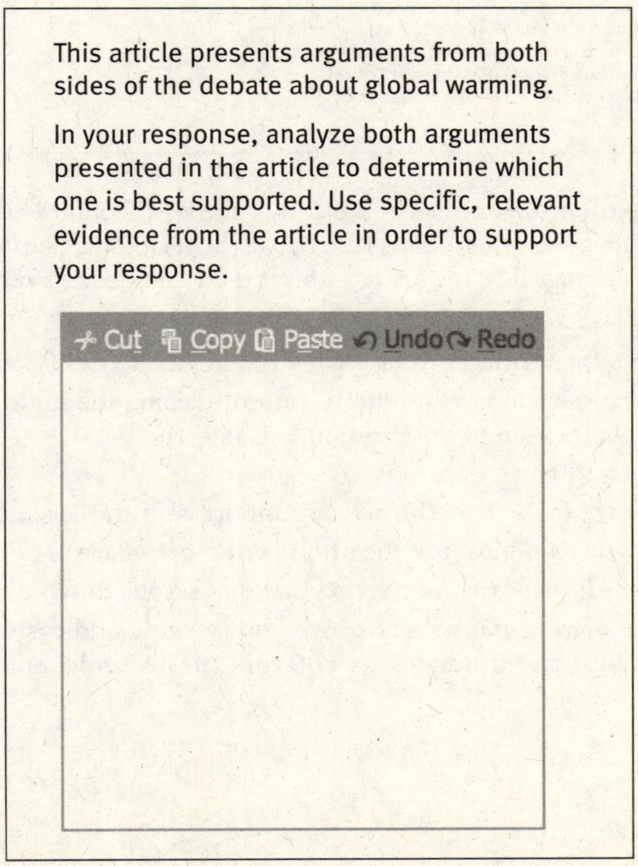

GED® TEST TIP

*The Extended Response will be the last question before the 10-minute break on the RLA Test. Carefully watch both the **Time Remaining** and **Question** bars at the top of the computer screen. Make sure you are allowing yourself 45 minutes for this task.*

Extended Response Question on the RLA Test

An important task on the RLA Test involves writing an extended response to a passage, two passages, or a passage accompanied by a graphic. This activity integrates reading and analytical skills with writing skills. The lessons in *Writing About Text,* on pages 116–141, give you a step-by-step approach to completing this task.

GED® TEST TIP

Preview the writing prompt before you read the passage(s). This will help you focus your reading to select key details and evidence that you will use to support your position.

Look at how a sample passage and writing prompt will appear on the computer screen. You will need to **tab** through the reading passage or passages and **compose** your response in the word processing **text box**.

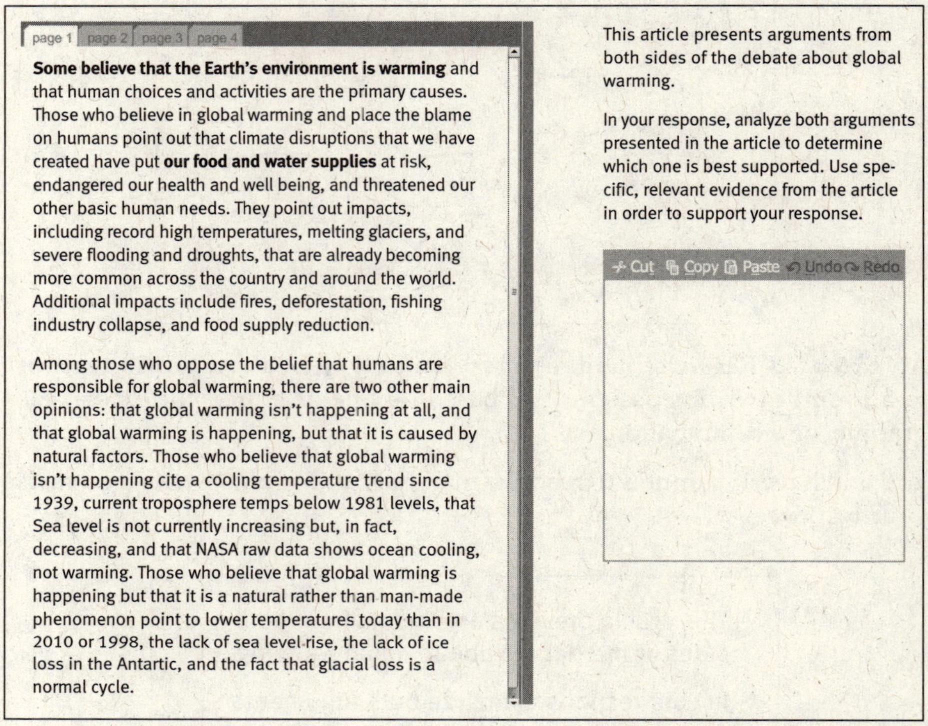

You can take up to 45 minutes at the end of the first section of the RLA Test to complete the assignment. This task has its own clock to help you manage your time. See page 124 for a suggested time management plan to do the following:

- ***Preview*** the writing prompt.
- ***Read*** the selection or selections, carefully using the **highlighter tool** to draw attention to information for later use.
- ***Compose*** a thesis statement.
- ***Gather evidence*** from the text to support your thesis statement.
- ***Plan*** your response (use the offline **wipe-off board**).
- ***Draft*** your response (in the **text box** that scrolls down).
- ***Review your response*** to improve your writing and correct any errors with the editing tools—**cut, copy, paste, undo,** and **redo**.

The Qualities of a Successful Extended Response

Your response can earn up to 6 points. It is reviewed for three different "traits" or qualities, and each trait is assigned a score from 0–2. So, *3 traits times a maximum of 2 points each equals a maximum of 6 points.*

Unlike other writing that you may have done in the past, this task is **"evidence-based writing,"** meaning that you need to base your position on the **information and arguments** in the reading materials.

<u>Trait 1:</u> **Creation of Arguments and Use of Evidence** To earn a score of 2 on Trait 1 you need to do the following:

- Create an **argument** by making a logical claim that clearly **states your position.**
- Use 3 or more **specific references** from the text(s) to support the claim.
- Identify **valid arguments and/or fallacious claims** in the text(s).
- Point out **supported and/or unsupported claims** in the text(s).

<u>Trait 2:</u> **Development of Ideas and Organizational Structure** To earn a score of 2 on Trait 2 you need to accomplish these tasks:

- Create an **effective organizational structure.**
- Sequence ideas **logically** so that one idea leads to the next.
- Elaborate main ideas and tie them to **specific evidence** from the text.
- Make effective transitions to **cohesively link** ideas.
- Use accurate and advanced **word choice.**
- Employ an appropriate level of **formality** (no slang, etc.).

<u>Trait 3:</u> **Clarity and Command of Standard English Conventions** To earn a score of 2 on Trait 3, you need to have few errors that would interfere with a reader's understanding of what you wrote. You should also do the following:

- Use varied and correct forms of **sentence structure.**
- Maintain **subject-verb** and **pronoun-antecedent** agreement.
- Adhere to the rules of **capitalization, punctuation,** and **spelling.**
- Distinguish between commonly confused words, such as **possessives** and **homonyms.**
- Avoid **wordiness** and **awkward constructions.**

GED® TEST TIP

Keep in mind that your work on the test is considered to be a "strong first draft," in which you put forth your best effort without a chance for a revised second draft.

If you practice writing throughout this book and use the self-evaluation checklists in the answer keys to make continual improvements to your writing skills, you will be well prepared.

LESSON

1

Main Ideas and Details

Key Ideas

- The most important point of a passage is called the main idea.
- Sometimes a main idea is stated, but often you must figure it out.
- Supporting details point to and explain the main idea.

GED® TEST TIP

Be sure you don't confuse a supporting detail of a passage with the main idea. If you are asked for the main idea, choose the most important, general point.

The Main Idea

A writer has a message, or **main idea**, to get across. Sometimes the main idea is stated directly; often you have to figure it out yourself. You can find the main idea by asking, "What is the *most important* point the writer is making?" Most of the information in a passage will point to and explain the main idea.

As you read this passage, ask yourself what *main* point the writer is making. The answer will be the main idea.

> When I am reading a poem, I rarely feel alone in the room. The poet and I are together. It's as if the poet wrote a secret diary years ago. I am unlocking it as I sit alone and read.
>
> At times I don't understand what a poem means. I just like the way it sounds or the strange images that it provokes. The world is so peculiar in a poem. At the same time, it is so enticing. Sometimes I understand exactly, as if the poet is whispering to me, as if we shared the same experience.
>
> I must be fully concentrated on reading, or I cannot enter the world of a poem. There are too many daily tasks to attend to—tasks that are very far removed from the magic and imagination involved in a poem.
>
> On a cold, snowy day, I cuddle up inside my apartment and read and read. Then, I'm free to ride through the imagination of all those who came before me.

► Which of the following statements expresses the main idea?
(1) The writer has a love of poetry.
(2) The writer cuddles up on cold days to read.

You are correct if you chose **(1)**. While the passage mentions that the writer reads on cold days, the main point of all the information is how much the writer enjoys reading poetry.

Each paragraph has a main idea. To find the main idea of a passage with more than one paragraph, put together the ideas from all the paragraphs.

Supporting Details

A writer explains the main idea of a passage with supporting details. **Supporting details** include facts, examples, descriptions, and specific pieces of information. When you read, you need to identify details that support the main idea.

► Which detail helps you understand the writer's main point?
(1) At times, the writer does not understand a poem.
(2) The writer feels poetry is filled with magic and imagination.

You are correct if you chose **(2)**. That detail helps you see that the main idea is the writer's love of poetry. The fact that the writer doesn't always understand a poem is true, but it alone does not support the main idea.

PRACTICE 1

Questions 1 through 5 refer to the following passage from a diary.

EXCERPTED FROM *ARIADNE'S THREAD*

1 I feel I have never had a home. All my life moving from place to place. The only thing that remained the same, that was stable, was Oklahoma. Even the landscape never changed. The towns there never grew up into cities. The people were the same each year, wearing the same clothing, saying the same things.

2 The search for a homeland is part of the Chickasaw migration legend. It was ordained by the deities and began in the past when the people lived in the land of the "setting sun." During the days they would walk over the land, searching for their home. The priests carried a pole. They carried it in their hands by day and planted it each night. During the night it moved about and by morning it would be pointing the direction they were to travel. For a while it commanded the people to journey east, toward the morning sun. They crossed the Mississippi River eventually, and on the other side, the pole finally ceased to move during the night. The land was settled, crops were planted. It became known as the Old Fields. But one morning the pole leaned westward. The people gathered together and began the long journey back. They abandoned their village but did not feel sorrow because the pole had commanded it.

3 And I am still moving, looking for a home. I don't know if I will ever escape my tradition, my past. It goes with me everywhere, like a shadow.

By Linda Hogan from *Ariadne's Thread*, edited by Lyn Lifshin, New York: Harper & Row, 1982.

1. How does the author describe herself?

She feels as if she is

A. searching for a place to call home
B. doomed to stay in Oklahoma
C. tired of the sameness in her life
D. being shadowed by failure

2. Who do the Chickasaw believe are responsible for making them move?

A. the priests
B. white people
C. themselves
D. the gods

3. Why did the Chickasaw not feel sad when they left their homes in the east?

A. They knew they were headed to a better place to live.
B. They had been forced to move east to begin with.
C. They were returning to their ancient homeland.
D. It was simply part of their beliefs to follow the pole.

4. Which of the following best summarizes the main idea?

The writer

A. has always lived in Oklahoma and plans to stay there
B. feels trapped by tradition and wants to move far away
C. understands that her tendency to search is part of her Chickasaw heritage
D. believes that people in Oklahoma are all the same

5. How does the statement "I don't know if I will ever escape my tradition" (paragraph 3) support the main idea?

It shows that the writer

A. is trying to escape by moving around
B. lives in a more modern time
C. believes in the power of Indian legends
D. accepts that she is Chickasaw

Answers and explanations start on page 182.

LESSON 2

Restatement and Summary

Key Ideas

- To restate an idea, put it in your own words.
- To summarize, choose the most important details that explain the main idea of a piece.

Restating Ideas

Restating an idea means putting it into your own words. For example, a friend may tell you that a movie wasn't worth the eight dollars she spent on it. You might then tell a co-worker that your friend said the movie was no good.

As you read the passage below, restate in your mind what you are reading.

> In Canton, Ohio, we take our desserts seriously. There are two local candy stores that receive over 90 percent of the city's candy business: Heggy's and Baldwin's. Those who prefer Heggy's won't befriend anyone who buys their sweets at Baldwin's.
>
> My family has always patronized Heggy's. At the Heggy's factory, Gerty wraps by hand each large chocolate candy in clear cellophane wrap. She's in the back of the store with her hairnet, seated at a table filled with hundreds of chocolates. My favorite chocolates at Heggy's are the dark chocolate creams, peanut clusters, and caramels.
>
> Heggy's aficionados point out that their candy of choice is a larger size and therefore superior. The rivalry runs deep . . . at Easter, Hanukkah, Christmas, Thanksgiving, and all occasions. Baldwin's loyal followers claim its sweets are sweeter. It's a feud over the best chocolate in town.

► How do the people of Canton feel about chocolate candy?
(1) They consider it a serious health issue.
(2) They feel it's important enough to take a stand on.

You are correct if you chose **(2)**. The phrase "take our desserts seriously" means that the candy is important to people.

On the *Reasoning Through Language Arts* Test, the correct answer will not always use the exact words from the passage. You will have to recognize that the idea has been restated.

GED® TEST TIP

As you read a GED® passage, check your understanding by pausing occasionally to see if you can restate and summarize what you are reading.

Summarizing

If you want to tell a friend about a movie you liked, you might **summarize** what happens in the movie. You certainly will not give all the details—that would take too long. A summary includes only the most important facts and ideas.

► Which of the following statements best summarizes the difference in opinion over the candy?
(1) Some people prefer Heggy's candy because it's bigger, while others prefer Baldwin's because it's sweeter.
(2) People argue whether to buy Heggy's or Baldwin's candy for different holidays.

You are correct if you chose **(1)**. The last paragraph sums up the difference in people's opinions. Statement (2) merely states a detail in the last paragraph.

PRACTICE 2

Questions 1 through 3 refer to the following business letter.

EXCERPTED FROM *THE ENCYCLOPEDIA OF BUSINESS LETTERS*

Dear Richard,

1 Attached is a copy of my June 8th letter to Customer Service. After having my car serviced on June 30th, the list of problems has grown. These matters need your immediate attention.

2 Although I did finally receive my copy of the warranty after waiting two months, it is not bumper-to-bumper as Mr. Schecht promised. It also requires service at your facility unless the warranty administrator waives that requirement. I purchased the car from you at a premium price with the expectation that I would have a bumper-to-bumper warranty that I could use at any dealer. I never would have bought this car from you if I knew about these limitations. I expect two things: A written waiver from the warranty administrator that allows me to have warranty service performed at any dealer, and a wrap-around warranty, provided at your cost, that turns this limited warranty into the promised "bumper-to-bumper" warranty.

3 I expect an itemized list of registration costs, and the exact amount of credit I received from the Department of Motor Vehicles for the canceled plates voucher I gave to Mr. Schecht. If there is a refund due, I expect it within 15 days.

4 I expect a proper bill of sale that itemizes and describes the payments for the alarm system and the extended warranty, and includes all the items on the original bill of sale.

5 Your mechanic was unable to locate a cause for the burning smell. The smell persists. I expect your written assurance that if and when the cause for this smell becomes known, you will repair the problem at your cost.

6 The mechanic did *not* repair the left front marker light, although he promised he would. Enclosed is a copy of your invoice for this repair, which wasn't made, as well as an invoice from another dealer who actually made the repair. I expect reimbursement for $22.90.

cc: Joe Smith, Department of Consumer Affairs

1. The problems that the writer mentions in the first paragraph and outlines in his letter include which of the following?

A. receiving repairs the writer did not ask for
B. rude treatment
C. lack of proper paperwork
D. the premium price paid for the car

2. What does the customer want done about the burning smell?

A. the mechanic to find the cause of the smell
B. the car to be repaired free of charge if the cause of the problem is discovered
C. a refund of the money that was paid to have the problem fixed
D. reimbursement for having the problem fixed by another dealer

3. Which of the following statements best summarizes this letter?

A. A letter to customer service was never responded to and is being attached.
B. Mechanics have been unable to fix one problem and did not fix a second.
C. The service and warranty on the customer's car have been unacceptable.
D. Some dealers and garages are better than others.

Answers and explanations start on page 182.

LESSON

3

INTERPRETING NONFICTION AND INFORMATIONAL TEXT

Application of Ideas

Key Ideas

- Applying ideas means using information in a new but similar situation.
- To apply ideas, ask yourself, "How is this new situation just like the situation in the passage?"

GED® TEST TIP

Remember that you can tab backward or forward in a passage on the computer screen to find information you need to answer a question.

When you **apply ideas**, you use information you already know in a new but similar situation. For example, suppose you know that a friend loves country music. When you need to buy a gift for that friend, you walk past the jazz and rock sections in the music store and head straight for the country. You're applying what you've learned about your friend to help you choose a gift.

To apply ideas when reading, look for elements in the new situation that are similar to elements in the passage you have read. Read this selection and then see if you can apply some of the ideas in it.

When the delivery truck pulled up to my house the day before my mother's birthday, I knew her gift had finally arrived. I was excited. Not only had I ordered a beautiful art book for her, but I'd also ordered a mystery novel for myself and a book each for my nephew and niece. I couldn't resist buying them while I was choosing my mother's gift from an online bookstore. The carton looked bigger than I expected, but perhaps it had a lot of filler to keep the books from becoming damaged.

I lugged the huge box into the kitchen so I could open it and begin wrapping my mother's gift. I tugged at the industrial staples and then tore open the carton. To my surprise, it was filled with many copies of the same book. To make matters worse, it was a book I had not ordered. *Who Moved My Cheese?* What kind of book was that? And who would order *one* copy of that book, let alone 11? I certainly didn't want these books. I knew my family wouldn't want them either. They wanted *The Art of Diego Rivera, Harry Potter,* and Dr. Seuss. So much for buying online. I'm sticking to in-store buying.

► Which of the following situations is most like the situation that happened to the writer?
(1) buying groceries only to discover you brought someone else's bag home
(2) buying 11 boxes of the same pasta at the store

Option **(1)** is correct. It shares the elements of intending to buy something and getting the wrong thing by mistake. The second option is wrong because the writer did not intentionally buy 11 copies of the book. Now try this question.

► If the writer attended an auction, she would be most likely to
(1) decide which item to bid on and how much she would bid
(2) get involved in the excitement and bid on many things

You are correct if you chose **(2)**. The writer states that she couldn't resist buying additional items when she was shopping online. Therefore, she seems the type to get caught up in buying things. If she had carefully chosen which book to buy her mother and had ordered only that one, then option (1) would be correct.

PRACTICE 3

Questions 1 through 4 refer to the following excerpt.

EXCERPTED FROM *MAKING THE MOST OF YOUR MONEY*

1 Once you stop using credit cards, three things will happen.

2 You will buy less—and whatever you do buy will probably be a less expensive model or make. Studies have found that people spend more when they pay with plastic, because it doesn't feel like real money. When it is real money, you're more sensible.

3 Your total debt will shrink rapidly. You are paying *off* back bills, you are not adding new ones, and you have extra money because you're buying less. That surplus cash will reduce your debt faster than you could imagine.

4 You will grow incredibly smug. You're the first on your block to get out of debt. Others will follow, but you'll be the first.

5 I'm not against credit cards. They're easy to use. They're handy. If your card has a low annual fee and a 25-day, interest-free grace period for paying your bills, you're getting monthly loans for practically nothing. What I'm against is buying more on your credit cards than you can pay for at the end of the month.

6 Once you've fought your way out of debt you can start using credit cards again—but only for the convenience of not carrying cash. Your days of debt are done. A big expense may sometimes drive you over the limit. A stereo. A llama. A hot-air balloon. Whenever you limp home, back in debt, recite your mantra: "From now on, I'm not going to put down a charge card for anything." Stick with it until you're free again.

From *Making the Most of Your Money* by Jane Bryant Quinn, New York: Simon & Schuster, 1991.

1. According to the writer, becoming debt free is a behavior most similar to

A. overcoming a bad habit
B. learning a new trick
C. forgetting a friend's birthday
D. setting a good example

2. If you have five credit cards with high interest rates and no grace periods, how can you become debt free?

A. pay your debt off slowly so that you have extra cash for necessities
B. never use the credit cards
C. use them only when it is not convenient to carry cash
D. cut up four of the credit cards right away

3. Which of the following situations is most like the process of becoming debt free?

A. driving a car
B. wearing a patch to give up smoking
C. losing weight by avoiding all-you-can-eat buffets
D. running a marathon race

4. Earlier in the book, the author made the statement "It's so simple that I'm almost embarrassed to mention it. Don't borrow any more."

Based on this information and the information in this passage, with which of the following statements would the author most likely agree?

A. "Money is the root of all evil."
B. "You can never have enough money."
C. "Live within your means."
D. "You deserve only the best."

Answers and explanations start on page 182.

LESSON

4

Cause and Effect

When one event or idea influences another, there is a cause-and-effect relationship. For example, if you forget to fill your car with gas, the car will stall. The lack of gas is the **cause**, or the reason. The stalled car is the **effect**.

As you read this passage, look for cause-and-effect relationships.

> He is deceptively sweet upon waking up, and lets out a large yawn, showing his thin pink puppy tongue, and simultaneously letting out a high-pitched squeaking sound. Not two minutes later, he's eaten my favorite magazine and stuffed his entire head in the kitchen wastebasket to find a leftover turkey bone. The pup searches under the bed, on top of the dresser, and beside the nightstand for anything to chew. He's on a rampage in the morning—it's just his puppy nature.
>
> To calm him down, we head to the park for one hour of exercise with the other neighborhood dogs. Afterwards, he plays with his stuffed animal squeaky toy, sleeps for an hour, then finds his favorite bone. He lies down like an angel, chewing with contentment.

► What causes the puppy's owners to take him to the park?
(1) They like to see the other neighborhood dogs.
(2) The puppy is acting too wild and energetic.

You are correct if you chose **(2)**. The first paragraph describes wild behavior, and the second paragraph says, "To calm him down, we head to the park . . ."

► Why is the puppy so wild and energetic?
(1) It is just the way a puppy is.
(2) He has a behavioral problem.

You are correct if you chose **(1)**. The writer doesn't indicate that the puppy's behavior is a problem. In fact, she clearly states that it's just the puppy's nature.

► What effect does the activity in the park have on the puppy?
(1) It calms him and tires him out.
(2) It teaches him to obey his owner.

You are correct if you chose **(1)**. When they get back from the park, the puppy plays quietly, sleeps for an hour, and then lies down to chew.

► Why does a walk in the park have a calming effect on the puppy?
(1) because the puppy enjoys seeing the other dogs
(2) because the puppy gets plenty of exercise

You are correct if you chose **(2)**. The exercise brings on the effect—calm behavior. This cause is not directly stated. You have to apply what you know about exercise and its effects in order to understand the relationship.

Key Ideas

- To determine the cause of an event, answer the question "Why did this happen?"
- To determine an effect, ask yourself, "What was the result?"

ON THE GED® TEST

In a GED® passage, a writer might discuss one cause and all its effects, one effect and all its causes, or a chain of events in which each effect becomes the cause of another event.

PRACTICE 4

Questions 1 through 5 refer to the following excerpt from an essay.

EXCERPTED FROM "THE DEPRESSION"

1 Some events are so important that their influence cuts across class lines, affects all races and ethnic groups, and leaves no region untouched. The depression of the 1930s was such an event. No one who lived through those years in the United States could ever completely forget the bread lines, the millions of unemployed, or the forlorn and discouraged men and women who saw their mortgages foreclosed, their dreams shattered, their children hungry and afraid.

2 The depression was precipitated by the stock market crash in October 1929, but the actual cause of the collapse was an unhealthy economy. While the ability of the manufacturing industry to produce consumer goods had increased rapidly, mass purchasing power had remained relatively static. Most laborers, farmers, and white-collar workers, therefore, could not afford to buy the automobiles and refrigerators turned out by factories in the 1920s, because their incomes were too low. At the same time, the federal government increased the problem through economic policies that tended to encourage the very rich to over-save.

3 Herbert Hoover, a sensitive and humane engineer, had the misfortune of being President when the depression began. Even though he broke with the past and used the power of the federal government to stem the tide of depression, especially through loans to businesses and banks, his efforts proved to be too little and too late.

From "The Depression" from *Generations: Your Family in Modern American History*, 2nd ed., edited by James Watts and Allen F. Davis, New York: Alfred A. Knopf, 1974, 1978.

1. According to the authors, why was the depression of the 1930s so important?

A. It could have been prevented.
B. It was a time of economic hardship.
C. It affected nearly everyone.
D. It was unforgettable.

2. According to the passage, which of the following was an effect of the depression?

A. Many people lost the mortgages on their homes.
B. The stock market collapsed in October 1929.
C. Herbert Hoover was elected president.
D. The rich began to save too much of their money.

3. According to the passage, which of the following was one cause of the depression?

A. a static stock market
B. low worker incomes
C. not enough productivity
D. laborers refusing to buy products

4. In the early part of the depression, what effect did government policies have on the economy?

A. Banks and businesses began to need loans.
B. They had little effect.
C. Some of the poorer people were helped.
D. The very rich were helped.

5. One person who lived during the depression stated, "I can remember one time, the only thing in the house to eat was mustard. . . . And we can't stand mustard till today."

This account supports which of the following ideas from the passage?

A. Workers should have been paid more.
B. The depression touched everyone.
C. Herbert Hoover could have done more to help the economy.
D. The depression left people emotionally scarred.

Answers and explanations start on page 182.

LESSON

5

Compare and Contrast

Key Ideas

- To compare ideas or things, find out how they are alike.
- To contrast ideas or things, find out how they differ.
- A writer might compare two things, contrast two things, or compare and contrast in one passage.

ON THE GED® TEST

In a GED® passage, a writer may (1) compare in one paragraph and contrast in the next or (2) go back and forth, discussing similarities and differences on different points.

You are probably familiar with comparing and contrasting whenever you go shopping. If you are looking at two cars or even two bottles of aspirin, you want to know if the price of the two is the same or different.

Writers **compare** to point out what is similar and **contrast** to point out what is different about ideas or things.

As you read this passage, look for things being compared and contrasted.

> In December, it seems everyone is hurrying to bake holiday treats, decorate, and buy gifts. Some holiday shoppers trek through store after store, while others prefer catalog or online shopping. Just two of the holidays that keep everyone so busy this time of year are Christmas and Hanukkah.
>
> These holidays are, of course, times of celebration. People plan parties and family get-togethers. Both involve gift giving. Both also coincide with the winter solstice in the Northern Hemisphere, a time when many ancient cultures rejoiced.
>
> Christmas is a celebration of the birth of Jesus, though celebrating Christmas on December 25 did not become common until the fourth century.
>
> Hanukkah, the Jewish Festival of Lights, celebrates the belief that a flask of oil sufficient for only one day miraculously burned for eight days in a temple in the second century B.C.E. That's why on Hanukkah an additional candle is lit each evening until, on the eighth night of the holiday, eight candles are burning.

► What is the writer comparing and contrasting?

(1) methods of shopping
(2) Christmas and Hanukkah

You are correct if you chose **(2)**. The similarities and differences between the two holidays are the focus of the discussion. Two methods of shopping are merely mentioned.

► What is one basis on which the writer compares the two?

(1) time of year celebrated
(2) kinds of meals served

You are correct if you chose **(1)**. The similarities discussed in this passage include the time of the winter solstice in the Northern Hemisphere, close to when each holiday is celebrated.

► What is one basis on which the writer contrasts the two?

(1) gift giving
(2) their histories

The correct answer is **(2)**. The two holidays have very different histories. Both holidays involve gift giving, so that is not a point of contrast.

Practice 5

Questions 1 through 5 refer to the following excerpt from a diary.

EXCERPTED FROM *DIARIES OF THE WESTWARD JOURNEY*

1 Mr. West from Peoria, Ill. had another man, his wife, a son Clay about 20 years of age and his daughter, America, eighteen. Unfortunately Mr. West had gone to the extreme of providing himself with such a heavy wagon and load that they were deemed objectionable as fellow argonauts. After disposing of some of their supplies they were allowed to join us. They had four fine oxen. This wagon often got stalled in bad roads much to the annoyance of all, but as he was a wagon maker and his companion a blacksmith by trade and both were accommodating there were always ready hands to "pry the wheel out of mire."

2 A mule team from Washington, D.C. was very insufficiently provisioned . . . [by] Southern gentlemen "unused to work. . . ." They deserted the train at Salt Lake as they could not proceed with their equipment and it was easier to embrace Mormonism than to brave the "American Desert."

3 Much in contrast to these men were four batchelors Messers Wilson, Goodall, Fifield and Martin, who had a wagon drawn by four oxen and two milch cows following behind. The latter gave milk all the way to the sink of the Humboldt where they died, having acted as draught animals for several weeks after the oxen had perished. Many a cup of milk was given to the children of the train and the mothers tried in every way possible to express their gratitude.

By Catherine Haun from *Women's Diaries of the Westward Journey*, edited by Lillian Schlissel, New York: Schocken Books, 1982.

1. What did Mr. West do that allowed his group to join the wagon train?

A. make wagons for the others
B. bring four fine oxen
C. offer milk to the children
D. leave some of his possessions behind

2. What purpose did the cows serve?

A. They led the oxen through rough terrain.
B. They carried children when wagons were full.
C. They provided milk and pulled wagons.
D. They provided food and replaced the mules.

3. Which of the following is contrasted in this excerpt?

A. the provisions of each group of travelers
B. the stability of each of the wagons
C. the number of people in each group
D. the ability of each group to feed the children

4. Suppose the writer were comparing a woman with five children who could sew and cook to one man with an old ox. Which of the following would be her most likely response?

The writer would

A. be happy to have people who could cook and sew
B. prefer to add fewer people to the group of travelers
C. feel sorry for the man and welcome him
D. offer the man one of her own animals

5. Based on the information in this excerpt, how is this trip similar for all the travelers?

A. They must cooperate and work together.
B. They will be rewarded for their efforts.
C. They have similar backgrounds and relate to each other.
D. They have all been forced to go on the journey.

Answers and explanations start on page 182.

LESSON

6

Conclusions and Generalizations

Conclusions

A detective draws a **conclusion** when he looks at different pieces of evidence and figures out who committed a crime. A doctor draws a conclusion when she looks at different symptoms and figures out what illness a patient has. You, as a reader, can draw a conclusion when you take pieces of information and put them together to figure out something that the writer has not directly stated.

See what conclusions you can draw from this notice sent by an employer.

> Thank you for sending your resume in response to our newspaper advertisement. We consider our company—and especially our employees—to be the best. And we want to keep it that way. For that reason, we carefully review each resume that is sent to us. We want to ensure that our company and the new employee we hire are a perfect match.
>
> This process, of course, takes some time. We want to assure you that your resume is part of this process and will be reviewed. If we feel we have an opening that matches your qualifications, we will contact you. If you have not heard from us within ten business days of the postmark of this notice, be assured that we will keep your resume on file for one year and review it when future openings arise.

► If a job applicant has not heard from this company three weeks after reading this notice, what can she conclude?
(1) The review process is taking longer than expected.
(2) She did not get the job that she applied for.

Option **(2)** is correct. The notice says that the review process takes some time. It also says that the company will contact the applicant if it feels she matches the opening. Finally, if she doesn't hear from it within ten business days, her resume will go on file. You can conclude that the review process takes about ten business days, and if she hasn't been contacted in that time, she didn't get the job.

► What kind of notice can you conclude this is?
(1) a personal note sent to this individual applicant
(2) a form notice sent to all applicants

Again, you're correct if you chose **(2)**. The way the notice is worded, with no personal details, lets you conclude this. You can also use your knowledge of the real world and business form letters to conclude that this, too, is a form.

► What conclusion can you draw about the company's attitude?
(1) It cares about its employees and their job satisfaction.
(2) It cares only about profits and employee productivity.

You are correct if you chose **(1)**. The fact that the company states not only that it considers its employees to be the best but also that it takes the time to communicate sincerely with potential employees lets you conclude that.

Key Ideas

- A conclusion is an idea figured out from different pieces of information.
- You can use your knowledge of the real world to help you draw conclusions when you read.

GED® TEST TIP

Be sure to read an entire passage before answering the questions about it. That way, you'll take all the information into account and won't "jump to conclusions."

PRACTICE 6.1

<u>Questions 1 through 5</u> refer to the following excerpt from an autobiography.

EXCERPTED FROM *THE STORY OF MY LIFE*

1 Once there were eleven tadpoles in a glass globe set in a window full of plants. I remember the eagerness with which I made discoveries about them. It was great fun to plunge my hand into the bowl and feel the tadpoles frisk about, and to let them slip and slide between my fingers. One day a more ambitious fellow leaped beyond the edge of the bowl and fell on the floor, where I found him to all appearance more dead than alive. The only sign of life was a slight wriggling of his tail. But no sooner had he returned to his element than he darted to the bottom, swimming round and round in joyous activity. He had made his leap, he had seen the great world, and was content to stay in his pretty glass house under the big fuchsia tree until he attained the dignity of froghood. Then he went to live in the leafy pool at the end of the garden, where he made the summer nights musical with his quaint love-song.

2 Thus I learned from life itself. At the beginning I was only a little mass of possibilities. It was my teacher who unfolded and developed them. When she came, everything about me breathed of love and joy and was full of meaning. She has never since let pass an opportunity to point out the beauty that is in everything, nor has she ceased trying in thought and action and example to make my life sweet and useful.

3 It was my teacher's genius, her quick sympathy, her loving tact which made the first years of my education so beautiful.

From *The Story of My Life* by Helen Keller.

1. What can you conclude about the writer's view of learning?

A. It is rewarding and one of life's joys.
B. It is better with a strict teacher.
C. It happens very slowly, if at all.
D. It happens most often when you are alone.

2. What conclusion can you draw about the writer's character?

The writer is

A. self-centered and demanding
B. confused and searching
C. fearful and shy
D. insightful and grateful

3. If Helen's teacher was trying to teach her addition, what method would the teacher most likely use?

A. make Helen stand and recite addition facts for one hour every day
B. assign an abundance of addition homework
C. show Helen how addition is used in everyday life
D. ask a well-known mathematician to teach the subject

4. How are the thoughts in this personal account organized?

A. as a comparison with a frog followed by a contrast
B. as a problem followed by its solution
C. in chronological order, or time sequence
D. as an anecdote followed by a generalization based on the anecdote

5. Later in her story, Helen compares a child's mind to a shallow brook "which ripples and dances merrily over the stony course of its education. . . ." Based on this information and the excerpt above, what is similar about the tadpole and a child?

A. They learn from others.
B. They are eager to grow into adulthood.
C. Youth can make them do dangerous things.
D. Their development is not entirely smooth.

Answers and explanations start on page 183.

Generalizations

A **generalization** is a broad statement about a group of people, objects, or things or about a type of event. Usually, it takes something that is true in one specific case and extends it to every possible case. For example, "My hometown celebrated Independence Day with fireworks last summer," is a fact about a specific Fourth of July in a specific town; a generalization could be "Every Independence Day, my hometown celebrates with fireworks."

► Identify one statement with *F* for a fact and the other with *G* for generalization.

(1) Every clerk in the store focuses on customer service more than any other aspect of the job.

(2) Tina, the manager of the women's shoe department, helps customers select just the right pair of shoes.

If you identified option **(2)** as being a fact and option **(1)** as being a generalization, you were correct. One hint that **(1)** is the generalization is the word "every." Words like *all, never,* and *always* show up in sentences that make broad, sweeping statements. The sentence about Tina, on the other hand, gives specific information about a specific person and so is not a generalization.

Generalizations can be valid and true when properly made. A writer can support a generalization with an example (like Tina, above) and information that shows why the example represents the whole group. Often, a generalization is too broad to apply to every member of a group, and a good writer will acknowledge that there are exceptions.

"Dogs are typically more attached to their owners than cats are, due in part to their evolution as pack animals. My dog will jump up to meet me as soon as I get home from work, while my cat will continue napping serenely until hunger motivates him to do otherwise."

► What example is given to support the generalization that "Dogs are typically more attached to their owners than cats"?

(1) Dogs evolved as pack animals.

(2) The author's dog jumps up to meet her, while her cat ignores her.

The example of the author's dog's attachment to her, **(2)**, illustrates and supports the generalization that most dogs show greater attachment to their owners. The specific example helps to show that the statement is based on experience.

Writers sometimes make the mistake of drawing **faulty generalizations** based on too little information. Imagine a person who bites into an apple, finds a worm, and concludes that all apples have worms in them. Since a generalization is a broad statement, a **valid generalization** requires broad knowledge to justify it. A generalization about American cities is more likely to be faulty if the writer bases on it only one city but more likely to be valid if the writer supports it with knowledge of 20 cities. With a larger sample, the writer is also better able to know whether to qualify a generalization as something that is true in most, but not all, cases.

► Identify one statement with *FG* for a faulty generalization and the other with *VG* for a valid generalization.

(1) Every breed of dog has four legs, so almost all dogs have four legs.

(2) Some dogs bark at kids, so all dogs must dislike or fear children.

You are correct if you chose **(1)** as the valid generalization: the writer shows awareness of many different types of dogs. Choice **(2)** is a faulty generalization; dogs may bark at children for reasons other than fear or dislike.

Key Ideas

- A generalization is a broad statement about a group or class.
- When assessing a generalization, evaluate the writer's evidence.
- An important factor in thoughtful reading is distinguishing between faulty and valid generalizations.

GED® TEST TIP

If you see a generalization, look for supporting evidence that may be introduced by phrases such as "for example," "such as," or "for instance."

PRACTICE 6.2

<u>Questions 1 through 3</u> are based on the following newspaper editorial.

OPINION: DOUBTS ABOUT GLOBAL WARMING

1 Shady Hollow was hit yesterday with record cold temperatures. And yet, despite this deep freeze, we'll continue to be subjected to the doctrine of global warming.

2 There is plenty to be said for fuel economy—anyone who lived through the energy crisis of the 1970s learned that lesson the hard way—but it's time we dispense with the terror campaign of doomsday climatology and recognize it for the pseudoscience that it is. Whenever Shady Hollow gets a big hit of winter weather, common sense tells us that the idea of "warming" seems fishy, yet climatologists insist on playing the same tune. More and more, this tune is taken up by policy-makers and government bodies, who steer our administrations accordingly. It must be the case that ivory towers have good weather stripping and excellent heating systems; as for the man on the street, he's finding his street a chilly one these days.

3 The simple fact is that it is logically impossible to reconcile a record cold temperature with the idea that it's getting warmer. A record cold temperature, and this may be worth spelling out, means exactly this: it has never been colder on this date in recorded history. If "warming" means what it sounds like it means—that temperatures are rising, not falling—then there is a real problem here, because that is quite simply not what is happening.

4 It may take years to get out from under the orthodoxy of the accepted opinion on climate change, but the facts themselves will not go away. Sooner or later, we'll be forced to acknowledge that we're still bundling up, and when that happens, we can stop building policy discussions around fictions.

1. What is a generalization that is made in paragraph 3?

A. Shady Hollow has the coldest temperatures in the region.
B. Global warming can only be valid if it predicts high temperatures.
C. On the whole, temperatures are not rising.
D. If children are taught a simpler theory, then a more complex theory should be set aside.

2. What evidence does the author give to support his generalization about global warming?

A. Shady Hollow was hit with a record cold temperature yesterday.
B. Ivory towers have good weather stripping.
C. It may take years to change opinions on climate change.
D. There is plenty to be said for fuel economy.

3. Which of the following pieces of information would put the author in a better position to make a generalization about climate change?

A. an account of the energy crisis of the 1970s
B. minutes of policy discussions from the 1970s through today
C. interviews with the "man on the street" from the 1990s through today
D. nationwide data tables of temperatures from the 1980s through today

Answers and explanations start on page 183.

LESSON

7

INTERPRETING NONFICTION AND INFORMATIONAL TEXT

Word Choice

Key Ideas

- Writers choose words carefully to make an impact on the reader.
- They deliberately choose words with positive, negative, or neutral connotations.
- Writers also use figurative language such as similes, metaphors, and personification to enhance descriptions.

GED® TEST TIP

Read closely to see how a writer's word choice affects how you picture something or feel about it. You may have to answer questions that require an awareness of the impact of both words' connotations and figurative language.

Writers make careful decisions to select words that will impact their audience. One choice that writers make is to select words that have a **connotation** associated with a particular image or feeling. Think of the different connotations of *dog*, *mutt*, and *man's best friend*. The word *dog* has a neutral connotation; it just describes the animal. To some, the word *mutt* would have a negative connotation, and the phrase *man's best friend* would have a positive connotation.

► Assign a *P* (positive) or an *N* (negative) to the following words to indicate the connotation that might be associated with them:
(1) shack
(2) villa

You are correct if you assigned an *N* to **(1)** and a *P* to **(2)**. The word *shack* probably brings to mind a small, poorly built or run-down building. On the other hand, the word *villa* might be associated with a house in the countryside or a vacation destination.

Writers use **figurative language** to make their descriptions clearer and more vivid. They use **similes**, which use the words *like* or *as* to compare two things; for example, "His voice was like velvet." This indicates that his voice was smooth. Another type of figurative language is a **metaphor**, which implies a comparison between two things. One familiar metaphor is "Life is a journey"; this compares two dissimilar things in order to describe life. A third figure of speech is **personification**, by which a writer assigns human characteristics to something that is not human. For example, a writer may describe a storm as "slashing at the windows and knocking on the door."

> If you look very carefully, you can find the island of Ascension on a map about midway between Angola, in Africa, and Brazil, in South America. This South Atlantic island has a population of about 1,000 people and is home to an important GPS ground antenna and a British air force base. Its volcanic terrain greets visitors with a forbidding aspect; place names like "Comfortless Cove" indicate how rocky and uninviting Ascension Island may appear. Even so, with its dry subtropical weather, excellent sport fishing, and unique wildlife, this barren outpost attracts about 1,000 tourists each year.

► What does the personification in the third sentence suggest about Ascension Island?
(1) Tourists are forbidden to visit the island.
(2) The island doesn't look like a good place to visit.

You are correct if you chose **(2)**. The writer refers to the island as if it were a person with an unfriendly appearance. Since the last sentence states that tourists do visit the island, you know that they are not forbidden to do so.

PRACTICE 7

Questions 1 through 5 refer to the following product description.

A COOL NEW BLANKET

1 Many people rely on electric blankets to keep warm on winter nights without turning on expensive central heating. In summer, though, there's no alternative to noisy fans and energy-hogging air conditioners if you want to stay cool . . . until now. The Starlight company recently introduced its newest product: an electric blanket that keeps you cool even on sweltering summer nights.

2 The CoolForter blanket works like an electric blanket, but it feels like a dream. The blanket contains a full tenth of a mile of flexible hose, fully insulated between layers of soft cotton. A small, quiet compressor refrigerates the safely enclosed cooling chemical and circulates it continuously through the coils. The CoolForter coddles you in refreshing comfort, and you never have to worry about waking up shivering. That's because your sleeping temperature is precisely controlled by the built-in thermostat, which can be adjusted to your exact temperature preference.

3 Your CoolForter blanket also matches your decorating preferences: the replaceable cover comes in a wide variety of bland colors to suit any décor. If you decide to redecorate, choose from a selection of fun and gaudy prints to liven up your room.

4 Best of all, the CoolForter saves you money every time you use it. Consuming an average of just 80 watts, the twin-size blanket is like a regular household lightbulb, costing just pennies per day to run. It's an investment in comfort that will pay for itself many times over the lifetime of its generous ten-year warranty and beyond.

1. In paragraph 2, what is compared to a dream?

A. an electric blanket
B. the flexible hose used in the CoolForter blanket
C. the cotton insulating layers
D. the CoolForter blanket

2. What could be a reason that the writer used the word "coddles" in paragraph 2?

A. to show that the blanket keeps its user warm
B. to show that the blanket is a pleasant indulgence
C. to show that the blanket keeps its user cool
D. to show that the user can wrap herself up in the blanket

3. What word could the writer have used instead of "chemical" in paragraph 2 that would have a less negative connotation?

A. fluid
B. antifreeze
C. contaminant
D. water

4. Which word in paragraph 3 means "neutral" and has a negative connotation?

A. decorating
B. replaceable
C. bland
D. gaudy

5. Why is "like a regular household lightbulb" from paragraph 4 an effective use of a comparison using figurative language?

A. It reminds the consumer that, while a lightbulb generates heat, the CoolForter blanket keeps its user cool.
B. It makes the CoolForter blanket seem ordinary.
C. It emphasizes the difference in cost between running a regular lightbulb and operating a compact fluorescent lightbulb.
D. It allows the consumer to compare the CoolForter's energy usage to that of a familiar item.

Answers and explanations start on page 183.

LESSON

8

Writer's Tone and Point of View

Key Ideas

- The writer's attitude toward a subject is conveyed by the tone of the writing.
- To determine tone, look at word choice and manner of expression. How would the writer sound reading the piece?
- The writer's point of view is the position she is writing from.

ON THE GED® TEST

Some kinds of tone you might see in GED® passages are formal or informal, positive or negative, objective, sarcastic, arrogant, concerned, affectionate, or nostalgic.

Tone

A writer usually has a certain attitude toward the subject he or she is writing about. This attitude is the **tone** of the piece. The tone is not directly stated. You have to sense it by the writer's choice of words and manner of expression.

As you read this drama review, ask yourself, "What tone of voice would the author have if she were reading this aloud to me?"

> Watching actor Brian Dennehy as Willy Loman in the stage production of *Death of a Salesman* was transforming. I know intellectually that live theater is better than movies. Movie actors reshoot scenes until they are perfect. An actor on stage has one chance to get it right. It is immediate. The actors are breathing human beings in the same room with you. Theater provides the opportunity for strong emotions to surface, right there, in the moment. Seeing a play often envelops me in energy.
>
> But I've never gone so far as to cry at a theater performance until now. I cried because Dennehy's Loman reminded me of my father, of the brevity of our lives, of how easy it is to waste our lives. This was not an intellectual response. I suddenly heard what this man on stage was saying—his life wasn't worth living, though he had tried hard, had a devoted wife and two sons. It didn't matter that this play was written in the 1940s. Mr. Dennehy stood on stage and roared at us about our lives now. It was hard-hitting, emotional drama.

► Which of the following best describes the tone of this piece?
(1) positive and somewhat awed
(2) cool and objective

The correct response is **(1)**. The writer states positive opinions. She also chooses short, clipped expressions—"It is immediate" and "right there, in the moment"—that by themselves create a sense of drama and awe. If the tone were cool and objective, you would not sense the writer's emotional attitude toward the play.

Point of View

The **point of view** of a piece is "where the author is coming from"—that is, the writer's background and experiences that may affect her opinions. For example, when you read a column in a newspaper, you can usually tell whether the writer has a liberal or a conservative point of view.

► What point of view does the writer of the review above have?
(1) that of a person who prefers sitting at home watching TV
(2) that of an enthusiastic theatergoer

You are correct if you chose **(2)**. You can conclude that the writer goes to the theater ("Seeing a play often envelops me") and enjoys it ("theater is better than movies"). Knowing this helps you evaluate the merits of the review.

PRACTICE 8

Questions 1 through 5 refer to the following review.

EXCERPTED FROM "TALKING BACK TO THE TUBE"

1 CBS delivered a television low mark called *Big Brother.* Focusing on ten fame-seeking, people-pleasing, hair-teasing losers willing to submit to surveillance by a nation of snoops for three months, it was so bad that it wasn't even good. Forget about camp reversals that transform trash into the perversely fascinating, forget about the Cheese Factor, which allows a pop-cultural product to be moldy and musty and stinky and still taste good. *Big Brother* was so bad that even Jean-Paul Sartre would have yawned, and the dude wrote hundreds of pages about useless passion in *Being and Nothingness.*

2 But something good did come of *Big Brother,* something wicked and warped and witty, something created by people with way too much time on their hands and way too much venom in their bite. While the reality series was channeling banality through the cable cords and over the airwaves six nights a week, a small crew of writers were deconstructing and eviscerating the tedium on the Internet. They were taking hours and hours of prime-time dross and turning it into decadent, amoral, sharp, electronic gold.

3 Internet sass.

4 You gotta love it, if only because it keeps razor-tongued fanatics and uncensored savants off the streets and out of trouble.

5 Not only was there a site devoted entirely to the ridiculing of CBS, *Big Brother,* its ten cast members, their families, host Julie Chen, and the gaseous *Big Brother* house pug, but a number of other general interest sites, notably Salon.com, spent the summer providing wry daily updates on the non-goings-on of the non-people in the non-house. They, too, took the non-pulse of a DOA television series and gave it a semblance of life on the Internet.

1. Who are referred to as "razor-tongued fanatics and uncensored savants" (paragraph 4)?

A. the television writers
B. the television cast of *Big Brother*
C. the Internet writers
D. the Internet audience

2. Which of the following best summarizes the reviewer's point about *Big Brother*?

A. The Internet reviews were much more interesting than the TV show.
B. The TV show was so bad that it was funny.
C. Internet writers are better than TV writers.
D. The main problem was with the ten people on the TV show.

3. What opinion is supported by the statement "even Jean-Paul Sartre would have yawned, and the dude wrote hundreds of pages about useless passion" (paragraph 1)?

A. The show was boring.
B. The show should have been longer.
C. The show needed more passion.
D. The show was incomprehensible.

4. Which of the following best describes the tone of this review?

A. apologetic
B. nostalgic for earlier shows
C. informal and hip
D. objective

5. From whose point of view is this piece likely written?

A. a television script writer
B. a person who hates watching TV
C. someone knowledgeable about the media
D. a disgruntled fan

Answers and explanations start on page 183.

LESSON

9

Text Structure

Writers make choices about how to organize informational and nonfiction materials based on their purpose. You have already seen two text structures: cause and effect, which shows how one thing made another happen, and compare and contrast, which illustrates similarities and differences.

There are other **text structures** often used for informational text:

- **Example**—introduces an unfamiliar topic and then follows with common examples to aid understanding.
- **Pros and Cons**—explains a situation by first presenting its benefits and then portraying its deficiencies in order to present both sides.
- **Chronological Order** or **Process**—presents details in the order in which they occur; also referred to as a **sequence** of events.
- **Elaboration**—makes a statement and indicates that additional information or an explanation will follow.

These text structures use different types of **transitions** to guide the reader from one idea to the next. Many of these are familiar to you.

Text Structure	Purpose	Sample Transitions
Example	Organizes illustrations that support a concept	for example, for instance, such as, to illustrate
Pros and Cons	Shows benefits and drawbacks	on the one hand, on the other hand
Chronological Order or Process	Describes events and procedures	before, after, next, following, meanwhile, until
Elaboration	Expands with additional details	additionally, furthermore, moreover

Key Ideas

- Writers may use different text structures depending on what they are writing about.
- One of the main tools writers use to create different text structures is transition words, which create relationships between ideas.

GED® TEST TIP

You will need to be aware of different types of text structure to answer questions, but you will not need to identify any structures by their names.

Practice using an understanding of text structure by reading the paragraph and answering the question below.

> Today, there are millions of workers who are not employees in the traditional sense; they are called "contract workers." These are self-employed individuals who have contracts with different businesses. For example, a graphic artist may have several different clients and design a newsletter for one and a website for another. Contract workers pay for their own equipment, supplies, and benefits—such as health insurance.

► What is an example that explains the concept of "contract workers"?
(1) They are not employees in the traditional sense.
(2) They may have contracts with several businesses.

Choice **(2)** illustrates the concept of contract workers by explaining that they have several different clients rather than one employer. Choice **(1)** is not an example that helps to explain contract work; it just explains what contract workers are not.

PRACTICE 9

<u>Questions 1 and 2</u> **refer to this scientific experiment.**

COWPOX, SMALLPOX, AND IMMUNITY

In 1796, British physician Edward Jenner conducted an experiment intended to help develop a viable treatment for the deadly smallpox disease. Some time before, he had noticed that dairymaids in his village commonly became infected with cowpox. Cowpox is an illness that is very similar to smallpox, but it is not deadly. The dairymaids who caught cowpox later turned out to be immune to smallpox. This led Jenner to experiment with whether he could make a test subject immune to smallpox by first infecting that person with cowpox. His test subject was a young boy named James. First, Jenner made small cuts on James's skin and inserted liquid from the cowpox sores of a local dairymaid. After being exposed to the disease, James caught cowpox and later recovered. After the boy's recovery from cowpox, Jenner exposed James to smallpox and found that the boy was immune. Today, scientists and medical professionals know that the cowpox and smallpox viruses are so similar that the body's immune system cannot tell them apart.

1. What step in the process came before James's recovery from cowpox?

A. his immunity to smallpox
B. exposure to the cowpox disease
C. scientists' discovery that cowpox and smallpox are similar
D. Jenner exposing James to smallpox

2. Which of the following phrases from the passage helps to understand the order of the steps in the process?

A. "cannot tell them apart"
B. "Jenner made small cuts"
C. "After being exposed to the disease"
D. "make a test subject immune"

<u>Question 3</u> **refers to this discussion of gardening.**

THE UPS AND DOWNS OF GARDENING

Planting and maintaining a backyard garden can have many benefits, but it also brings challenges. On the one hand, successful gardeners often express deep feelings of accomplishment and satisfaction in their gardens. Gardening can involve good exercise and fresh air, and spending time outdoors can be a healthy escape from everyday responsibilities and concerns. A flower garden provides a beautiful view that often attracts delightful visitors, including butterflies and hummingbirds. A vegetable garden provides nutritious food and can add up to significant savings on your grocery bill. An herb garden can supply alternatives to unhealthy ingredients such as salt and oil.

On the other hand, planting and maintaining a garden can be very expensive and time-consuming, and a garden may fail despite your best efforts. Proper soil and fertilizers must be bought, and plants or seeds must be chosen. It is also important to consider the watering and feeding of the garden to ensure proper growth. A number of factors beyond your immediate control may affect the success of your garden. If the season's weather is extreme in any way—too dry, too rainy, too hot, or too cold—it can damage tender plants and undo your hard work, wasting your investment of time and money. Similarly, invasive pests and diseases can be devastating to your home garden and can be difficult and expensive to control.

3. Which of the following is one of the writer's arguments against planting and maintaining a backyard garden?

A. Time outdoors often alleviates stress.
B. A number of factors can damage a garden.
C. Having too many daily chores is stressful.
D. Rain is bad for a garden.

Answers and explanations start on page 183.

Interpreting Nonfiction and Informational Text Practice Questions

Questions 1 through 4 refer to the following excerpt from an autobiography.

EXCERPTED FROM *THE LIAR'S CLUB*

1 That fall my school career didn't go much better. I got suspended from my second-grade class twice, first for biting a kid named Phyllis who wasn't, to my mind, getting her scissors out fast enough to comply with the teacher, then again for breaking my plastic ruler over the head of a boy named Sammy Joe Tyler, whom I adored. A pale blue knot rose through the blond stubble of his crew cut. Both times I got sent to the principal, a handsome ex-football coach named Frank Doleman who let Lecia and me call him Uncle Frank. (Lecia and I had impressed Uncle Frank by both learning to read pretty much without instruction before we were three. Mother took us each down to his office in turn, and we each dutifully read the front page of the day's paper out loud to him, so he could be sure it wasn't just some story we'd memorized.)

2 He let me stay in his office playing chess all afternoon with whoever wandered in. He loved pitting me against particularly lunkheaded fifth- and sixth-grade boys who'd been sent down for paddlings they never got. He'd try to use my whipping them at chess to make them nervous about how dumb they were. "Now this little bitty old second-grader here took you clean in six plays. Don't you reckon you need to be listening to Miss Vilimez instead of cutting up?" When Mrs. Hess led me solemnly down the hall to Frank Doleman's office, I would pretend to cry, but thought instead about Brer Rabbit as he was being thrown into the briar patch where he'd been born and raised, and screaming *Please don't throw me in that briar patch!*

From *The Liar's Club* by Mary Karr, New York: Penguin Books, 1995.

1. If the writer had attended an elementary school dance, which of the following might she have done?

   A. made fun of everyone as they danced
   B. sat and played chess with the boys
   C. been too shy to dance with anyone
   D. hit a boy in the arm to get his attention

2. What is meant by the statement "I . . . thought instead about Brer Rabbit as he was being thrown into the briar patch where he'd been born and raised and screaming *Please don't throw me in that briar patch!*" (paragraph 2)?

   A. She was so upset that she wanted to scream.
   B. She was just pretending she didn't want to go to the principal's office.
   C. She hoped the teacher would let her back in class if she pleaded with her.
   D. She was afraid of what would happen in the principal's office.

3. What type of principal was Frank Doleman?

   A. strict
   B. ineffective
   C. unusual
   D. mean

4. Later in the autobiography, the narrator describes herself as "small-boned and skinny, but more than able to make up for that."

   Based on this description and the excerpt, which of the following best describes the narrator?

   A. confident
   B. serious
   C. friendly
   D. hopeful

<u>Questions 5 through 9</u> refer to this article about soda.

TURNING BACK A SUGARY TIDE

1 The popular soft drinks known as soda, pop, or both trace their origins all the way back to 1767, when English chemist Joseph Priestley invented a method for carbonating water. Over the last two and a half centuries, soda has risen to prominence primarily as a sweet beverage for social occasions. By the mid-1990s, soda had become the beverage of choice for adolescents. This increase in consumption has not been without negative consequences. Since the early 1980s, obesity rates for young Americans have risen steadily, as has the incidence of juvenile diabetes, heart disease, and myriad other ailments related to poor diet.

2 To counteract the harmful effects of overindulging in soda, federal, state, and local governments have taken steps in recent years. First Lady Michelle Obama promotes healthier diet choices and campaigns against childhood obesity. Several states now require that restaurants post calorie information next to all menu items, including beverages. In a controversial move, New York City mayor Michael Bloomberg proposed banning the sale of sodas over 16 ounces in city eateries. Additionally, many school districts around the country have banned the sale of soda in school vending machines.

3 These efforts appear to be paying off: latest statistics indicate that the percentage of teens who consume soda daily has fallen from 75 percent in the 1990s to 62 percent in 2009. However, most teens who abandon soda as a daily beverage replace it with other high-sugar choices, such as juice or energy and sport drinks. While many of these products have slightly less sugar than soda, the net impact of regular consumption is likely to be just as damaging in the long term. Regulating the sale of soda is a step in the right direction, but more can be done to educate young people about the dangers of a diet overflowing with sugary beverages.

5. Which of the following best describes the tone of this article?

   A. playful but informative
   B. pessimistic and sarcastic
   C. concerned but hopeful
   D. neutral and inquisitive

6. Which of the following best describes the author's point of view on reducing consumption of sugared beverages?

   A. The sale of soda should be outlawed due to the beverage's negative impact on health.
   B. Consuming diet soda is healthier than consuming regular soda.
   C. A young person's decision to consume soda is a personal choice that must be respected.
   D. Young people will choose healthier beverages if they are better educated about the dangers of consumption of sugared beverages.

7. According to paragraph 3, what will likely be the "net impact" of regularly consuming juice, energy, and sport drinks instead of soda?

   A. Teenagers who consume these beverages instead of soda will avoid the health hazards associated with soda.
   B. Soda manufacturers will likely go out of business since fewer consumers will be purchasing their products.
   C. Young people who drink these beverages regularly will eventually suffer from the same ailments as those who drink soda regularly.
   D. Many of the teenagers who drink juice, energy, and sport drinks will choose healthier food options to supplement their diets.

8. According to the passage, the author most likely regards the steps to curb soda consumption described in paragraph 2 as

   A. disruptive but essential
   B. effective to some extent
   C. invasive and extreme
   D. well-intentioned but unenforceable

9. In the beginning of paragraph 3, the words "These efforts" refer to which of the following?

   A. creating soda from carbonated water
   B. recommending energy and sport drinks instead of soda
   C. reducing excessive consumption of soda
   D. increasing educational programs about the effects of soda

Questions 10 through 12 refer to the following business document.

EXCERPTED FROM *INDEPENDENT CONSULTANT'S BROCHURE AND LETTER HANDBOOK* BY HERMAN HOLTZ

1 The National Association of Temporary Services (NATS), which represents the nation's temporary help employers, testified today before the House Ways and Means Committee on the employer mandate and related provisions of the President's Health Security Act (H.R. 3600).

2 Edward A. Lenz, NATS senior vice president, legal and government affairs, said that the temporary help industry supports the principle of universal coverage, but has serious concerns that the cost of mandates could weaken the ability of the temporary help industry to act as a "jobs bridge" to regular, full-time employment.

3 According to Lenz, the temporary help industry has recently "assumed a new and vital role—by helping to ease the burden on individuals during the current restructuring of the American work force. Temporary work offers displaced workers a critical safety net of income, benefits, and skills training and often provides a bridge back to regular, full-time employment."

4 In addition, the Association is concerned that the mandates, as currently structured, would "also impose enormous administrative burdens" due to annual temporary employee turnover in the range of 400 to 600 percent. If employer mandates are adopted, Lenz urged Congress to create a mechanism that relates premium payments to hours worked, such as a simple payroll tax.

10. Which of the following states one of the main concerns of NATS?

A. NATS won't be able to offer skills training to temporary employees if the government mandates coverage.
B. There will be an increase in turnover of temporary employees if the government mandates coverage.
C. The cost of mandated coverage will lessen the ability of NATS to hire and supply temporary workers.
D. Restructuring the work force is a burden to all Americans.

11. According to the press release, why have businesses supplying temporary help become even more necessary?

A. Many workers are losing their jobs and need temporary jobs until they find permanent work again.
B. There is not enough work for everyone to have a full-time permanent job.
C. The job turnover rate has gone as high as 400 to 600 percent.
D. More and more workers do not want permanent full-time work.

12. What is the overall purpose of this piece?

A. to stimulate debate over universal health insurance coverage
B. to impress both the Congress and the president
C. to describe various alternatives to mandated coverage
D. to raise awareness of an issue

Questions 13 through 16 refer to the following excerpt from a historical feminist speech.

EXCERPTED FROM *A TREASURY OF THE WORLD'S GREAT SPEECHES*

1 We have met here today to discuss our rights and wrongs, civil and political, and not, as some have supposed, to go into the detail of social life alone. We do not propose to petition the legislature to make our husbands just, generous, and courteous, to seat every man at the head of a cradle, and to clothe every woman in male attire. None of these points, however important they may be considered by leading men, will be touched in this convention. As to their costume, the gentlemen need feel no fear of our imitating that, for we think it in violation of every principle of taste, beauty, and dignity; notwithstanding all the contempt cast upon our loose, flowing garments, we still admire the graceful folds, and consider our costume far more artistic than theirs. Many of the nobler sex seem to agree with us in this opinion, for the bishops, priests, judges, barristers, and lord mayors of the first nation on the globe, and the Pope of Rome, with his cardinals, too, all wear the loose flowing robes, thus tacitly acknowledging that the male attire is neither dignified nor imposing. No, we shall not molest you in your philosophical experiments with stocks, pants, high-heeled boots, and Russian belts. Yours be the glory to discover, by personal experience, how long the kneepan can resist the terrible strapping down which you impose, in how short time the well-developed muscles of the throat can be reduced to mere threads by the constant pressure of the stock, how high the heel of a boot must be to make a short man tall, and how tight the Russian belt may be drawn and yet have wind enough left to sustain life.

2 But we are assembled to protest against a form of government existing without the consent of the governed—to declare our right to be free. . . .

From a speech at a woman's-rights convention by Elizabeth Cady Stanton, as reprinted in *A Treasury of the World's Great Speeches*, edited by Houston Peterson, New York: Simon & Schuster, 1954, 1965.

13. Which of the following best restates the lines "Yours be the glory to discover . . . how long the kneepad can resist the terrible strapping down which you impose" (paragraph 1)?

   A. Men do not understand how uncomfortable women's clothes are.
   B. Women will not resort to wearing pants or other restrictive men's clothing.
   C. Men will only understand women when women dress like them.
   D. Men and women will be equal only when they both wear belts and collars.

14. What is a "stock" (paragraph 1)?

   A. a man's jacket
   B. a wooden frame holding a prisoner
   C. a loose shirt
   D. a cloth worn around the neck

15. If the speaker attended a fancy tea party, which of the following would she be most likely to do?

   A. be on her best behavior
   B. speak up about current events
   C. treat the hostess like royalty
   D. comment on everyone's clothing

16. Later in the speech, Stanton states that "over the horns of bigotry and prejudice will be our way." Based on this and the excerpt, you can conclude that Stanton is giving this speech for what reason?

   A. Women are fighting for the right to vote.
   B. Women are tired of being made to wear dresses.
   C. Husbands need to be made just and generous.
   D. Many people mistakenly judge others by their appearance.

Answers and explanations start on page 183.

LESSON

1

ANALYZING NONFICTION AND INFORMATIONAL TEXT

Purpose of Text

Key Ideas

- Writers have different reasons, or purposes, for writing.
- The main purposes for writing are to narrate a story, to inform, to persuade, and to entertain.

GED® TEST TIP

As you are reading passages on the test, ask yourself, "Why did the author write this story, article, or speech?" That will help you to understand the purpose.

When you read *GED® Reasoning Through Language Arts* passages, it is important that you comprehend not only what the author is writing about but also the **purpose**—the reason *why* he or she is writing this passage. Authors of nonfiction passages have one or more of the following purposes:

- **Narrate**—Narrative passages typically recount events chronologically, that is, in the order in which they happened. Examples include a person's life story and hour-by-hour developments in a news story.
- **Inform**—The author seeks to present facts and data to explain a subject, situation, or idea. Examples include news articles, financial summaries, and scientific findings.
- **Persuade**—The author seeks to change readers' minds, and the passage includes the author's opinions, recommendations, or conclusions. Examples are political speeches, newspaper editorials, and entertainment reviews.
- **Entertain**—Authors writing to entertain are trying to amuse or interest their readers. Examples include a humorous memoir or articles about celebrities.

Read the paragraph and answer questions about the writer's purpose.

According to market research, video game sales—including digital downloads and apps—in the United States topped $15 billion in 2010. The most popular game genres were Action (21.7 percent of sales), Sports (16.3 percent), and Shooter (15.9 percent). Family Entertainment games accounted for only 9.1 percent of sales.

► What is the writer's purpose for this paragraph?
(1) to present facts about video game sales
(2) to convince readers that Family Entertainment games' sales should be increased

► Imagine there is an additional sentence at the end of the paragraph. "Because popular games in the Action and Shooter genres may contain extremely graphic violence, parents must be educated about how to monitor their children's purchases and game play." What would be the purpose of the revised paragraph about video games?
(1) to entertain readers with an amusing fact about video games
(2) to persuade parents to become more involved in their children's use of video games

In the first question, choice **(1)** is correct because the writer gives facts and not persuasive information. In the second question, once the information about violence has been added, choice **(2)** is correct because the statement offers a recommendation to persuade, not entertain, parents.

Practice 1

After an explosion damaged critical systems on the spacecraft of the Apollo 13 mission, the three astronauts aboard were forced to make the journey back to Earth inside the Lunar Module (LM), the small vessel originally designed to land on the Moon's surface. Using the LM as a "lifeboat" provided the astronauts with enough oxygen and water for the return trip, but it also introduced a new problem: there was no way to recycle used air. To solve the problem, engineers back on Earth cataloged all of the spare parts and detachable pieces inside the Apollo modules. From these, they prototyped various devices the astronauts might use to make filters to use inside the LM. The Earth-based engineers talked the astronauts through the process of constructing and installing the makeshift filters. The engineers' quick thinking and creativity provided the astronauts with a way to maintain breathable air throughout their journey back to Earth.

1. The purpose of the paragraph above is to

- A. explain how the Lunar Module worked
- B. tell how creative engineers saved astronauts
- C. inform about the space program's value
- D. convince that engineers are essential workers

Our state should cut all sales taxes on the purchase of new automobiles to encourage buying new cars. Older cars do not run as cleanly as new vehicles and, thus, contribute to air pollution. Additionally, older cars are less safe to operate. One study estimates that last year, as many as 500 deaths or serious injuries from accidents in our state could have been prevented by the sorts of safety features that are standard on newer-model cars.

2. The writer most likely includes the fact about preventable deaths or serious injuries in automobile accidents because it

- A. is the conclusion the writer is trying to prove
- B. supports the writer's main recommendation
- C. may shock readers into becoming safer drivers
- D. will encourage legislators to cut sales taxes

Questions 3 and 4 are based on this passage.

SILK: NOW AND THEN

Modern consumers do not appreciate the historical importance of the fabric silk. Silk fabric is valued for its smooth texture and shimmering appearance. It is also highly absorbent, making silk clothing comfortable in both high and low temperatures. Today, silk fabrics remain somewhat more expensive than cotton cloth and synthetic textiles, but many would be surprised to learn that silk was arguably the most important product in Asia and Europe for nearly 1,000 years.

Originally, sericulture—the technology of making silk cloth from silkworm cocoons—was known only in China. Around 2,000 years ago, nomads from Central Asia would travel to China to trade horses and other goods for silk cloth. As these nomads ventured West, silk became known to people in the Middle East and Europe. Over time, traders established routes over 4,000 miles long from China to Europe that became known as the Silk Road. Throughout the ancient and medieval world, silk was the preferred fabric for the robes of royalty and the very wealthy.

3. This purpose of this passage is to

- A. criticize ancient peoples for overvaluing silk
- B. explain how silk fabrics are made
- C. entertain readers who enjoy historical travel
- D. inform about the historical importance of silk

4. How does the information in the second paragraph support the purpose of the passage?

- A. It illustrates why silk remains an expensive product today.
- B. It refutes the notion that silk is a valuable product in the modern world.
- C. It provides examples of silk's historical importance in trade and culture.
- D. It compares the value of silk to that of other products from Asia.

Answers and explanations start on page 184.

LESSON

2

Effectiveness of Argument

Key Ideas

- An argument is a statement that takes a position.
- An argument consists of a conclusion about the issue and supporting evidence.
- Critically reading an argument involves understanding the stated or implied assumptions behind the claim.

You may think of an argument as being a quarrel between people. However, in reading and writing, an **argument** consists of the following:

- A statement, which is a **conclusion** about something
- The **evidence**, which is support that is given for the argument
- The **premises** (and unstated premises, called assumptions) behind the argument

Writers should provide supporting evidence for their argument; otherwise, they are just making an unsupported claim. Sometimes writers clearly state the premises behind their argument, but in other cases, you may need to read carefully to **infer** their assumptions.

Read the argument below and answer the questions that follow.

> In the past few years, the majority of state governments have passed laws making it illegal to send text messages while driving. These laws are clearly a good decision for which legislators should be praised. Drivers are 23 times more likely to have accidents while texting than they are while driving undistracted. It is common sense that the government has a responsibility to protect its citizens from the recklessness of a careless few.

1. What is the writer's argument about anti-texting laws?
   (1) Such laws are a good idea because drivers are prone to accidents while texting.
   (2) The majority of state governments have passed laws making it illegal to text while driving.

2. What evidence is given in support of the author's argument?
   (1) Drivers are 23 times more prone to accidents while texting.
   (2) Members of state legislatures should be praised.

3. Which of the following is likely one of the author's unstated premises?
   (1) Drivers must police themselves to avoid dangerous situations.
   (2) A state government has a responsibility to ensure citizens' safety.

The answer to Question 1 is **(1)**. The author's opinion is that anti-texting laws are "good" and "should be praised." The rest of the argument supports that opinion. The answer to Question 2 is **(1)**. A statistic such as "23 times more likely" is typical of the factual evidence you can expect to see on the GED® Test. The answer to Question 3 is **(2)**. We know that the assumption that governments should protect citizens is a premise of the author because he praises legislators for passing these laws to make roads and highways safer.

GED® TEST TIP

On some passages, writers may use terms such as "for these reasons," "it follows that," or "therefore" to indicate their conclusion. In other cases, you may have to carefully analyze the passage to find the argument.

PRACTICE 2

Questions 1 through 4 refer to this passage about the minimum wage.

MAKING MINIMUM WAGE WORK FOR WORKERS

1 The minimum wage is the lowest salary that a company can legally pay its employees. The federal minimum wage is the lowest allowed in the nation, but many states have set minimum wages higher than the national number.

2 Several states have taken the sensible step of automatically raising their minimum wage to adjust for inflation and consumer price increases. This policy ensures that low-paid workers are paid a stable, livable income over the long term. Raising the federal minimum wage, however, requires direct action by lawmakers. As a result, over the past 40 years, the federal minimum wage has not kept pace with the rate of inflation. Nowadays, full-time minimum-wage workers earn so little money that many have fallen below the poverty line. In the case of the minimum wage, the federal government should follow the lead of the states. Congress needs to establish automatic wage increases triggered by increases in inflation and changes to the consumer price index. That is the only way to ensure sustainable earnings for hard-working citizens.

1. Which of the following is the main point of the passage?

A. States' minimum wages differ from the federal minimum wage.
B. The federal government should automatically raise the minimum wage to match price increases.
C. The federal minimum wage ensures a comfortable living for people earning it.
D. State minimum wages are the result of political games played with people's livelihoods.

2. What is the writer's argument about states that automatically raise their minimum wages?

A. Those states' wages have not kept pace with the rate of inflation.
B. People earning more than minimum wage in those states are wealthy.
C. Those states have many workers in poverty.
D. Those states have systems superior to the federal system of manual increases.

3. What evidence is given to support the author's argument?

A. Some states have minimum wages lower than the federal minimum wage.
B. The federal government should adjust its minimum wage automatically.
C. Over the past 40 years, the federal minimum wage has not kept pace with inflation.
D. As a result of inflation, $1 in 1972 was worth more than $5 is worth today.

4. Which of the following is most likely to be one of the author's assumptions?

A. Employees under the age of 18 might be paid less than the minimum wage.
B. Ensuring sustainable incomes for hardworking citizens is a responsibility of lawmakers.
C. Employees earning the federal minimum wage cannot support themselves and their families.
D. The past 40 years have experienced significantly higher inflation than was expected.

Answers and explanations start on page 184.

LESSON

3

ANALYZING NONFICTION AND INFORMATIONAL TEXT

Validity of Arguments

Key Ideas

- An argument may or may not be valid.
- For the argument to be valid, it needs to be supported by relevant and provable evidence.
- Critical thinking requires questioning both the method of argument and the source of supporting evidence.

GED® TEST TIP

When you are reading a writer's argument, don't evaluate it based on what you already believe. Think critically about whether or not the writer adequately and validly supports the argument.

Just because a writer makes an argument does not mean you have to accept it as **valid**, or convincing. You need to analyze the supporting evidence. Below are some types of **support for arguments** and ways that you can question their legitimacy.

Type of Support	Description	Questions to Ask
Facts	Objective facts that can be tested or measured	Is the information complete, or is it partial or selectively chosen?
Data or Statistics	Numerical data that have been gathered or sampled	Do the numbers accurately represent the subject? How were they gathered?
Examples or Anecdotes	Stories to demonstrate the "truth"	Are the stories true? Are they relevant?
Authority	Testimonials from a recognized authority	Does the person really know the issue, or is he or she a spokesperson or celebrity?
Causality	Assertions that one thing caused another	Is this really a cause, or is it just a related factor?

In addition to analyzing the evidence, you need to be aware that sometimes writers use **emotional appeals** based on fear, pity, or getting you to "jump on the bandwagon."

> Gasoline prices spiked suddenly in the Weston metropolitan area last week when the local oil refinery went offline due to a facility-wide computer malfunction. Shortly thereafter, the average number of miles driven daily by Weston residents fell by a whopping 55 percent. Clearly, the higher gas prices were responsible for the decline in miles driven.

► What is the argument in the paragraph?
(1) Higher gas prices were responsible for the decline in miles driven.
(2) The spike in gas prices was due to a computer malfunction at the local refinery.

► Which of the following undermines the writer's argument?
(1) Oil refineries have stopped production in the past.
(2) Last week, a blizzard struck the Weston area, causing a state of emergency that required all nonemergency vehicles to stay off the roads.

For the first question, choice **(1)** is correct. The writer concludes that high gas prices caused the decline in driving and uses the background about the refinery shutdown as support. For the second question, choice **(2)** is correct. The writer's argument is faulty because she assumes that the high price of gasoline was the only cause of the reduction in driving. Choice **(2)** supplies another reasonable explanation for the reduced driving, thereby weakening the argument.

PRACTICE 3

Questions 1 through 4 refer to this passage about voting technology.

DIGITAL VOTING: A BETTER WAY TO COUNT

1 The large-scale adoption in 1996 of direct-recording electronic (DRE) voting marked the beginning of an era of superior voting technology. For as long as elections have been held, voting systems have been flawed in various ways. In mid-18th century America, voters called out their selections publicly. This assured an accurate count but meant voting could not be private. Paper ballots, on the other hand, were anonymous but could be easily forged or miscounted.

2 The next innovation was the mechanical-lever voting machine, introduced in the late 19th century. The use of this voting system peaked in the 1960s. Over the next several decades, the mechanical-lever machines were replaced by two early electronic voting systems: bubble sheets recorded by optical scanner and punch cards processed electronically. All of these systems were prone to glitches, such as the notorious "hanging chads" and unreadable ballots in Florida after the 2000 U.S. presidential election.

3 Now, many jurisdictions use all-electronic DRE systems. Every step of the voting process is electronic: the ballot appears on a screen, the voter indicates his or her selection via buttons or touch-screen technology, and results are stored on a memory card. In DRE voting, there is always a record of a voter's choices, and there is no chance of voters filling in the wrong bubble or of poorly punched cards that cause votes to go uncounted. For all of these reasons, DRE is clearly the most secure and accurate voting system available.

1. The main point of the passage is that

A. unlike optical-scanning and punch-card voting systems, DRE voting is completely electronic
B. punch-card voting systems caused a problem in the 2000 presidential election
C. DRE systems offer more security and accuracy than other voting systems
D. elections in America have changed greatly over the years

2. Which of the following is evidence to support the writer's argument?

A. When technology changes, voting systems change along with it.
B. DRE voting avoids problems associated with other voting systems.
C. Several voting systems have become obsolete because they violated voters' privacy.
D. No modern-day election would ever be conducted using a public voice vote.

3. What evidence is given to support the writer's argument?

A. Each voter's choices are recorded in the DRE voting system.
B. Mechanical-lever voting machines were replaced by other mechanical voting devices.
C. Punch-card voting involves electronic processing.
D. In the mid-18th century, public votes were popular.

4. Which of the following is an example of faulty reasoning that weakens the argument?

A. The writer claims that punch-card systems contributed to problems in the 2000 presidential election without providing any support for the claim.
B. The writer suggests that DRE voting was responsible for the demise of older voting systems, overlooking the possibility that there might have been another cause.
C. The writer fails to consider that even if DRE voting addresses all the flaws of previous systems, it may introduce other flaws of its own.
D. The author fails to provide evidence that voters in 18th-century America were wary of elections.

Answers and explanations start on page 185.

LESSON

4

Text Related by Theme or Topic

On the GED® Test, you may need to read related **paired passages** and answer questions based on your understanding of both of them. The two texts will be related by **topic** (what the passages address) or **theme** (the writer's message about a topic). You will need to understand each passage on its own and be able to **synthesize** (blend) information to draw a conclusion.

Below are two paragraphs about the same topic. One is a news story, and the other is an opinion piece. Read both selections and answer the questions based on your understanding and analysis of both texts.

News Story

Candy, greasy meals, and high-calorie sodas may be banned in U.S. elementary and high schools. According to news reports, new standards proposed by the Department of Agriculture would replace such items as fried potato chips with baked chips and sugary sodas with lower-calorie sport drinks. These regulations are a result of a child nutrition law, passed by the U.S. Congress to combat childhood obesity.

Response Letter

The paper announced that the government will be mandating "healthier food" in school cafeterias. Doesn't the government have anything better to do than to "babysit" our schools? Shouldn't the schools be focused on improving education, not monitoring behavior? Where is the research to show that school meals account for childhood obesity? This is just one more government intrusion into our personal lives.

► What is the topic of both of these selections?
(1) greasy food in school cafeterias
(2) new guidelines for healthy school meals

► What information is given in the news story?
(1) The government is "babysitting" our schools.
(2) Certain unhealthy foods may be banned from public schools.

► Which relevant argument is made in the response letter?
(1) The new regulations are a good way to help combat childhood obesity.
(2) The new regulations are a poor idea because monitoring student behavior is not a school's responsibility.

The correct choice in the first question is **(2)** because the news story reports on the regulations while the response letter criticizes them. In the second question, choice **(2)** is correct because it summarizes the factual information in the news story. The correct choice in the third question is **(2)** because the writer of the response letter clearly states her opposition to the new regulations.

Key Ideas

- The GED® Test will present two selections on a related topic or theme.
- Some questions will require comprehension and analysis of each piece on its own.
- Other questions will require a synthesis of information from the two sources.

GED® TEST TIP

When you answer questions related to two selections, skim the questions before you read the selections. That way, you can be thinking about how the test requires you to relate the pieces as you read them.

PRACTICE 4

Questions 1 through 4 refer to the paired passages below.

Passage 1

The online piracy of digital files is a major problem for the music industry. From 2004 to 2009, 30 billion songs were downloaded illegally, representing a loss of billions of dollars of revenue. Recent legislation, along with the shutdown of certain major file-sharing websites, has begun to stem the tide of piracy. The organization representing the music and recording industry, however, reports that the annual harm to the economy from piracy may be as high as $12.5 billion dollars a year. More must be done.

Passage 2

Online piracy is harmful to the music industry, but not only for the reasons the industry claims. The financial harm caused by piracy is often exaggerated. The recording industry's estimates are based on the prices of songs and the number of songs downloaded; in reality, a person who illegally downloaded 10,000 songs would download only a fraction of that number if forced to pay for each file. As a result, the actual loss of revenue caused by piracy is certainly much lower than the industry estimates. However, a fear of piracy has made investors cautious about signing new, experimental artists. That in itself is a cause for concern and a reason more needs to be done to halt illegal downloading.

---

1. The topic of both passages is

A. ways in which industries can exaggerate financial harm
B. examples of recent legislation to protect an industry
C. online piracy of music files
D. the signing of new, experimental musicians

2. The main argument of Passage 1 is that

A. new, experimental artists are necessary for the music industry to succeed
B. additional action to combat online piracy is warranted because piracy causes financial losses to the music industry
C. the shutdown of major file-sharing websites was a positive development because they contributed to $12.5 billion per year in damages
D. from 2004 to 2009, 30 billion songs were downloaded illegally

3. Which claim in Passage 2 supports the conclusion drawn in Passage 1?

A. Fear of piracy makes it difficult for new, experimental acts to get signed.
B. Recent legislation has begun to reduce the amount of online music piracy.
C. A person who downloads music illegally would likely download fewer songs if he or she had to pay for them.
D. Financial harm from illegal music downloads is often exaggerated.

4. With which of the following statements would the writers of both passages agree?

A. Online piracy of digital files has a harmful effect on the music industry.
B. Online piracy of digital files causes serious damage to the economy.
C. The main reason to combat online piracy is to ensure that new, experimental artists can find investors.
D. Music is important for a healthy society to function properly.

Answers and explanations start on page 185.

LESSON 5

Texts with Opposing Arguments

Key Ideas

- The GED® Test may present opposing arguments on the same topic.
- Some arguments will reach different conclusions because they use different types of evidence.
- Other opposing pairs of arguments may use the same evidence but have different underlying assumptions.

You have learned about writers' arguments and have seen how the GED® Test requires you to work with two related texts. In some cases, you may read two selections that have **opposing arguments** about the same topic. Read the selections below and think about the authors' claims, the **assumptions** or the thinking behind their positions, and the supporting evidence for each.

Argument

Coal, the source of half the energy in the United States, has been the dirtiest of all fossil fuels because it creates harmful emissions when burned. Help is on the way with the development of new "clean coal" technologies that reduce coal's environmental impact. These new technologies purify exhaust gases as coal burns (wet scrubbers) and prevent the formation of harmful emissions in the first place (low-NO*x* burners). There is even gasification, which avoids burning coal altogether.

Opposing Argument

"Clean coal" amounts to just an advertising slogan. Don't be fooled by claims about new technologies making coal a clean-burning fuel. The hazards to our environment start well before that. Coal mining wastes huge amounts of water—70 to 260 million gallons daily. Today's mining companies now use mountaintop removal, instead of traditional mining, to extract coal. Forty-nine states have issued fish intake advisories due to high mercury concentration in water, much of it due to run-off from coal mining.

GED® TEST TIP

When you read two selections with opposing viewpoints, carefully analyze each writer's arguments. Don't let your opinions on the topic influence how you answer the questions.

► What is the topic of both of these selections?
  (1) preventing air pollution from coal
  (2) the usefulness of "clean coal" technologies

You were right to pick choice **(2)**. The Argument suggests that "clean coal" will reduce coal's environmental impact, while the Opposing Argument contends that coal will continue to harm the environment.

► What type of evidence is provided in the Argument?
  (1) statistics demonstrating the effectiveness of "clean coal" technologies
  (2) facts about new "clean coal" technologies

Here, choice **(2)** is correct. The Argument lists and briefly describes the new technologies.

► How does the Opposing Argument confront the underlying assumption of the Argument?
  (1) It points out environmental damage caused by coal before it is burned, when "clean coal" technologies are not used.
  (2) It cites studies showing that "clean coal" technologies are less effective than their advocates claim they are.

Choice **(1)** is correct. Impacts from mining, water waste, and mercury run-off are among the other harms cited in the Opposing Argument.

PRACTICE 5

<u>Questions 1 through 4</u> **refer to the Argument and Opposing Argument below.**

ARGUMENT: Rating Systems for Movies Are Beneficial

In 1968, the Motion Picture Association of America (MPAA) replaced the complicated, morals-based Hays Code with the current, user-friendly MPAA rating system. This system is designed specifically to help parents decide whether a movie is appropriate for their child. Every parent in America knows what G, PG, PG-13, and R mean and can use these ratings to quickly judge suitability. Moreover, ratings now include descriptions that give even more information that parents can use to assess content and make wise movie-viewing decisions for their children. MPAA ratings take the guesswork out of at least one aspect of parenting!

OPPOSING ARGUMENT: Movie Rating Systems Are a Joke

A movie's MPAA rating—G, PG, PG-13, or R—is a familiar tag that parents, in particular, use to make fundamental decisions about family entertainment. Sadly, the rating system is more a marketing tool for the industry than a useful guide for parents. Consider that, in the early 1980s, unknowing parents exposed their children to alarming gore and violence under the PG rating, prompting the creation of the PG-13 rating. The result is that now, a movie that includes violence, drug use, gore, and sexual content can be marketed as a family-friendly PG-13 experience. Parents are better off finding an unbiased source of realistic reviews than trusting the MPAA rating system.

---

1. The topic of both passages is
   A. violence in movies
   B. good and bad parenting decisions
   C. the MPAA movie rating system
   D. motion picture marketing strategies

2. Which of the following is the main point of the Argument?
   A. The MPAA rating system replaced the Hays Code.
   B. The MPAA rating system is a useful tool for parents.
   C. Parents should consult a variety of sources before deciding which movies to allow their children to watch.
   D. The G, PG, PG-13, and R ratings are familiar and easy to understand.

3. The writer of the Opposing Argument would agree with which of the following statements?
   A. Parents overreacted to movie content in the 1980s.
   B. The PG-13 rating introduced a helpful distinction to the system.
   C. Violence and drug use are examples of family-friendly movie content.
   D. The MPAA rating system should not be trusted.

4. Which of the following conclusions could be drawn about the writer of the Argument?
   A. She largely approves of the MPAA rating system as a guideline for parents.
   B. She allows her children to watch movies rated PG but not those rated PG-13.
   C. She is wary of how the MPAA rating system judges violent content in movies.
   D. She believes that the Hays Code was detrimental to the movie industry.

Answers and explanations start on page 185.

LESSON

6

ANALYZING NONFICTION AND INFORMATIONAL TEXT

Texts with Related Graphic Information

Key Ideas

- The GED® Test will present some selections with accompanying graphics.
- Read the passage carefully and analyze the graphic.
- Evaluate whether each question is based on the text, the graphic, or a combination of the two.

GED® TEST TIP

When you see that a graphic accompanies a selection, ask yourself, "Is this graphic providing supporting material, or is it providing additional information?" If you understand that, you will be better able to answer the test questions.

When you read nonfiction and informational text in a textbook, magazine, or website, it is often accompanied by a **graphic**—an illustration, photograph, or diagram—that helps you to understand the information. On the GED® Test, you will need to combine information from text and graphics to draw conclusions and to make observations about how the graphic supports the information in the text. Practice with the text and graphic below.

"Mayfield" No More? The Changing American Household

Although *Leave It to Beaver* was a fictional television show, many advertisements, politicians, and movies still echo its portrayal of the typical American household of the 1950s: a married couple with children. A closer look at government statistics shows that it might be time to retool that image; today, fewer than half of American households are husband-wife households. In fact, more than a quarter of American households are now occupied by one person living alone—a significant group for marketers to target, as those who live alone are entirely responsible for all household purchases.

Percent Distribution of Households by Type

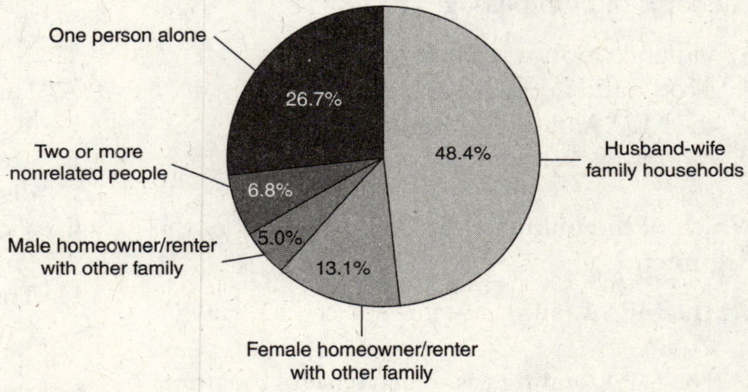

Source: U.S. Census Bureau

► What is the topic of the story and the graphic?
(1) the composition of American households
(2) advertising on *Leave It to Beaver*

If you answered **(1)**, you were correct. The story outlines the current make-up of American households, and the graphic supplies factual detail.

► How does the pie chart support the information in the story?
(1) It provides statistics comparing American households in the 1950s with American households today.
(2) It confirms the story's point about current household composition and provides additional details not discussed in the story.

Choice **(2)** is correct. The pie chart supplies statistics about husband-wife households (48.4%) and single-resident households (26.7%) that match the article's assertions and show the proportion of Americans living with other family and with roommates to whom they are not related.

PRACTICE 6

Questions 1 through 3 refer to the following passage and the two figures.

Gerrymandering: An Electoral Advantage

1 The term *gerrymander* is used to describe the process by which electoral districts are given curious shapes in order to favor the interests of the party in power of a state legislature. Through this process, the governing political party tailors the electoral map to group unfavorable neighborhoods into a few districts likely to vote for the opposition while configuring the majority of districts to favor the party in power.

2 Figures 2(a) and 2(b) show how a governing political party can benefit from gerrymandering. In both figures, there are 40 gray squares and 60 white squares, and the area is divided into four equal-sized districts. In Figure 2(a), the white-square party will win only two seats out of four, but in Figure 2(b), the white-square party will take three of the four districts, as most of the gray votes are consolidated into one oddly shaped and geographically divided district. In fact, Illinois's 4th Congressional District is similar in shape to the gray district in Figure 2(b).

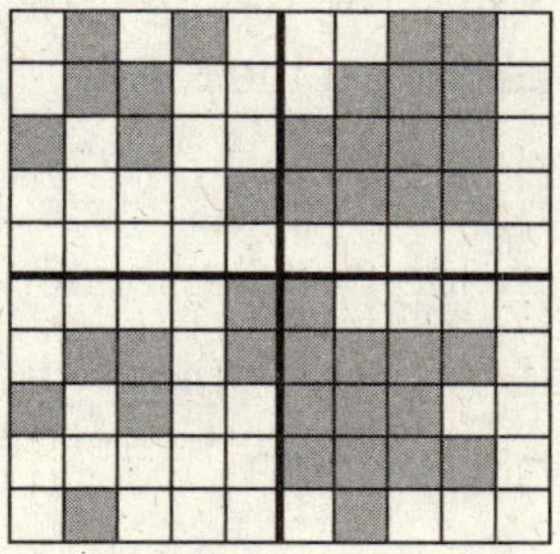

Fig. 2(a)

Geographically Uniform Districts.

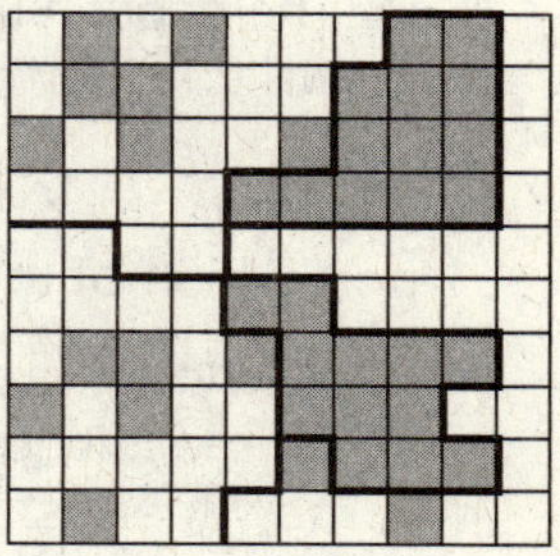

Fig. 2(b)

Gerrymandered Districts.

1. Which of the following is the main point of the passage and figures?
   A. Illinois's 4th Congressional District has now been in existence for over 200 years.
   B. Curiosity is the most important ingredient in the democratic process.
   C. Gerrymandered congressional districts are a major threat to the democratic system.
   D. Governing parties can use their power to shape electoral districts to their advantage.

2. Which of the following conclusions can be drawn from the passage and the figures?
   A. Gerrymandering is more common in Illinois than in other American states.
   B. Through gerrymandering, a governing party can be elected to a greater number of seats than its voter support might otherwise allow.
   C. Through gerrymandering, impartial committees draw boundaries to keep elections fair.
   D. Gerrymandering convinces citizens who would ordinarily be unfavorable to a party to change their votes.

3. In what way do the figures support the passage?
   A. They illustrate the advantages a party can obtain through gerrymandering.
   B. They predict victory for the gray party in the upcoming election.
   C. They are more relevant to Chicago than to rural Illinois.
   D. They show that voter turnout will continue to decline if governing parties continue to gerrymander districts.

Answers and explanations start on page 185.

ANALYZING NONFICTION AND INFORMATIONAL TEXT PRACTICE QUESTIONS

Questions 1 through 4 refer to the following passage about communication technology and the accompanying cartoon.

SOCIAL NETWORKING AT WHAT COST?

1 Sit in any restaurant or coffee shop long enough, and you're bound to witness a familiar scene: a couple, a family, or a group of friends gathered to enjoy a meal, but instead of conversing, each person at the table sits staring at his or her cell phone. In this age of social media, the question arises: does technology enhance or limit our ability to make strong emotional connections with other people?

2 Social networks have broadened with the expansion of communication technology. We connect easily with new acquaintances, old friends, potential clients, and complete strangers. For loved ones who are separated by distance, technology provides an important lifeline. Soldiers, deployed for long tours of duty, meet their newborn children over video chat. Grandparents, limited by ill health, watch their grandchildren grow through pictures and videos posted to social media sites.

3 With all the benefits of social media, however, come considerable costs. Each new connection we make (and old acquaintance we maintain) demands time, energy, and emotional investment. This often comes at the expense of time we could give to the most important people in our lives. Moreover, much of what we share through social media is superficial or entertaining. Only when technology is used to enhance our deepest, most valuable connections can it be considered real progress for humankind.

"A bunch of friends are coming over to stare at their phones."

1. What is the purpose of the passage and the graphic?

   A. to discuss different forms of social media
   B. to suggest a new form of communication technology
   C. to examine ways in which modern families use technology to communicate
   D. to discuss whether communication technology helps or hurts relationships

2. What is the topic of the passage and the graphic?

   A. maintaining long-distance relationships
   B. how technology affects interpersonal connections
   C. the limits of social media
   D. the expense of new technologies

3. Which of the following details in the graphic supports the author's point of view in the passage?

   A. The caption reveals that the woman is expecting friends to visit.
   B. The woman in the cartoon is speaking on the phone with a computer nearby.
   C. The woman in the cartoon is alone.
   D. The caption reveals that the woman's friends will use their phones during their visit.

4. Together, the graphic and the passage support which of the following conclusions?

   A. New communication technologies may offer exciting ways for people to establish new friendships.
   B. New communication technologies may adversely impact important human relationships.
   C. New communication technologies may offer positive solutions for friends who are separated by distance.
   D. New communication technologies may help people to complete several tasks at once.

<u>Questions 5 through 8</u> refer to this passage about the giant squid.

THE GIANT SQUID: MORE THAN COLOSSAL?

1 The giant squid is the world's longest cephalopod. Based on measurements of over 100 full specimens (including adult and adolescent individuals) recovered from the stomachs of sperm whales and other predators, scientists have determined that the giant squid can reach a length of 13 meters.

2 Some have argued that the honor of longest cephalopod should instead go to the colossal squid, a distant relative of the giant squid, but this belief is incorrect. It is true that the colossal squid may outweigh its giant cousin. However, of the few specimens of the colossal squid (all of them juveniles) described in the scientific literature, the longest measured ten meters. Therefore, the giant squid wins the length contest.

3 No other cephalopod is even close in length to either of these animals. For example, the giant Pacific octopus, the world's longest octopus species, has a maximum arm span of only about six meters. The giant squid's status as the world's longest cephalopod remains uncontested.

5. The main point of the passage is that

   A. the colossal squid weighs more than the giant squid
   B. the giant squid is the world's longest cephalopod
   C. the giant Pacific octopus is the world's longest octopus species
   D. the giant squid can reach a length of 13 meters

6. Which of the following best summarizes the writer's argument in paragraph 2?

   A. The colossal squid is the world's longest cephalopod.
   B. The colossal squid is a distant relative of the giant squid.
   C. The giant Pacific octopus is not as long as the giant squid.
   D. The giant squid is longer than the colossal squid.

7. What evidence is given to support the writer's argument in paragraph 2?

   A. The colossal squid can weigh more than the giant squid.
   B. The giant squid is the world's longest cephalopod.
   C. The length of the longest known colossal squid specimen is ten meters.
   D. The giant Pacific octopus has a maximum arm span of only about six meters.

8. Which of the following is an example of faulty reasoning that weakens the writer's argument?

   A. The longest known colossal squid is ten meters long, so there is no colossal squid longer than the longest giant squid.
   B. The giant Pacific octopus is the world's longest species of octopus, but it is not as long as the giant squid.
   C. Many specimens of the giant squid have been measured.
   D. Because sperm whales prey on giant squid, they must also prey on colossal squid.

Questions 9 through 15 refer to these two passages about mercury.

Passage 1

The use of mercury amalgam for dental fillings has already been banned in several European nations, and it should also be banned in the United States. The mercury contained in amalgam fillings slowly leaches into the mouth and is swallowed. It is then absorbed by the small intestine and accumulates in various body tissues, including the brain, kidney, and liver. This accumulated mercury causes a variety of health problems. In 2001, a study reported that patients with a higher number of amalgam fillings also had higher occurrences of cancer, respiratory disease, and diseases of the nervous system.

In addition to its health impact, the mercury released from dental amalgam has a number of damaging environmental consequences. Mercury waste produced by dental offices is sometimes directly disposed of into sewage water or landfills. Mercury can leach from landfills into groundwater and get into rivers and lakes. It has been estimated, for example, that dental amalgam is the source of 4 percent of the mercury found in the water of Lake Superior.

Due to the alarming health and environmental consequences of mercury amalgam, dental fillings should be made from resin composites instead. These composites are already becoming popular due to their cosmetic appeal, so banning mercury amalgam will create no consumer backlash. There are demonstrable advantages (and no disadvantages) to banning mercury dental amalgam in the United States.

Passage 2

In recent years, uneducated consumers have expressed a growing fear of the mercury commonly found in dental fillings. The environmental impact of mercury is serious, and the release of mercury into the environment must be better controlled. However, the health risks associated with mercury amalgam fillings are minimal.

It is well known that people who have mercury amalgam fillings absorb small amounts of mercury. However, most of this mercury is excreted in the urine. To date, no convincing scientific study has demonstrated that mercury absorbed from dental fillings causes any serious health problems. Because mercury amalgam fillings tend to last longer than resin composite fillings, amalgam is preferable for use whenever there is no cosmetic need for a tooth-colored filling.

However, the disposal of mercury amalgam in dental offices absolutely must be regulated. The Environmental Protection Agency estimates that 40 to 50 percent of the mercury in the wastewater processed at public treatment plants comes from dental amalgam. This is inexcusable, especially because devices that remove mercury from wastewater are inexpensive and easy for dental offices to use. While mercury amalgam should remain available because it is more durable than composites, every dental office must have a device to remove mercury from wastewater.

9. The topic of both passages is

A. groundwater contamination
B. mercury dental amalgam
C. resin composite fillings
D. dental health risks

10. What is the main argument of Passage 1?

A. Mercury amalgam fillings are not unhealthy, but their disposal should be regulated for environmental reasons.
B. Resin composite should replace mercury amalgam for dental fillings because it tends to last longer.
C. Mercury amalgam fillings should be banned because they are unhealthy and bad for the environment.
D. Mercury dental amalgam leaches mercury into a patient's mouth and can damage the liver.

11. Which statement best describes the supporting evidence in paragraph 3 of Passage 2?

A. It appears convincing at first glance, but no source is cited.
B. It is a seemingly convincing statistic, but the source is untrustworthy.
C. It is an unconvincing statistic from an untrustworthy source.
D. It is a convincing statistic from a reliable source.

12. In paragraph 3, the author of Passage 1 states that "These composites are already becoming popular due to their cosmetic appeal, so banning mercury amalgam will create no consumer backlash." Which of the following is an assumption the author of Passage 1 makes about consumers?

A. Consumers have no other reason, such as cost or durability, to prefer mercury amalgam to composite fillings.
B. Consumers will be happy with whatever material they are offered for dental fillings.
C. Consumers are not generally vocal about their preferences.
D. Consumers never discuss the choice of filling material with their dentists.

13. The writer of Passage 2 would be most likely to agree with which of the following statements?

A. Mercury amalgam fillings should be banned because they are unhealthy.
B. Resin composite fillings look better than mercury amalgam fillings when each is used on visible tooth surfaces.
C. Mercury contamination of public wastewater is an unimportant issue.
D. Resin composite fillings are preferable to mercury amalgam in all cases.

14. Which of the passages has weaker supporting evidence and why?

A. Passage 1, because it cites no sources for the study or the statistic it cites
B. Passage 1, because it argues that mercury should be banned in dental fillings
C. Passage 2, because it cites the Environmental Protection Agency as the source of a statistic it cites
D. Passage 2, because it argues that mercury used by dental offices should be better regulated

15. Which of the statements in Passage 1 is an example of faulty reasoning?

A. Resin composites are already gaining in popularity.
B. The use of mercury dental amalgam has already been banned in several European nations.
C. The mercury released from dental amalgam has damaging environmental consequences.
D. Mercury that accumulates in body tissues causes a variety of health problems.

Answers and explanations start on page 186.

LESSON

1

INTERPRETING FICTION

Plot Elements

Plot refers to the events in a story. Generally, the events are told in order—what happened first, next, and so on. Understanding the order of events, the sequence, can help you see which events caused or affected others.

A story usually contains at least one **conflict**, or problem. The conflict may be between characters, within a character, or between a character and nature. Conflict creates tension. When it is resolved, the tension ends.

The following excerpt is about a brother and sister whose mother has a tumor. As you read it, look for the order of events and the conflict.

> Robert didn't phone until evening. His voice was fatigued and thin. "I've moved her to the university hospital," he said. "They can't deal with it at home."
>
> Kate waited, saying nothing. She concentrated on the toes of her shoes. They needed shining. *You never take care of anything*, her mother would say.
>
> "She has a tumor in her head." He said it firmly, as though Kate might challenge him.
>
> "I'll take a plane tomorrow morning," Kate answered, "I'll be there by noon."
>
> Robert exhaled. "Look," he said, "don't even come back here unless you can keep your mouth shut and do it my way."
>
> "Get to the point."
>
> "The point is they believe she has a malignancy and we're not going to tell her. I almost didn't tell you." His voice faltered. "They're going to operate but if they find what they're expecting, they don't think they can stop it."
>
> For a moment there was no sound except an oceanic vibration of distance on the wire. Even that sound grew still. Robert breathed. Kate could almost see him, in a booth at the hospital, staring straight ahead at the plastic instructions screwed to the narrow rectangular body of the telephone. It seemed to her that she was hurtling toward him.

From "Souvenir" by Jayne Anne Phillips, from *Black Tickets*, NY: Delacorte Press, 1979. Reprinted with permission of Jayne Anne Phillips.

► When did Robert decide not to tell his mother about the tumor?

(1) before talking to Kate
(2) after discussing the issue with Kate

(1) is correct. Robert has already decided what to do when he calls Kate.

► Which of the following identifies a conflict in this excerpt?

(1) Kate tells Robert she will fly there tomorrow.
(2) Robert tells Kate that she must do as he says.

(2) is correct. Robert challenges Kate. That creates tension.

Key Ideas

- The plot is the series of events in a story. Understanding the order of the events helps you see how they are related.
- The conflict is a problem between characters, between a character and nature, or within a character.

GED® TEST TIP

To understand the events and conflict in a story, pay attention to the dialogue. Remember that every time the speaker changes, a new paragraph begins.

PRACTICE 1

Questions 1 through 4 refer to the following excerpt from a short story.

EXCERPTED FROM "THE PIECE OF STRING"

1 The countryman looked at the Mayor in astonishment, already terrified by this suspicion resting on him without his knowing why.

2 "Me? Me? I picked up the pocketbook?"

3 "Yes, you, yourself."

4 "On my word of honor, I never heard of it."

5 "But you were seen."

6 "I was seen, me? Who says he saw me?"

7 "Monsieur Malandain, the harness-maker."

8 The old man remembered, understood, and flushed with anger.

9 "Ah, he saw me, the clodhopper, he saw me pick up this string, here, Mayor." And rummaging in his pocket he drew out the little piece of string.

10 But the Mayor, incredulous, shook his head.

11 "You will not make me believe, Maître Hauchecorne, that Monsieur Malandain, who is a man we can believe, mistook this cord for a pocketbook."

12 The peasant, furious, lifted his hand, spat at one side to attest his honor, repeating:
"It is nevertheless God's own truth, the sacred
13 truth. I repeat it on my soul and my salvation."

14 The Mayor resumed:

15 "After picking up the object, you stood like a stilt, looking a long while in the mud to see if any piece of money had fallen out."

16 The old fellow choked with indignation and fear. . . .

17 He was confronted with Monsieur Malandain, who repeated and maintained his affirmation. They abused each other for an hour. At his own request, Maître Hauchecorne was searched. Nothing was found on him.

18 Finally the Mayor, very much perplexed, discharged him with the warning that he would consult the Public Prosecutor and ask for further orders.

1. What was the peasant doing when he "lifted his hand, spat at one side to attest his honor" (paragraph 12)?

A. thinking of striking the Mayor
B. swearing that he was telling the truth
C. pleading to the Mayor for mercy
D. performing a peasant ritual

2. How did the peasant react when confronted with Malandain, the harness-maker?

He

A. became choked with fear and indignation
B. tried to explain what had actually happened
C. became respectful and subdued
D. confronted him and then asked to be searched

3. Which of the following statements best describes the conflict in this excerpt?

A. A town mayor is abusing his authority.
B. A peasant leads a harsh life and is often at odds with others.
C. A peasant is accused of taking a pocketbook.
D. Someone has lost a pocketbook with a great deal of money in it.

4. Place the numbers next to the actions to indicate the order in which the actions occurred in the excerpt.

The peasant and the harness-maker argue.	
The peasant explains that he picked up a piece of string, not a pocketbook.	
The mayor issues a warning to the peasant.	
The mayor states that the harness-maker witnessed the peasant stealing the pocketbook.	

1.
2.
3.
4.

Answers and explanations start on page 186.

LESSON

2

INTERPRETING FICTION

Inferences

Key Ideas

- To understand a story, you must make inferences.
- Making inferences means that you look closely at the details in the story, think about your knowledge of the real world, and then ask yourself, "What does this information point to?"

GED® TEST TIP

Do not leave a question unanswered. If you read a tough question, do your best to think about it, look back at the passage for information you may need, and then choose the best answer.

To understand a story, you can't just rely on what is directly stated. You also need to "read between the lines," or make **inferences**. An inference is based on information you are given *plus* what you have learned about the real world—the way things happen and the way people act.

As you read this excerpt from a story, look for suggested meanings behind people's actions and words.

> "Last night?" The old blue eyes looked blank, then brightened. "Ah no, I must have taken one of my Seconals. Otherwise I'd have heard it surely. 'Auntie,' my niece always says—'what if there should be a fire, and you there sleeping away?' Do what she says, I do sometimes, only to hear every pin drop till morning." She shook her head, entering the elevator. "Going up?"
>
> "N-no," said Mrs. Hazlitt. "I—have to wait here for a minute." She sat down on the bench, the token bench that she had never seen anybody sitting on, and watched the car door close on the little figure still shaking its head, borne upward like a fairy godmother, willing but unable to oblige. The car's hum stopped, then its light glowed on again. Someone else was coming down. . . .
>
> The car door opened. "Wssht!" said Miss Finan, scuttling out again. "I've just remembered. Not last night, but two weeks ago. And once before that. A scream, you said?"
>
> Mrs. Hazlitt stood up. Almost unable to speak, for the tears that suddenly wrenched her throat, she described it.

From "The Scream on Fifty-Seventh Street" by Hortense Calisher, from *Tales for the Mirror,* reprinted in *Women and Fiction,* edited by Susan Cahill, New York: New American Library, 1975.

► What happened before the beginning of this excerpt?
  (1) Mrs. Hazlitt heard a scream the night before and asked Miss Finan if she heard it too.
  (2) Mrs. Hazlitt asked Miss Finan about her health and whether she is sleeping well.

The correct answer is **(1)**. You can infer it from details such as "Last night?" and "Not last night, but two weeks ago. And once before that. A scream, you said?"

► What is the most likely reason that "tears suddenly wrenched" Mrs. Hazlitt's throat?
  (1) She was upset at Miss Finan's inability to remember.
  (2) She was relieved that Miss Finan had heard a scream too.

You are correct if you chose **(2)**. Mrs. Hazlitt is so relieved that someone else heard the scream that she has to fight back tears.

PRACTICE 2

Questions 1 through 4 refer to the following excerpt from a short story.

EXCERPTED FROM "THE STORY OF AN HOUR"

1 She knew that she would weep again when she saw the kind, tender hands folded in death; the face that had never looked save with love upon her, fixed and gray and dead. But she saw beyond that bitter moment a long procession of years to come that would belong to her absolutely. And she opened and spread her arms out to them in welcome.

2 There would be no one to live for during those coming years; she would live for herself. There would be no powerful will bending her in that blind persistence with which men and women believe they have a right to impose a private will upon a fellow creature. A kind intention or a cruel intention made the act seem no less a crime as she looked upon it in that brief moment of illumination.

3 And yet she had loved him—sometimes. Often she had not. What did it matter! What could love, the unsolved mystery, count for in face of this possession of self-assertion, which she suddenly recognized as the strongest impulse of her being!

4 "Free! Body and soul free!" she kept whispering . . .

5 Some one was opening the front door with a latchkey. It was [her husband] Brently Mallard who entered, a little travel-stained, composedly carrying his grip-sack and umbrella. He had been far from the scene of accident, and did not even know there had been one. He stood amazed at [his wife] Josephine's piercing cry; at Richards' quick motion to screen him from the view of his wife.

6 But Richards was too late.

7 When the doctors came they said she had died of heart disease—of joy that kills.

From "The Story of an Hour" by Kate Chopin.

1. How did Brently Mallard generally feel toward his wife?

He

A. had always loved her
B. kept her at arm's length
C. liked to play practical jokes on her
D. had cruel intentions toward her

2. Which detail best expresses Josephine's vision of her future?

A. that bitter moment
B. she'd weep again
C. spread her arms out in welcome
D. blind persistence

3. What was the doctors' meaning when they said that Josephine died of "joy that kills" (paragraph 7)?

They thought that

A. she was overcome and thrilled to see her husband
B. she was excited about her upcoming life of freedom
C. her heart was worn out from giving so much love
D. her heart was weakened from the strain of living

4. Why did Josephine die?

A. She was overcome with relief.
B. She was shocked that she would not be free.
C. She was confused by feelings of love and hate.
D. She thought there would be no one to live for.

Answers and explanations start on page 187.

LESSON

3

INTERPRETING FICTION

Character

Key Ideas

- Characters are the people in the story.
- You can understand a character by noting what the narrator tells you directly as well as by inferring from the character's appearance, actions, words, and thoughts.

ON THE GED® TEST

A common kind of question asks you to choose how a character would act in a different situation, based on what you know about the character's personality.

Characters are the people who inhabit a story. The personalities and motivations of characters are often stated directly by the **narrator**—the person telling the story. Sometimes you can also infer characters' personalities or motivations by what they do, what they think, and what they say.

As you read this excerpt, look for details that describe each character.

> Axel Olsen was going to paint Helga Crane. Not only was he going to paint her, but he was to accompany her and her aunt on their shopping expedition. Aunt Katrina was frankly elated. Uncle Poul was also visibly pleased. Evidently they were not above kow-towing to a lion. Helga's own feelings were mixed; she was amused, grateful, and vexed. It had all been decided and arranged without her, and, also, she was a little afraid of Olsen. His stupendous arrogance awed her.
>
> The day was an exciting, not easily to be forgotten one. Definitely, too, it conveyed to Helga her exact status in her new environment. A decoration. A curio. A peacock. Their progress through the shops was an event; an event for Copenhagen as well as for Helga Crane. Her dark, alien appearance was to most people an astonishment. Some stared surreptitiously, some openly, and some stopped dead in front of her in order more fully to profit by their stares. "*Den Sorte*" dropped freely, audibly, from many lips.
>
> The time came when she grew used to the stares of the population. And the time came when the population of Copenhagen grew used to her outlandish presence and ceased to stare. But at the end of that first day it was with thankfulness that she returned to the sheltering walls of the house on Maria Kirkplads.

From "Quicksand" by Nella Larsen, in *The Norton Anthology of African American Literature*, edited by Henry Louis Gates, Jr., and Nellie Y. McKay, New York: W.W. Norton, 1997.

► Which of the following describes Helga?
(1) attractive, down-to-earth, embarking on a new life
(2) self-centered, smug, enjoys being watched

Choice **(1)** is correct. An artist is painting her, suggesting she is attractive. Yet she prefers not to be the center of attention (see the end of the last paragraph).

► Which of the following would Olsen most likely do at a party?
(1) snub the hostess if the wine was below his expectations
(2) offer to drive anyone home who needed a ride

Choice **(1)** is correct. Apply what you know about people with "stupendous arrogance" (see the end of the first paragraph) to answer this question.

PRACTICE 3

Questions 1 through 3 refer to the following excerpt from a story.

EXCERPTED FROM "HIZAKURIGE"

1 "I shall never forget it," the witch went on. "When you were ill you gave your sickness to me. Our only child, who had to carry on our name, grew weak and thin because there was no rice to fill his empty stomach. Every day the bill collectors were knocking at the door and the rent remained unpaid. Yet I did not complain—not even when I slipped in the dogs' dirt in the lane."

2 "Don't talk of it," said Yaji. "You'll break my heart."

3 "And then, when through my labors I had saved enough money to buy a kimono, I had to pawn it for your sake and never saw it again. Never again did it come back to me from the pawnbroker's."

4 "At the same time you must remember what a pleasant place you are in now," said Yaji, "while I have to worry along down here."

5 "What? What is there pleasant about it? It is true that by the help of your friends you erected a stone over my grave, but you never go near it, and you never contribute to the temple to get the priests to say prayers for my soul. I am nothing to you. The stone over my grave has been taken away and put into the wall, where all the dogs come and make water against it. Not a drop of water is ever placed on my grave. Truly in death we suffer all sorts of troubles."

6 "True, true," said Yaji.

7 "But while you thus treat me with neglect," the witch went on, "lying in my grave I think of nobody but you and long for the time when you will join me in the underworld. Shall I come to meet you?"

8 "No, no, don't do that," said Yaji. "It's really too far for you."

9 "Well then, I have one request to make."

10 "Yes, yes. What is it?"

11 "Give this witch plenty of money."

12 "Of course, of course."

13 "How sad the parting!" cried the witch. "I have yet much to tell you, countless questions to ask you, but the messenger of Hell recalls me!"

14 Then, recovering from her trance, the witch twanged her bow.

From "Hizakurige" by Jippensha Ikku in *The Longwood Introduction to Fiction,* Boston: Allyn and Bacon, 1992.

1. Why does Yaji say, "No, no, don't do that . . . It's really too far for you" (paragraph 8)?

A. He is trying to be more considerate than he had been in the past.
B. He is frightened about seeing the ghost of his wife.
C. He has no real interest in seeing his wife again.
D. His wife can't really travel to him anyway.

2. Which of the following is the best description of the witch?

A. caring
B. straightforward
C. untrustworthy
D. thoughtful

3. Earlier in the story the witch, speaking as Yaji's wife, says, "Ah, what agony I went through when I was married to you—time and again suffering the pangs of hunger and shivering with cold in the winter."

Based on this information and the excerpt, what kind of husband did Yaji seem to be?

A. angry
B. kind-hearted
C. responsible
D. neglectful

Answers and explanations start on page 187.

LESSON

4

INTERPRETING FICTION

Theme

Every story has a subject. The subject might be about fighting a war or growing up in poverty. But there is more to a story than its subject. As a reader, look for what the author is trying to say about the subject. That is the **theme**—the message the author wants the reader to understand. In fiction, the theme is often a statement about life. For example, the theme might be that fighting in a war changes a person's life forever.

The theme may be directly stated. If it is not, you can infer the theme from the characters' thoughts and actions and from the things that happen in the story.

As you read the following excerpt, ask yourself what message about the people and their lives the author is trying to tell you.

> While the boys were getting the Doctor's horse, he went to the window to examine the house plants. "What do you do to your geraniums to keep them blooming all winter, Mary? I never pass this house that from the road I don't see your windows full of flowers."
>
> She snapped off a dark red one, and a ruffled new green leaf, and put them in his buttonhole. "There, that looks better. You look too solemn for a young man, Ed. Why don't you git married? I'm worried about you. . . ."
>
> Sometimes the Doctor heard the gossipers in the drugstore wondering why Rosicky didn't get on faster. He was industrious, and so were his boys, but they were rather free and easy, weren't pushers, and they didn't always show good judgment. They were comfortable, they were out of debt, but they didn't get much ahead. Maybe, Doctor Burleigh reflected, people as generous and warmhearted and affectionate as the Rosickys never got ahead much; maybe you couldn't enjoy your life and put it into the bank, too.

From "Neighbor Rosicky" by Willa Cather, from *Obscure Destinies.*

► Which of the following statements is the theme of the story?
(1) A good life is measured in terms of love, not money.
(2) People should not gossip about others.

You are correct if you chose **(1).** Doctor Burleigh's thoughts at the end of the excerpt help you understand that this is the author's main message.

► Which of the following details supports the theme?
(1) Mary Rosicky lovingly "worries" about the doctor.
(2) The Rosickys keep out of debt.

Again, you are correct if you chose **(1).** The flowers Mary grows, the fact that she snaps off one to give the doctor, and her expressed concern for him all show her warmth and happiness. They help support the theme that the doctor reflects on.

Key Ideas

- The subject of a story is what the story is about.
- The theme of a story is different from the subject. The theme goes beyond the subject and often expresses a point of view about life.

GED® TEST TIP

Read the whole passage carefully but not too slowly before you begin to answer the questions. If you read a question that really stumps you, skip it and go on. You can come back to it.

PRACTICE 4

Questions 1 through 5 refer to the following excerpt from a short story.

EXCERPTED FROM "GONE FISHIN'"

1 Early morning is the best time. You're fully rested but not awake enough to remember how hard it all is. Morning is like being a child again, and morning before the sun is out is like those magic times that you hid under the bed and in between the clothes hanging in your mother's closet. Times when any kind of miracle could come about just as normal as a spider making her web.

2 I remember waking up in the dark once when I was very small. I jumped right out of bed and went up next to the screen door on the back porch to see what kind of fantastic thing was going on outside. At first I couldn't see anything but there was a clopping sound, nickering, and a deep voice that made me feel calm and wondering. Slowly, coming out from the darkness, I saw a gray shimmering next to a tall black pillar. The shimmer turned into a big horse and the pillar became my father holding out an apple and cooing in his bass voice, "Ho! Yeah, boy," even though the horse was tame and eating from his hand.

3 I drifted into sleep thinking that we were poor and didn't own a horse. When I woke up it was light and there was no horse to be seen. I asked my father about it but he told me that I was dreaming—where were poor people like us going to find big gray stallions?

4 But there were horse chips behind the barn and hoofprints too.

5 I decided that it was a magic horse and man that I'd seen. From that day on I believed that magic hides in the early morning. If you get up early enough you might find something so beautiful that it would be all right if you just died right then because nothing else in life could ever be better.

From "Gone Fishin'" by Walter Mosley, Baltimore: Black Classic Press, 1997.

1. In the story, the boy __________ after hearing his father's explanation.

A. feels confused
B. finds a new explanation
C. no longer trusts his father
D. tries to convince his father

2. Which of the following is the best description of the boy?

A. hard-hearted
B. imaginative
C. skeptical
D. chatty

3. What is the most likely reason the boy decides he saw a magic horse and man?

A. He wants to reconcile what he saw with what his father told him.
B. He enjoys magic and likes to make up stories.
C. He wants to prove his father was mistaken.
D. This kind of miracle can happen.

4. Which of the following would the father probably enjoy most?

A. daydreaming about the future
B. having enough money to pay some bills
C. keeping his son's hopes up about getting a new bicycle for his birthday
D. sharing ghost stories around a campfire

5. Which of the following statements fits the theme of this story?

A. False hopes will not get you anywhere.
B. Dreams really can come true.
C. Adults cannot see what children see.
D. Morning and youth are full of possibility.

Answers and explanations start on page 187.

LESSON

5

INTERPRETING FICTION

Style and Point of View

Key Ideas

- The style of a piece of writing is determined by the choices a writer makes in words, sentence structure, images, and other devices.
- A story is written from a narrator's point of view. The narrator may be an "outsider" or a character who can reveal only what he or she sees and thinks.

ON THE GED® TEST

You will not have to identify and use terms such as third person *and* first person, *but you should be able to understand and appreciate the effect of the writers' choices.*

Style

A writer has many choices when deciding how to write a story. A writer may use long, complex sentences; short, clipped sentences; or anything in between. A writer may use flowery or formal language, slang, or spoken dialect. One writer may use vivid images or symbols, while another writes a plain, spare story. The individual characteristics that a writer chooses—sentence structure, choice of words, use of images, and other devices—are all part of the writer's **style.**

As you read this excerpt, look for the characteristics that this particular author chose. Ask yourself what effect they have on your understanding of the writing.

> The only part of the night I recall without feeling anger or sadness is loading the horses. Andy and I hardly had the fencing up before Brett came along with the first ten or twelve. . . . A couple of roans and an Appaloosa stood out in that first bunch in the starlight, and a bay with a roached mane. Then Ed brought up a second bunch, about fifteen mostly dark but a palomino and two paints in there, I remember. Andy and I shooed them up the ramp, which clattered and thundered under their hooves. It was a cool night, still. I could feel the horses on my skin, their body heat swirling around us. I could . . . hear their nostrils fluttering. I felt hard muscle ripple under my hand when I clapped a hip to steer them around. I felt their tails slap my back, and caught a glint in their bared eyes.

From "Stolen Horses" by Barry Lopez, from *Writers Harvest 3,* edited by Tobias Wolff, copyright © 2000 by Share Our Strength. Used by permission of Dell Publishing, a division of Random House, Inc.

► What is the effect of the author's description of the horses?
  (1) It creates a depth of feeling for the horses' vitality.
  (2) It provides insight into what the characters are doing.

You are correct if you chose **(1).** The vivid, descriptive details allow you to imagine the horses and sense their vitality and strength.

Point of View

Another choice a writer makes is which **point of view** to write from. Will the narrator be outside the story, watching and revealing the characters' actions and perhaps even their thoughts and feelings? If so, the writer will use *third person* point of view. Or will the narrator be a character in the story, able to report only what he or she thinks? In that case, the writer will use *first person* point of view.

► Which of the following indicates that the narrator is a character and so we can know only his thoughts?
  (1) "The only part of the night I recall . . ."
  (2) "Then Ed brought up a second bunch . . ."

(1) is correct. The narrator tells his own thoughts. A clue is the word *I.*

PRACTICE 5

Questions 1 through 4 refer to the following excerpt from a short story called "Coach."

EXCERPTED FROM *AN AMATEUR'S GUIDE TO THE NIGHT*

1 "This apartment your mom found is like an office or something. A studio for her to go to and get away every now and then. . . ."

2 "She wants to get away from us," Daphne said.

3 "Definitely not. She gave me a list, is how this whole thing started. She's got stuff she wants to do, and you with your school problems and me with the team—we're too much for her, see? She could spend her entire day on us, if you think about it, and never have one second for herself. If you think about it fairly, Daphne, you'll agree." . . .

4 She made a sigh and marched over to a trash can to deposit her slumping cone. Then she washed up at the children's drinking fountain and rejoined Coach, who had finished his Brown Cow but had kept the plastic spoon in the mouth.

5 "What was on this list of Mom's?" Daphne asked.

6 "Adult stuff," Coach said.

7 "Just give me an example."

8 Coach removed the plastic spoon and cracked it in half.

9 "Your mother's list is for five years. In that time, she wants to be speaking French regularly. She wants to follow up on her printmaking."

10 "This is adult stuff?" Daphne said.

11 Coach raised a hand to Bobby Stark. Stark had three malt cups in a cardboard carrier and he was moving toward the parking lot.

12 "Hey, those all for you?" Coach called out.

13 "I got a month to get fat, Coach. You'll have five months to beat it off me," the boy called back.

14 The people at some of the tables around Coach's lit up with grins. Bobby Stark's parents were grinning.

15 "Every hit of that junk takes a second off your time in the forty—just remember that!" Coach shouted.

16 Stark wagged his head ruefully, his cheeks blushing. He pretended to hide the malts behind his arm.

1. What is Bobby Stark's attitude?

A. He worries about his weight problem.
B. He takes things in stride.
C. He is looking forward to the sports season.
D. He feels unfairly criticized by the coach.

2. Because of the narrator's point of view, what does the reader know?

A. only Bobby Stark's actions
B. thoughts and feelings of the characters
C. the actions and speech of the characters
D. only Daphne's thoughts and feelings

3. Through their dialogue, what kind of relationship can you conclude the characters have with each other?

A. informal
B. tense
C. suspicious
D. deteriorating

4. Later in the story, Coach has this discussion with his wife, Sherry: "'It's like my apartment,' Sherry said. 'A place apart.' Coach cut her off. 'Don't go on about how much you love your apartment.'"

Based on this information and the excerpt, which of the following best describes Coach in his discussion with Daphne?

A. brutally frank
B. angry and hostile
C. loving and warm
D. not entirely honest about his feelings

Answers and explanations start on page 187.

LESSON

6

Figurative Language

Key Ideas

- Fiction writers and poets use figurative language—words that do not have their literal meaning—to compare different things.
- Some comparisons are introduced by *like* or *as*; others are not. Some comparisons give human characteristics to nonhuman things.

GED® TEST TIP

You are not penalized for wrong answers on the GED® Test, so do not leave any answers blank. If you return to a skipped multiple-choice question and still cannot determine the answer, narrow the choices to the two most reasonable and then select the one that makes the most sense.

Figurative language refers to words that are being used to mean something other than their actual, literal meaning. Writers and poets use figurative language to help paint a mental picture in the reader's mind. Instead of saying, "His voice was soothing and pleasing," for example, a writer might say, "His voice was like velvet."

Figurative language often compares two different things. Sometimes the comparison is signaled by the words *like* or *as*, but not always. A writer might also say, "His voice was velvet." Another favorite technique of writers and poets is to give a human characteristic to something nonhuman, such as, "The wind sighed."

As you read this poem, look for figurative language and what it might mean.

The School Children

The children go forward with their little satchels.
And all morning the mothers have labored
to gather the late apples, red and gold,
like words of another language.

And on the other shore
are those who wait behind great desks
to receive these offerings.

How orderly they are—the nails
on which the children hang
their overcoats of blue or yellow wool.

And the teachers shall instruct them in silence
and the mothers shall scour the orchards for a way out,
drawing to themselves the gray limbs of the fruit trees
bearing so little ammunition.

From "The House on Marshland" from *The First Four Books* by Louise Gluck. Copyright 1968, 1971, 1972, 1973, 1974, 1975, 1976, 1977, 1978, 1980, 1985, 1995.

▶ What is suggested by comparing apples to "words of another language" in the fourth line?

(1) a sense of strangeness, not a part of one's world
(2) useless things that have no meaning

You are correct if you chose **(1)**. A language different from your own can seem strange and removed. The mothers feel removed from the world of teachers and schoolchildren.

▶ What does the word *shore* in the fifth line refer to?

(1) the farthest edge of a lake
(2) the world of the classroom

You are correct if you chose **(2)**. The mothers in the poem think of school as far away from them.

PRACTICE 6

Questions 1 through 5 refer to the following poem.

EXCERPTED FROM "DÉJEUNER SUR L'HERBE" ("LUNCH ON THE GRASS")

1 It's pleasant to board the ferry in the sunscape
As the late light slants into afternoon;
The faint wind ruffles the river, rimmed with foam.
We move through the aisles of bamboo
Towards the cool water-lilies.

2 The young dandies drop ice into the drinks,
While the girls slice the succulent lotus root.
Above us, a patch of cloud spreads, darkening
Like a water-stain on silk.

3 *Write this down quickly, before the rain!*

4 Don't sit there! The cushions were soaked by the shower.
Already the girls have drenched their crimson skirts.
Beauties, their powder streaked with mascara, lament their ruined faces.

5 The wind batters our boat, the mooring-line
Has rubbed a wound in the willow bark.
The edges of the curtains are embroidered by the river foam.

6 Like a knife in a melon, Autumn slices Summer.

7 *It will be cold, going back.*

1. What is compared to "a water-stain on silk" (Stanza 2)?

A. foam on the edge of the river
B. rain clouds approaching
C. lotus root juice on a tablecloth
D. ice cubes dropping into cold drinks

2. What is meant by the statement "lament their ruined faces" (Stanza 4)?

A. They could no longer smile.
B. They were growing old.
C. The rain caused their makeup to run.
D. The wind was chapping their faces.

3. Why is "The edges of the curtains are embroidered by the river foam" (Stanza 5) an effective use of figurative language?

It helps the reader see that

A. the people forgot to close the windows and curtains
B. the wind is so strong that it is blowing spray from the river into the boat
C. the curtains are beautifully edged with lace
D. the river is rising quickly

4. According to the speaker, how was the change from summer to autumn (Stanza 6)?

A. quick and easy
B. halting and uncertain
C. slow and predictable
D. pleasant and smooth

5. Which of the following words best describe the tone of this poem?

A. gentle and calm
B. humorous and playful
C. wry and observant
D. dry and formal

Answers and explanations start on page 187.

Interpreting Fiction Practice Questions

Questions 1 through 3 refer to the following excerpt from a story.

EXCERPTED FROM *SHILOH & OTHER STORIES*

1 Leroy Moffitt's wife, Norma Jean, is working on her pectorals. She lifts three-pound dumbbells to warm up, then progresses to a twenty-pound barbell. Standing with her legs apart, she reminds Leroy of Wonder Woman.

2 "I'd give anything if I could just get these muscles to where they're real hard," says Norma Jean. "Feel this arm. It's not as hard as the other one."

3 "That's cause you're right-handed," says Leroy, dodging as she swings the barbell in an arc.

4 "Do you think so?"

5 "Sure."

6 Leroy is a truckdriver. He injured his leg in a highway accident four months ago, and his physical therapy, which involves weights and a pulley, prompted Norma Jean to try building herself up. Now she is attending a body-building class. Leroy has been collecting temporary disability since his tractor-trailer jackknifed in Missouri, badly twisting his left leg in its socket. He has a steel pin in his hip. He will probably not be able to drive his rig again. It sits in the backyard, like a gigantic bird that has flown home to roost. Leroy has been home in Kentucky for three months, and his leg is almost healed, but the accident frightened him and he does not want to drive any more long hauls. He is not sure what to do next. In the meantime, he makes things from craft kits. He started by building a miniature log cabin from notched Popsicle sticks. He varnished it and placed it on the TV set, where it remains. It reminds him of a rustic Nativity scene. Then he tried string art (sailing ships on black velvet), a macramé owl kit, a snap-together B-17 Flying Fortress, and a lamp made out of a model truck, with a light fixture screwed in the top of the cab. At first the kits were diversions, something to kill time, but now he is thinking about building a full-scale log house from a kit. It would be considerably cheaper than building a regular house, and besides, Leroy has grown to appreciate how things are put together. He has begun to realize that in all the years he was on the road he never took time to examine anything. He was always flying past scenery.

1. Which of the following best describes Leroy's wife, Norma Jean?

   A. shy
   B. loving
   C. self-concerned
   D. grumpy

2. By comparing Leroy's truck to a bird that has flown home to roost, the author suggests that Leroy

   A. comes and goes as he pleases
   B. always preferred to be at home "nesting"
   C. won't be driving his truck for a while
   D. is a bit "flighty" and unpredictable

3. Why might Leroy be continually making things from craft kits?

   Because he

   A. is impatient with his leg healing
   B. has always enjoyed working with his hands
   C. grew tired of bodybuilding
   D. doesn't want to face what to do next

Questions 4 through 7 refer to this excerpt from a story.

EXCERPTED FROM *WINTER'S TALES*

1 A small sailor-boy, named Simon, stood on the wet, swinging deck, held on to a shroud, and looked up towards the drifting clouds, and to the upper top-gallant yard of the main-mast.

2 A bird, that had sought refuge upon the mast, had got her feet entangled in some loose tackle-yarn of the halliard, and, high up there, struggled to get free. The boy on the deck could see her wings flapping and her head turning from side to side.

3 Through his own experience of life he had come to the conviction that in this world everyone must look after himself, and expect no help from others. But the mute, deadly fight kept him fascinated for more than an hour. He wondered what kind of bird it would be. These last days a number of birds had come to settle in the barque's rigging: swallows, quails, and a pair of peregrine falcons; he believed that this bird was a peregrine falcon. He remembered how, many years ago, in his own country and near his home, he had once seen a peregrine falcon quite close, sitting on a stone and flying straight up from it. Perhaps this was the same bird. He thought: "That bird is like me. Then she was there, and now she is here."

4 At that a fellow-feeling rose in him, a sense of common tragedy; he stood looking at the bird with his heart in his mouth. There were none of the sailors about to make fun of him; he began to think out how he might go up by the shrouds to help the falcon out. He brushed his hair back and pulled up his sleeves, gave the deck round him a great glance, and climbed up. He had to stop a couple of times in the swaying rigging.

5 It was indeed, he found when he got to the top of the mast, a peregrine falcon. As his head was on a level with hers, she gave up her struggle, and looked at him with a pair of angry, desperate yellow eyes.

6 He had to take hold of her with one hand while he got his knife out, and cut off the tackle-yarn. He was scared as he looked down, but at the same time he felt that he had been ordered up by nobody, but that this was his own venture, and this gave him a proud, steadying sensation, as if the sea and the sky, the ship, the bird and himself were all one.

From *Winter's Tales* by Isak Dinesen, Random House, Inc ©1942.

4. What can you infer about the boy's decision to climb the rig?

   A. It took some courage.
   B. It was a familiar task.
   C. It felt like a chore.
   D. He was ordered to do it.

5. Which of the following best describes both the boy and the bird at the beginning of the excerpt?

   A. confident
   B. alone
   C. scared
   D. wary

6. Which ideas are most clearly contrasted in this excerpt?

   A. love and hate
   B. youth and experience
   C. fear and fearlessness
   D. loneliness and sense of belonging

7. The word ____________ best describes the mood created by the author in this excerpt.

   A. mournful
   B. nostalgic
   C. peaceful
   D. triumphant

Questions 8 through 11 refer to this excerpt from a story.

EXCERPTED FROM "THE LEGEND OF SLEEPY HOLLOW"

1 "Who are you?" He received no reply. He repeated his demand in a still more agitated voice. Still there was no answer. Once more he cudgelled the sides of the inflexible Gunpowder, and, shutting his eyes, broke forth with involuntary fervor into a psalm-tune. Just then the shadowy object of alarm put itself in motion, and, with a scramble and a bound, stood at once in the middle of the road. Though the night was dark and dismal, yet the form of the unknown might now in some degree be ascertained. He appeared to be a horseman of large dimensions, and mounted on a black horse of powerful frame. He made no offer of molestation or sociability, but kept aloof on one side of the road, jogging along on the blind side of old Gunpowder, who had now got over his fright and waywardness.

2 Ichabod, who had no relish for this strange midnight companion, and bethought himself of the adventure of Brom Bones with the Galloping Hessian, now quickened his steed, in hopes of leaving him behind. The stranger, however, quickened his horse to an equal pace. Ichabod pulled up, and fell into a walk, thinking to lag behind—the other did the same. His heart began to sink within him; he endeavored to resume his psalm-tune, but his parched tongue clove to the roof of his mouth, and he could not utter a stave. There was something in the moody and dogged silence of this pertinacious companion, that was mysterious and appalling. It was soon fearfully accounted for. On mounting a rising ground, which brought the figure of his fellow-traveller in relief against the sky, gigantic in height, and muffled in a cloak, Ichabod was horror-struck, on perceiving that he was headless!—but his horror was still more increased, on observing that the head, which should have rested on his shoulders, was carried before him on the pommel of the saddle: his terror rose to desperation; he rained a shower of kicks and blows upon Gunpowder, hoping, by a sudden movement, to give his companion the slip—but the spectre started full jump with him.

3 Away then they dashed, through thick and thin; stones flying, and sparks flashing at every bound. Ichabod's flimsy garments fluttered in the air, as he stretched his long lank body away over his horse's head, in the eagerness of his flight.

From "The Legend of Sleepy Hollow" by Washington Irving.

8. What is meant by "he endeavored to resume his psalm-tune" (paragraph 2)?

   Ichabod Crane tried to

   A. remind himself to stay calm
   B. ride more steadily
   C. start singing again
   D. think of a realistic solution

9. What is the effect of the author's use of words such as "dashed," "stones flying," and "sparks flashing" (paragraph 3)?

   The words create a feeling of

   A. panic
   B. clumsiness
   C. playfulness
   D. magic

10. Which of the following best describes the mood of this excerpt?

   A. angry
   B. sorrowful
   C. suspenseful
   D. sentimental

11. Later in the story, the narrator implies that the horseman had a pumpkin on the pommel of his saddle. Given this additional information, Ichabod can best be described as ____________ given his actions in the excerpt.

   A. brave in the face of great danger
   B. too scared to think rationally
   C. moving too quickly
   D. quick thinking in his escape

Questions 12 through 16 refer to this excerpt from a story.

EXCERPTED FROM "THE WEDDING OF HENRY MARKOWITZ"

Those sprawling universities Henry left behind long ago. America, with its mass-produced undergraduates processed through seedy lecture halls where, under flickering lights, they slump with their knees up and take in lectures as they might see movies. Where the familiar passes into the wide pupils of their eyes and the rest dribbles down the aisles to collect with the dirt and candy wrappers at the professor's feet. Has he not been a professor at Queens College and then NYU? And the graduate students. Hasn't he seen them at Princeton clustering at the office doors? Young Calibans eager for praise. They can tear open the Italian Renaissance before lunch, strangle a Donne sonnet and crush its wings, battering away with blunt instruments. As for the older scholars—like students at a cooking school, they cook up Shakespeare, serve him up like roast goose, stuffed with their political-sexual agendas, carve and quarter him with long knives. For Henry, reading had always been a gentle thing, a thing as delicate as blowing eggs. Two pinpricks and the meaning came, whole, unbroken, into the bowl. Now reading is a boiling and a breaking, something to concoct. It's a deviling of art, history, social theory, politics—all mixed and piped back in and served up on a platter. These are the scholars in the journals now. They are at war with the beautiful. . . .

12. Which of the following is Henry most interested in?

    A. teaching
    B. reading
    C. students
    D. history

13. Based on the passage, it is most likely that Henry would use the term/phrase ____________ to describe younger college students.

    A. bright
    B. open to new ideas
    C. a dime a dozen
    D. insightful about literature

14. When the author compares Shakespeare to a roast goose in the middle of the paragraph, what is she suggesting about the older students?

    The older students

    A. dissect literature too much and ruin the meaning
    B. enjoy literature as they would a fine meal
    C. throw Shakespeare back in Henry's face
    D. have trouble finding meaning in literature

15. What is the tone of this excerpt?

    A. upbeat
    B. scholarly
    C. disapproving
    D. sentimental

16. Later, Henry refers to his brother as a "shaper himself of the tawdry yellow thing they sell now as the humanities."

    Based on this information and the excerpt, what is Henry's attitude toward college education?

    A. indifferent
    B. appreciative
    C. admiring
    D. disapproving

Answers and explanations start on page 188.

LESSON

1

WRITING EFFECTIVE SENTENCES

Simple Sentences

Key Ideas

- Make sure each sentence has a subject and verb and expresses a complete thought.
- If a sentence doesn't express a complete thought, you may need to add a subject, verb, or other words.
- Use correct end punctuation.

A complete simple sentence has at least one subject and one verb. The **subject** is the person, place, or thing that the sentence is talking about. The subject performs an action or is described. The **verb** is the word that tells what action the subject is doing or links the subject to a modifier.

Action verb: Elaine (subject) took (verb) notes on the meeting.

Linking verb: They (subject) were (verb) long (modifier).

If a sentence is missing either the subject or the verb, it is incomplete. An incomplete sentence is called a **fragment.**

EXAMPLES

No subject: Typed up her notes.
Complete sentence: Elaine typed up her notes.

No verb: The computer in the main office.
Complete sentence: The computer in the main office crashed several times.

A complete sentence must also express a complete thought. The reader should not be left asking questions.

Incomplete thought: When she lost her work. (What happened when she lost her work?)
Complete thought: Elaine was very frustrated when she lost her work.

Incomplete thought: The person in charge of computer support. (What about that person?)
Complete thought: Elaine called the person in charge of computer support.

Incomplete thought: By replacing the hard drive.
Complete thought: Elaine can fix the computer by replacing the hard drive.

Finally, a complete sentence should have correct end punctuation. A statement should end with a period, and so should a command. A question should end with a question mark. An exclamation should end with an exclamation point.

Statement: Elaine has lost several files this way.
Command: Turn off the computer.
Question: Will the computer ever be fixed?
Exclamation: What a mess we're in!

If you find a fragment in your writing, rewrite to make it a complete sentence.

- If the sentence does not have a subject, add a subject.
- If the sentence does not have a verb, add a verb.
- If the thought is incomplete, add words or combine the incomplete thought with a complete sentence.

GED® TEST TIP

Read each sentence in a GED® passage to yourself and pause at its end. That may help you "hear" whether the sentence is actually an incomplete thought or a sentence fragment.

PRACTICE 1

A. Directions: Write *C* if the sentence is complete or *F* if the sentence is a fragment. Rewrite any fragments to make them complete.

EXAMPLE

Talks all the time on the telephone. *F Dave talks all the time on the telephone.*

1. Drives his girlfriend crazy. ______

2. As soon as he comes home from work. ______

3. He calls everyone he knows. ______

4. Dave's sister and his best friend. ______

B. Questions 5 through 7 refer to the following advertisement.

What Is Three-Way Calling?

Three-way calling is a unique service that enables you to conduct a conference [Select...] the privacy of your own home. You can talk to your sister in Florida and your mother in Nebraska at the same time. It's even possible to seek a third person's advice when you're in the middle of a regular call. For instance, [Select...].

Why wait? This useful and convenient [Select...] be yours for only pennies a month.

5. Three-way calling is a unique service that enables you to conduct a conference [Select...] the privacy of your own home.

A. call. And from
B. call. It from
C. call from
D. calling from

6. For instance, [Select...].

A. if you're closing a deal, can bring in your lawyer into the conversation
B. if you're closing a deal, can be bringing your lawyer into the conversation
C. if you're closing a deal, you can bring your lawyer into the conversation
D. if you're closing a deal, you might could bring your lawyer into the conversation

7. This useful and convenient [Select...] be yours for only pennies a month.

A. service is
B. service it can
C. service can
D. service. That can

Answers and explanations start on page 188.

LESSON

2

WRITING EFFECTIVE SENTENCES

Compound and Complex Sentences

Key Ideas

- You can join two independent clauses into one compound sentence.
- Use a coordinating conjunction preceded by a comma.
- Choose a conjunction that correctly relates the two ideas.

Compound Sentences

The simple sentences described in Lesson 1 are also called **independent clauses.** An independent clause has a subject and a verb and expresses a complete thought. You can join two or more independent clauses in one **compound sentence.** To make a compound sentence, you should:

- Choose a logical **coordinating conjunction** to join the independent clauses. The coordinating conjunctions are *and, but, or, nor, for, so,* and *yet*.
- Insert a comma before the coordinating conjunction.

EXAMPLES

Two independent clauses: Sam saw a design flaw. He wrote a memo.
Joined correctly: Sam saw a design flaw, so he wrote a memo.

No coordinating conjunction: Sam asked his boss, she told him to send it.
Correct: Sam asked his boss, and she told him to send it.

No comma: Sam's boss was busy so she asked Sam to write the memo.
Correct: Sam's boss was busy, so she asked Sam to write the memo.

Be sure the coordinating conjunction expresses the correct relationship between the ideas in the two independent clauses.

Relationship between Ideas	Coordinating Conjunction
join two equally important ideas	and
contrast two ideas	but, yet
show a cause	for
show an effect	so
give a choice	or
give no choice	nor

GED® TEST TIP

Be sure that a coordinating conjunction separates two independent clauses before you choose the option that inserts a comma before the conjunction.

Incorrect conjunction: Sam showed initiative, **yet** his boss praised him.
Correct conjunction: Sam showed initiative, **and** his boss praised him.

Be sure that you are actually joining two independent clauses and not just two subjects or two verbs.

Incorrect: The designers, and the builders got the memo.
Correct (no comma): The designers and the builders got the memo.

Incorrect: The designers needed the information, and appreciated the memo.
Correct (two independent clauses): The designers needed the information. They appreciated the memo.
Correct (no comma): The designers needed the information and appreciated the memo.

PRACTICE 2.1

A. Directions: Using the list on page 88, choose a coordinating conjunction for each sentence. Rewrite the sentence using the conjunction preceded by a comma.

EXAMPLE

I didn't want to seem timid, ____*so*____ I didn't tell anyone about my experience.

1. It was late ______________________ I was walking home from work.
2. My coworker, Judy, had offered to drive me ______________ I had refused.
3. It was a warm night ______________ I decided to get some fresh air.
4. It was really my choice. I could have taken a cab ______________ I could have walked.
5. I heard a loud noise ______________ I ran the last block to my house. Later, I learned that it was only a car backfiring.

B. <u>Questions 6 through 8</u> refer to the following paragraph.

Air Couriers

If you want to travel abroad but don't have a lot of money, one option is to be an air courier. [Select...] gets a cheap ticket in return. Companies use couriers because it often costs less to check freight as baggage than to ship it as cargo. Air couriers fly on the major [Select...] sometimes they can't check any baggage of their own. Couriers usually book their trips [Select...].

6. [Select...] gets a cheap ticket in return.

   A. An air courier carries shipping documents on an international flight, and
   B. An air courier carries shipping documents on an international flight and
   C. An air courier, carries shipping documents on an international flight, and
   D. An air courier carries shipping documents, on an international flight, and

7. Air couriers fly on the major [Select...] sometimes they can't check any baggage of their own.

   A. airlines, but
   B. airlines but
   C. airlines nor
   D. airlines, or

8. Couriers usually book their trips [Select...].

   A. in advance but they get their tickets on the day of the flight
   B. in advance, but they get their tickets on the day of the flight
   C. in advance getting their tickets on the day of the flight
   D. in advance, but they get their tickets, on the day of the flight

Answers and explanations start on page 188.

Complex Sentences

A **complex sentence** is made up of an independent clause and a **subordinate clause.** A subordinate clause has a subject and verb, but it does not express a complete thought.

Key Ideas

- Join a subordinate and an independent clause to form a complex sentence.
- Use a subordinating conjunction that shows the correct relationship between ideas.
- Put a comma after the subordinate clause when it comes at the beginning of a sentence.

EXAMPLES

Subordinate clause: Because their pay was too low.
Complex sentence: Teachers went on strike because their pay was too low.
independent clause — subordinate clause

Every subordinate clause begins with a **subordinating conjunction** that shows the relationship between the subordinate clause and the independent clause. Below is a list of common subordinating conjunctions.

Relationship between Clauses	Subordinating Conjunction
cause/reason	because
effect/result	in order that, so that
time	after, as, before, once, since, until, when, whenever, while
place	where, wherever
choice	if, whether
contradiction	although, even though, though

ON THE GED® TEST

You may need to select the correct subordinating conjunction to link two clauses. Choose the word or phrase that correctly conveys the relationship between the ideas.

Choose the subordinating conjunction that conveys the meaning you are trying to express.

Incorrect meaning: The strike continued for more than a month once it finally ended.
Correct meaning: The strike continued for more than a month before it finally ended.

When a subordinate clause comes at the beginning of a sentence, put a comma after it. If the subordinate clause comes at the end of a sentence, you generally don't need a comma before it.

At beginning of sentence: While teachers were on the picket line, kids stayed home.
At end of sentence: Kids stayed home while teachers were on the picket line.

However, when a subordinate clause at the end of a sentence begins with *although, though,* or *even though,* put a comma before the clause.

At beginning of sentence: Even though the public supported the teachers, the school board did not concede to the teachers' demands.
At end of sentence: The school board did not concede to teachers' demands, even though the public supported the teachers.

A subordinate clause cannot stand independently. By itself, a subordinate clause is a sentence fragment. Make sure that every subordinate clause is joined to an independent clause.

Incorrect: After the strike finished. The school year began.
Corrected by joining independent and subordinate clauses: After the strike finished, the school year began.

PRACTICE 2.2

A. Directions: Join the clauses to form complex sentences. Use the subordinating conjunctions in parentheses.

EXAMPLE

(if) You buy a smoke detector. You can protect your family.

If you buy a smoke detector, you can protect your family.

1. Most fatal fires occur. (when) A family is asleep.

____

2. (because) A smoke alarm wakes you up. It can allow you to escape.

____

3. Try to replace the smoke detector's battery. (before) It goes dead.

____

4. (although) Smoke detectors cost money. The expense is worth it.

____

B. <u>Questions 5 through 7</u> refer to the following paragraph.

Phone Etiquette

When you [Select...] it's wise to keep a few key rules in mind. First of all, be prepared. Have paper and pencil ready so that you won't have to fumble for them. [Select...] the person whether this is a good time to talk. Get to the point quickly. Before you hang [Select...] the person for his or her time. Finally, put the phone down gently. Slamming down the receiver makes a poor impression.

5. When you [Select...] it's wise to keep a few key rules in mind.

A. are making a business call
B. are making a business call,
C. will make a business call
D. business call make

6. [Select...] the person whether this is a good time to talk.

A. After you identify yourself, ask
B. Whenever you identify yourself, ask
C. After you identify yourself ask
D. After identifying yourself and asking

7. Before you hang [Select...] the person for his or her time.

A. up and then Thank
B. up and thank
C. up thank
D. up, thank

Answers and explanations start on page 188.

LESSON 3

WRITING EFFECTIVE SENTENCES

Run-Ons and Comma Splices

Key Ideas

- A run-on sentence is two or more sentences that are connected without correct punctuation.
- In a comma splice, two sentences are joined with only a comma.
- To correct a run-on or comma splice, make a compound or complex sentence or separate the sentences.

Run-Ons

There are two errors people commonly make when they join independent clauses to form a sentence. The first type of error is called a **run-on.** In a run-on, two independent clauses are combined without proper punctuation.

Run-On: Banks offer many helpful services you should check them out.

You can correct a run-on in one of several ways:

- Break the run-on into two separate sentences.

  Correct: Banks offer many services. You should check them out.
- Make a compound sentence (add a coordinating conjunction and a comma).

  Correct: Banks offer many services, so you should check them out.
- Make a complex sentence (add a subordinating conjunction and, if necessary, a comma).

  Correct: Because banks offer many services, you should check them out.

A run-on can also consist of independent clauses strung together with *and.* Correct this kind of run-on by dividing it into one or more compound sentences or by combining ideas into one sentence.

Run-On: Banking is getting more and more convenient and you can check on your account using bank-by-phone services and it's even possible to do your banking on the Internet.
Correct: Banking is getting more and more convenient. You can check on your account using bank-by-phone services, and it's even possible to do your banking on the Internet.

Run-On: Friday I got paid and I went to the bank and I cashed my check.
Correct: Friday I got paid, went to the bank, and cashed my check.

GED® TEST TIP

When you read a run-on sentence or a comma splice, look for the place where you would pause if you read the sentence aloud. That is the place where you would make the correction.

Comma Splices

The second type of error people sometimes make when joining independent clauses is called a **comma splice.** A comma splice occurs when two sentences are joined with just a comma. To correct a comma splice, add a coordinating conjunction after the comma:

Comma splice: You can check on your account using bank-by-phone services, it's even possible to do your banking on the Internet.
Correct: You can check on your account using bank-by-phone services, and it's even possible to do your banking on the Internet.

You can also correct a comma splice using the methods described above for correcting a run-on. You can also join two related ideas with a semicolon.

Comma splice: There are fewer bank tellers today, banks do offer other services.
Corrected by creating a complex sentence: Although there are fewer bank tellers today, banks do offer other services.

PRACTICE 3

A. Directions: Correct the following run-ons and comma splices using the methods explained on page 92. Try to use each method at least once.

1. Jeff just got his driver's license, he's very excited.

____

2. He bought a car that has a lot of miles on it it wasn't very expensive.

____

3. He doesn't have a lot of free time, he'd like to take a car trip.

____

4. He needs to find out about car insurance and he needs to get a good map and he needs to join an auto club.

____

B. Questions 5 through 7 refer to the following paragraph.

Photography Tips

It's not hard to take great [Select...] keep these tips in mind. For one thing, you need to get close to your subject, or you won't get a good shot. [Select...] for the right moment to shoot. Make sure the lighting is sufficient. Even outdoors, you can use a flash to fill in shadows.

Think about what you want to emphasize in your picture. You don't have to use [Select...] allow you to select the focus point you prefer. For example, many photographs of people focus on the eyes.

5. It's not hard to take great [Select...] keep these tips in mind.

A. pictures if you just
B. pictures just
C. pictures, you just
D. pictures that just

6. [Select...] for the right moment to shoot.

A. Be patient, wait
B. Be patient and wait
C. Be patient wait
D. Be patient and you wait

7. You don't have to use [Select...] allow you to select the focus point you prefer.

A. the autofocus option, most cameras
B. the autofocus option most cameras
C. the autofocus option, because most cameras
D. the autofocus option most cameras therefore

Answers and explanations start on page 189.

LESSON

4

WRITING EFFECTIVE SENTENCES

Subordinate Ideas

Key Ideas

- Use smooth, flowing sentences rather than short, choppy sentences.
- Form compound or complex sentences from short sentences.
- Combine two predicates to make a compound predicate or combine two subjects to make a compound subject.

GED® TEST TIP

Read the passages on the test to yourself as if you could hear them in your mind. That "silent hearing" will help you notice sentences that are choppy or repetitive.

Writing is more effective when it flows smoothly. Therefore, try to eliminate short, choppy sentences whenever possible. You can do this by using **subordination** in a variety of ways.

You already know how to form a complex sentence with a subordinating clause. You also know how to create compound sentences. Either of these methods can be used to combine short sentences.

EXAMPLES

Short and choppy: Carla ran for the bus. She missed it.
Complex sentence: Although Carla ran for the bus, she missed it.
Compound sentence: Carla ran for the bus, but she missed it.

If two sentences have the same subject, you can combine them to form one sentence with a compound predicate. The **predicate** includes the verb plus anything else that is not part of the subject:

Short and choppy: Carla sat on the bench. She looked at her watch.
With compound predicate: Carla sat on the bench and looked at her watch.

Likewise, when two sentences have the same predicate, you can combine them to form one sentence with a compound subject. The resulting sentence will be less repetitive and wordy:

Short, choppy, and repetitive: Carla missed the bus. Dave missed the bus, too.
With compound subject: Carla and Dave missed the bus.

Finally, several short sentences that are related can be combined into one longer and more detailed sentence:

Short and choppy: Carla missed the bus. It was the 7:45 bus. She was on her way to work.
More detailed sentence: Carla missed the 7:45 bus on her way to work.

Sometimes, you can use two methods at the same time. For instance, in the sentence below, you can make a complex sentence with combined details:

Short and choppy: Carla found a pay phone near the bus stop. She called her boss. Then she called one of her coworkers.
Complex sentence with combined details: After Carla found a pay phone near the bus stop, she called her boss and one of her coworkers.

Repetitive: Her boss thanked her for calling. Her coworker thanked her for calling, and they both offered to pass along any messages.
With compound subject and compound predicate: Both her boss and her coworker thanked her for calling and offered to pass along any messages.

PRACTICE 4

A. Directions: Write each set of short, choppy sentences as one longer, smooth sentence.

EXAMPLE

If you are in a tornado, keep the windows closed. You should go to a safe place.

If you are in a tornado, keep the windows closed and go to a safe place.

1. Tornadoes can cause a lot of damage. Earthquakes are also capable of causing a lot of damage.

____

2. Earthquakes are somewhat common in California. Many Californians do not seem to mind.

____

3. On May 20, 2013, there was a tornado. It happened in Oklahoma. Twenty-four people were killed. Almost 400 people were injured.

____

4. Tornadoes can occur anywhere in the United States. They can happen any time of year.

____

B. Questions 5 through 7 refer to the following warranty.

Limited Warranty

If there is any defect, Pantronics will repair this unit free of charge. Audio components will be [Select...] to one year after the date of purchase. The unit [Select...]. A proof of purchase, such as a receipt, must be presented in order to receive service. This warranty does not cover damage [Select...] faulty installation.

5. Audio components will be [Select...] to one year after date of purchase.

A. repaired. Repairs will then take up
B. repaired and repairs will take place up
C. repaired, the repairs will take place up
D. repaired up

6. The unit [Select...].

A. may be brought or mailed to the service center
B. may be brought to the service center. Or it can be mailed
C. may be brought to the service center. It can be mailed, too
D. may be brought, or mailing it, to the service center

7. This warranty does not cover damage [Select...] faulty installation.

A. due to accidents. It does not cover damage due to mishandling or
B. due to accidents, nor it does not cover damage due to mishandling or
C. due to accidents or cover damage due to mishandling or
D. due to accidents, mishandling, or

Answers and explanations start on page 189.

LESSON

5

WRITING EFFECTIVE SENTENCES

Modify Ideas

Key Ideas

- Modifiers make writing clearer and more interesting.
- Correct a dangling modifier by turning it into a subordinate clause or by making the word that is modified the subject of the sentence.
- Place a modifier as near as possible to the word or phrase it describes.

GED® TEST TIP

When a modifying phrase is at the beginning of a sentence, use a comma to separate it from the rest of the sentence.

Modifiers are words and phrases used to add descriptive details. A modifier might be a word like *sweaty*, a verb phrase like *dragging the heavy box*, a prepositional phrase like *from the storage room*, or a clause like *that we packed this morning*. Modifiers make writing clearer, more specific, and more interesting.

EXAMPLES

Without modifiers: Our friends Jack and Tina helped us while we were moving.

With modifiers: Our good friends Jack and Tina helped us while we were moving, watching our baby in their home.

Without modifiers: We realized the weather would not cooperate.

With modifiers: Sweating profusely at 9 a.m., we realized the weather would be uncooperatively hot.

Use modifiers carefully, or your meaning will be unclear. A **dangling modifier** is a word or phrase at the beginning of the sentence that has no clear subject to describe. To correct a dangling modifier, turn it into a subordinate clause, or make the word that the modifier describes into the subject of the sentence.

Dangling modifier: Driving the truck, one of the boxes fell out. (Who was driving the truck—one of the boxes?)

Correct: As we were driving the truck, one of the boxes fell out.

Correct: Driving the truck, we heard one of the boxes fall out.

Dangling modifier: Parking in a tow zone, a police officer gave us a ticket. (It sounds as if the police officer were parking in the tow zone.)

Correct: Because we parked in a tow zone, a police officer gave us a ticket.

Dangling modifier: Never having planned a move before, the real estate agent gave us some tips. (It sounds as if the real estate agent is the one who had never planned a move.)

Correct: Never having planned a move before, we asked the real estate agent for some tips.

A **misplaced modifier** is poorly placed in the sentence. It is not clear which word it modifies, or it modifies the wrong word in the sentence. To correct a misplaced modifier, put the modifier next to the word it describes.

Misplaced modifier: The moving van was just large enough that we rented.

Correct: The moving van that we rented was just large enough.

Misplaced modifier: We hoisted and lugged all our furniture up two flights of stairs panting heavily. (What was panting heavily—*we* or *the stairs*?)

Correct: Panting heavily, we hoisted and lugged all our furniture up two flights of stairs.

PRACTICE 5

A. Directions: Revise each sentence, correcting the misplaced or dangling modifier.

1. Trent's sister encouraged him to become a nurse, who is a health professional.

____

2. Waking up the patients to take their blood pressure, they get rather annoyed.

____

3. He writes their temperature and blood pressure on their charts carefully.

____

4. Talking with the patients, it is hard to make visitors leave at 9 p.m.

____

B. **<u>Questions 5 through 7</u> refer to the following passage about adoption.**

Adoption

Adoption is a legal procedure that gives [Select...]. This practice dates back to ancient Greece. People without heirs used it to perpetuate their estates.

Adoptions may be handled through an agency or by independent placement. [Select...] whether prospective parents will be fit. In an independent placement, there is no study. Lawyers [Select...].

5. Adoption is a legal procedure that gives [Select...].

A. a person the rights of a son or daughter, who is not the adopter's birth child
B. a person who is not the birth child of the adopter the rights of a son or daughter
C. a person a son's or daughter's rights, who is not a birth child
D. a person the rights of a birth child, who is not a son or daughter of the adopter

6. [Select...] whether prospective parents will be fit is required.

A. Going through an agency, a "home study" is required to determine
B. Undergoing a "home study," an agency determines
C. An agency requires a "home study" to determine
D. Requiring a "home study," parents undergo such a study to determine

7. Lawyers [Select...].

A. handle these adoptions when parents ask them to frequently
B. handle these adoptions when frequently asked to do so by parents
C. handle these adoptions when parents ask them to, frequently
D. frequently handle these adoptions when parents ask them to

Answers and explanations start on page 189.

LESSON

6

WRITING EFFECTIVE SENTENCES

Parallel Structure

When you write a sentence that lists two or more words, phrases, or clauses, the elements in the list must be in the same grammatical form. In other words, the sentence must have **parallel structure.** Writing that has parallel structure is clearer and easier to follow.

Key Ideas

- Listed items should be parallel in form and structure.
- Each phrase should have the same elements as other phrases in the series.
- Don't put words and clauses together in the same series.

Examples

Not parallel: Jim wants to eat less, exercise more, and be getting more sleep.
Parallel: Jim wants to eat less, exercise more, and get more sleep.

Not parallel: Walking and to swim are good aerobic exercises.
Parallel: Walking and swimming are good aerobic exercises.

Not parallel: Try to lose weight slowly, sensibly, and be careful.
Parallel: Try to lose weight slowly, sensibly, and carefully.

To be sure that your sentences have parallel structure, follow the guidelines below.

Make sure that verbs in a list are in the same form and tense:

Not parallel: Jim went to the store, bought an exercise mat, and is doing exercises.
Parallel: Jim went to the store, bought an exercise mat, and did exercises.

Be sure that phrases in a list are parallel in form and wording. For example, if one phrase in a list begins with a preposition, the others should, too. If one phrase begins with the word *the*, the others should, too.

Not parallel: Avoid exercising on busy streets, near traffic jams, and polluted areas.
Parallel: Avoid exercising on busy streets, near traffic jams, and in polluted areas.

Not parallel: He left the gym shoes, sweatpants, and the shirt in the gym.
Parallel: He left the gym shoes, the sweatpants, and the shirt in the gym.

Each list must have single words, short phrases, or clauses. Don't put single words and clauses together in the same series:

Not parallel: The most effective fitness programs are low impact, informal, and you can do them at home.
Parallel: The most effective fitness programs are low impact, informal, and home based.

Finally, notice that a comma separates each item within a list of three or more: *low impact, informal, and home based.*

GED® TEST TIP

When you revise a sentence to use parallel structure, use the comma to separate each element as shown in these examples.

Practice 6

A. Directions: Rewrite each sentence to make the structure parallel.

EXAMPLE

Jenna works quickly, carefully, and is thorough.

Jenna works quickly, carefully, and thoroughly.

1. Jenna has worked in a factory, a store, and has a waitressed.

___

2. She would like putting her kids in a better school and to get a better job.

___

3. She thinks the kids' father is irresponsible, lazy, and doesn't care about them.

___

4. He doesn't have the time, the energy, or money to give them what they deserve.

___

B. Questions 5 through 7 refer to the following memo.

TO: All Employees

A new alarm system has been installed. It is designed to make our workplace [Select...]. However, we need everyone's cooperation.

If you are the last one to leave, turn off all lights, [Select...] coffee makers. Then go to the alarm system located by the door. Punch in [Select...]. Lock the door behind you.

5. It is designed to make our workplace [Select...].

   A. safer, more comfortable, and pleasant
   B. safer and make it more comfortable and pleasant
   C. safer, more comfortable, and more pleasant
   D. safer, more comfortable, and make it more pleasant

6. If you are the last one to leave, turn off all lights, [Select...] coffee makers.

   A. and computers, and the
   B. computers, and check the
   C. computers, and checking the
   D. computers, and

7. Punch in [Select...].

   A. the secret code, press ON, and leaving immediately
   B. the secret code, pressing ON, and immediately leaving
   C. the secret code, press ON, and leave immediately
   D. the secret code, press ON, and then you will leave immediately

Answers and explanations start on page 189.

WRITING EFFECTIVE SENTENCES PRACTICE QUESTIONS

Questions 1 through 5 refer to the following paragraphs.

Conserving Household Energy

According to the Department of Energy, many families spend an average of 14 percent of their yearly income on heating and cooling costs. Although you can't do much about high fuel prices, you can try some energy-saving measures.

To reduce wintertime energy costs, keep the shades drawn at night. [Select...] the cracks. You can use sealing material available at any hardware store. If you have an air conditioner, cover it with thick plastic. Keep your thermostat at 68°F [Select...].

In the summer, use fans and natural breezes rather than air-conditioning whenever possible. If you have windows that get direct [Select...] the shades down during the day. Don't leave your air conditioner running when you're not at [Select...] the filter every summer. With a clogged filter, the air conditioner's energy use can go up as much as 5 percent. Put your air conditioner on a low setting. Your home [Select...].

1. [Select...] the cracks.

   A. Sealing your windows, so that cold air can't get through
   B. Seal your windows so that cold air can't get through
   C. Seal your windows, so that cold air couldn't get out
   D. Your windows being sealed, cold air won't get through

2. Keep your thermostat at 68°F [Select...].

   A. day, and it should be kept at 62° at night
   B. day and 62° at night
   C. day. Keep it at 62° at night
   D. day. At night, it should be kept at 62°

3. If you have windows that get direct [Select...] the shades down during the day.

   A. sun and
   B. sun and to keep
   C. sun keep
   D. sun, keep

4. Don't leave your air conditioner running when you're not at [Select...] the filter every summer.

   A. home and change
   B. home change
   C. home, so change
   D. home. Do change

5. Your home [Select...].

   A. will not cool down any faster when your air conditioner is on full blast
   B. any faster will not cool down having your air conditioner on full blast
   C. will not cool down having your air conditioner on full blast any faster
   D. will not cool down when any faster your air conditioner is on full blast

Questions 6 through 10 refer to the following letter of complaint.

Cole Electronics
2514 Broadway
New York, NY 10057

Dear Manager:

On August 2, I purchased a television at your store. Select... that the picture was fuzzy. Select... be fixed easily. I assumed that there would be no problem because I had just purchased the set.

The customer service personnel said they had no time to handle my complaint. They were extremely rude and unprofessional. Finally, a salesman told me that I would have to send the TV to a service center in Detroit. At that point, I demanded a refund. Select... it could not be returned.

I am Select... . I would now like to receive a full Select... the TV repaired locally. Please contact me to let me know what action will be taken. My phone number is (212) 555-2719.

Sincerely,
Jeffrey Barnes

6. Select... that the picture was fuzzy.

   A. When I got the television home I discovered
   B. When I got the television home, I discovered
   C. When I got the television home. I discovered
   D. When I got the television home I discovered,

7. Select... be fixed easily.

   A. I returned to the store to see if the problem could
   B. Returned to the store, I wanted to see if the problem could
   C. Returning to the store, the problem could
   D. Returning to the store to see if the problem could

8. Select... it could not be returned.

   A. He claimed that because the TV had been used,
   B. Claiming that because the TV had been used,
   C. The TV was claimed to be used, and therefore
   D. Claimed that the TV had been used and said

9. I am Select... .

   A. angry and frustrated about the treatment I received
   B. angry about the treatment I received. I am also very frustrated
   C. angry about the treatment I received, I am also frustrated
   D. angry about the treatment I received I am also frustrated

10. I would now like to receive a full Select... the TV repaired locally.

   A. refund, getting
   B. refund, or getting
   C. refund or get
   D. refund to getting

Questions 11 though 15 refer to the following paragraphs.

Workplace Friendships

Should you make friends at work or keep your distance? Most experts agree that it's not wise to get too chummy with your boss. Relationships with coworkers, however, are a more complex matter. Although workplace friendships between peers can be beneficial, they can also cause problems.

Workplace friendships have many positive aspects. It's hard to [Select...]. Having friends at work [Select...]. Friends can serve as a sounding board for problems and help you succeed.

However, like any other friendship, workplace friendships can turn sour. [Select...] in plain view of your boss and coworkers. Discrimination and harassment suits have even been brought in some cases.

Experts recommend keeping your social life with work friends out of the workplace. For instance, don't exchange presents at [Select...] about your evening out. Avoid praising a friend publicly if it could make someone else resentful. Keeping your work life separate from your social life [Select...].

11. It's hard to [Select...].
    A. work productively if you feel alone
    B. work if you feel alone and in a productive way
    C. work in a productive way and feeling alone
    D. work, it isn't easy if you feel alone, productively

12. Having friends at work [Select...].
    A. can make your day more pleasant. And can give you energy
    B. can make your day more pleasant, and give you energy
    C. can make your day more pleasant and give you energy
    D. can make your day, giving you energy, more pleasant

13. [Select...] in plain view of your boss and coworkers.
    A. Things get messy, when the friendship unravels
    B. Things get messy when the friendship unravels
    C. Things are getting messy, when the friendship unravels
    D. Things getting messy when the friendship unravels

14. For instance, don't exchange presents at [Select...] about your evening out.
    A. work or talk
    B. work, or talk
    C. work, or talking
    D. working or talking

15. Keeping your work life separate from your social life [Select...].
    A. is worth the effort although it be hard
    B. may be hard, but it's worth the effort
    C. is worth the effort it may be hard
    D. may be hard but, it's worth the effort

Questions 16 through 19 refer to the following paragraphs.

Computer Virus Hoaxes

If you use email, you've probably received at least one message warning you of a terrible virus that will ruin your computer. Most of these messages are Select... to scare you. Though some messages about viruses are accurate, most are just inaccurate rumors.

Virus hoax messages are similar to one another. Frequently, they describe viruses that will destroy your hard drive or computer. These hoaxes also claim that a respected authority, such as a government agency, has issued a warning about the virus. You can Select.... Finally, hoaxes urge you to send the message to everyone you Select... just creates panic.

If you receive a virus warning, don't pass it on. However, you don't have to worry about opening the email message itself. Your computer can't get a virus that way. Don't open any suspicious attachments, though, as you might infect your computer with a real virus. By following these guidelines, you can Select....

16. Most of these messages are Select... to scare you.

    A. hoaxes and they are designed
    B. hoaxes and they designed
    C. hoaxes, designing
    D. hoaxes designed

17. You can Select....

    A. check a claim like this. Contacting the agency is a good way to check
    B. check a claim like this by contacting the agency
    C. check a claim like this, is contacting the agency
    D. check a claim like this, contact the agency

18. Finally, hoaxes urge you to send the message to everyone you Select... just creates panic.

    A. know and this
    B. know, this
    C. know. This
    D. know that this

19. By following these guidelines, you can Select....

    A. keep your computer equipment safe, and avoid spreading hysteria
    B. avoid spreading hysteria, keep your computer equipment safe
    C. avoiding spreading hysteria by keeping your computer equipment safe
    D. keep your computer equipment safe and avoid spreading hysteria

Answers and explanations start on page 189.

LESSON

1

Connecting Ideas

Organize Ideas into Paragraphs

Key Ideas

- Each paragraph should have one main idea. Each sentence in the paragraph should relate to the main idea.
- Break long paragraphs into two if possible.
- Join short paragraphs if they both relate to the same main idea.

GED® TEST TIP

If a paragraph is especially long, check to see if the main idea shifts at some point. If so, that is where the paragraph should be divided in two.

Effective Paragraphs

A **paragraph** is a group of sentences that relate to one main idea. If the sentences do not help develop the same main idea, the paragraph seems disorganized, and the writer's meaning is unclear.

Incorrect: Group of sentences that do not relate to the same main idea:

Houseplants make a home more beautiful, but many people find them difficult to take care of. I water my houseplants once a week. There are many different kinds of houseplants. If you are buying a houseplant as a gift, consider how much light the person's home gets.

In the example above, each sentence is about houseplants, but there is no main idea. In the paragraph below, however, each sentence supports one idea: *helping houseplants adjust to a new home.*

Correct: Paragraph with sentences that relate to one main idea:

Houseplants need help to adjust to a new environment. Your home is probably less bright and humid than a greenhouse or plant store. Therefore, when you get a new houseplant, keep it near a south-facing window at first. Move it away from the light over a period of four weeks. Use a humidifier to make the air in your home more humid. These actions will help avoid the loss of foliage that often occurs when plants change locales.

One paragraph should stop and a new one begin when the main idea shifts. In the example below, the first four sentences describe what road rage is, while the last four sentences tell how to react to road rage. The writer should have started a new paragraph with sentence 5.

Incorrect: One paragraph that should be divided into two paragraphs:

(1) Road rage is an episode of violent behavior that takes place when one driver's actions anger another driver. (2) Young males are the most likely to lose their cool on the road. (3) Most road rage incidents take place during rush hour, when people often get frustrated. (4) Warm weather is another factor in road rage. (5) If you're a victim of an aggressive driver, try to stay calm. (6) Don't react or make eye contact. (7) Try not to brake or swerve in retaliation. (8) These actions will only infuriate the other driver, and you might lose control of your car.

Sometimes the ideas in two paragraphs really belong in one:

Incorrect: Two paragraphs that should be combined:

To make chicken broth, boil a pot of water. Take some chicken, onions, parsnips, carrots, and herbs, and wrap them up in cheesecloth.

Make sure it is real cotton cheesecloth, or you won't be able to eat the broth! Simmer the cheesecloth-wrapped vegetables and chicken in the water for several hours; then remove them. Add salt and pepper to taste.

PRACTICE 1.1

A. Directions: Read each group of sentences. If there is a main idea, underline it. If there is no main idea, write "No MI."

____ 1. The pharmacist at the local drugstore is very helpful. She can always get the medicines we need. She arranges deliveries of our prescriptions when we're sick. When we don't have money, she lets us pay the next time. Many people have written to thank her.

____ 2. Keep your toolbox well equipped, and you'll always be able to make home repairs. Common home repairs include replacing lighting fixtures and fixing furniture. The community center offers a class on this subject. You can pay someone to do home repairs.

____ 3. Some people don't vote because they think their vote doesn't count. However, elections have been won by just a few hundred votes. If people don't vote, they are giving up their voice. Every vote counts, so let your voice be heard and vote!

____ 4. When you are traveling, it's a good idea to mark your luggage clearly. Put a luggage tag on every piece you intend to bring, including hand luggage like backpacks. To recognize your luggage quickly, put a brightly colored ribbon on it.

____ 5. Listening to music can benefit you in many ways. When you are feeling stressed, music can help soothe and relax you. When you need energy, rock 'n' roll or hip-hop can give you a boost. If you have a baby or small child, soft music can help lull the child to sleep.

B. Questions 6 and 7 refer to the following paragraphs.

The Common Cold

(A)

(1) How frequently you get colds depends on your age. (2) The average young adult gets two to four colds a year. (3) Adults over 60 have fewer than one cold a year, while children have six to ten colds annually. (4) Colds are caused by viruses. (5) Contrary to popular belief, being cold will not cause you to get a cold. (6) Vitamin C is thought to prevent colds, but there is no proof.

(B)

(7) Because there is no cure for the common cold, prevention is key. (8) Washing your hands is the best way to avoid getting a cold. (9) Encourage others who have colds to sneeze into a tissue and throw it away immediately.

(C)

(10) Refrain from touching your eyes and nose, and stay far from people who have colds.

6. Which revision would improve the effectiveness of the article?

Begin a new paragraph with

A. sentence 2
B. sentence 3
C. sentence 4
D. sentence 5

7. Which revision would improve the effectiveness of the article?

A. remove sentence (1)
B. remove paragraph B
C. remove paragraph C
D. join paragraphs B and C

Answers and explanations start on page 190.

Topic Sentences in Paragraphs

Every paragraph should have a **topic sentence** that states the main idea. The other sentences in the paragraph are **supporting details**. These details tell more about the topic sentence. The topic sentence usually appears at the beginning of the paragraph, though it may appear elsewhere.

A topic sentence must do two things:

- Identify the topic, or subject, of the paragraph
- State the central point that the writer wants to make about the topic

In the paragraph below, the topic sentence is underlined. Notice how the topic sentence tells the subject of the paragraph *(graffiti in our neighborhood)* and states the central point about the topic *(graffiti is a serious problem in the neighborhood and should be addressed).*

EXAMPLE

We need to do more to stop the problem of graffiti in our neighborhood. Recently, several bus stops and the exterior walls of many buildings have been defaced with unsightly graffiti. The neighborhood is fast becoming a much less desirable place to live. As a result, prospective renters feel frightened and look elsewhere.

A topic sentence should not be too specific or too general. If it is, readers won't know what the overall point is. A topic sentence like "The market is covered with gang symbols" would be too specific for the paragraph above. "There is graffiti in our neighborhood" would be too general.

Main Idea Statements in Essays

Just as every paragraph should have a topic sentence, so every essay should have a **main idea statement**. Whereas a topic sentence states the main idea, or "point," of a single paragraph, a main idea statement expresses the central point of all the paragraphs in an essay. In the essay below, the main idea statement is underlined. Notice that while the main idea statement appears in the first paragraph, it is not the first sentence.

EXAMPLE

While graffiti is indeed a serious problem facing our neighborhood, other issues also need to be addressed. Two of the most pressing neighborhood issues are the crime rate and the lack of decent housing.

In recent months, crime has increased. For example, a number of muggings have occurred. As a result, residents are nervous about going out at night. The number of apartment break-ins has increased as well. We need a stronger police presence to combat the crime problem.

In addition, much of the housing in this neighborhood is in poor condition. Every day, residents are put in danger by peeling paint, broken locks, and rundown fences. We must put pressure on landlords to resolve their tenants' complaints, perhaps by showing them that, in the long run, it is in their financial interest to do so.

If we do not act immediately, our neighborhood will decline even more. Therefore, I recommend that we form a community task force to tackle these issues. We should ask our city councilwoman to be an advocate for us. With full participation of community members, we will be on our way to a safer, more livable neighborhood.

Key Ideas

- A topic sentence states the main idea of a paragraph.
- Each sentence in a paragraph should provide details to support the main idea.
- An essay should have a main idea statement that states the main point of the entire essay.

GED® TEST TIP

Be sure that every paragraph has a clear topic sentence.

PRACTICE 1.2

A. Directions: Write topic sentences for each of the following paragraphs.

1. ____

Weather satellites send us information about weather around the world. Thanks to satellite TV, we have an ever-widening range of programs to choose from. Satellites even play a role in long-distance telephone communication.

2. ____

First of all, stock prices are falling. Second, home sales have slowed to a crawl. Finally, many consumers have cut back on big purchases such as cars, home improvements, and vacations.

3. ____

According to the new dress code, employees of the library may now wear "semi-casual" clothing. Khakis, blue jeans with no holes, and other slacks are acceptable for men and women. Skirts must be knee-length or longer. Sandals are acceptable in the summer. Employees are requested not to wear gym shoes.

B. Questions 4 and 5 refer to the following paragraphs.

Repetitive Strain Injury

(A)

Repetitive strain injury is a problem. The injury can affect factory workers, computer users, and meatpackers, among others. Anyone who uses his or her hands all day may be affected, even if the work does not seem to require a lot of physical effort. When fine hand movements are repeated for many hours a day, they eventually strain the forearms, wrists, and fingers.

(B)

Maintaining a stiff and constrained posture, as is required for working at a computer, places a lot of stress on the body. Likewise, holding muscles still for long periods causes fatigue and discomfort. In addition, many jobs require workers to work at top speed all day long. Consistently working quickly deprives the body of natural rest breaks, forcing workers to push themselves to the limit.

4. Which is the most effective revision of sentence 1?

A. Some workers get repetitive strain injury.
B. Just what, you may ask, is repetitive strain injury?
C. Workers suffer many injuries on the job, and repetitive strain injury is just one of them.
D. Repetitive strain injury is a painful condition resulting from repeated use of the hands.

5. Which sentence would be most effective if inserted at the beginning of paragraph B?

A. Repetitive movements cause muscle strain.
B. A number of factors contribute to repetitive strain injury.
C. Watch your posture as you work.
D. Repetitive strain injury is very common.

Answers and explanations start on page 190.

LESSON

2

CONNECTING IDEAS

Use Logical Order and Relevant Ideas

Key Ideas

- The sentences in a paragraph should follow a logical order.
- Keep reasons and examples close to the point you are making with them.
- Eliminate any irrelevant details.

When you are writing a paragraph, it is important to put your sentences in a logical order. For instance, you may choose to sequence supporting details from most important to least important, from least important to most important, or in time order. All the sentences in the paragraph should follow the same order. If not, your readers may get confused. Look at the sample paragraphs below:

Incorrect: Sentences not in time order:

To clear a clogged drain using a plunger, fill the sink with enough water to cover the plunger cup. Put petroleum jelly on the rim of the cup to form a tight seal. Before you begin, check to make sure that the plunger's suction cup is big enough to cover the drain. Block the sink overflow with rags. Plunge 15 or 20 times.

Correct: Sentences in time order:

To clear a clogged drain using a plunger, first check to make sure that the plunger's suction cup is big enough to cover the drain. Fill the sink with enough water to cover the plunger cup. Put petroleum jelly on the rim of the cup to form a tight seal. Block the sink overflow with rags. Plunge 15 or 20 times.

The reasons and examples you use to support your points should come immediately after you make each point. If they come later, they will be less effective.

Incorrect: Reason far from point:

Don't make a habit of using chemicals to clear your drain. Always wear rubber gloves to protect your hands when using chemical drain cleaners. These powerful cleaners can damage the pipes.

Correct: Reason close to point:

Don't make a habit of using chemicals to clear your drain. These powerful cleaners can damage the pipes. Always wear rubber gloves to protect your hands when using chemical drain cleaners.

ON THE GED® TEST

Make sure that every supporting sentence is relevant to the topic sentence. Ask yourself, "Does this support the main idea of the paragraph?" If not, delete it or move it to where it belongs.

Sometimes a sentence in a paragraph relates to the topic in a general way but does not support the topic sentence. This mistake is a type of **irrelevant detail**, as shown in the paragraph below:

In many cultures, blonde is considered a desirable hair color. Perhaps blonde hair is valued because few people are naturally blonde. The practice of bleaching one's hair blonde is very old, dating back to ancient Roman times, and it continues to be popular today. My sister dyed her hair last year. A number of hair-bleaching products are sold in drugstores and supermarkets.

The sentence "My sister dyed her hair last year," is an irrelevant detail. While it relates to the topic of bleaching one's hair, it does not support the idea that blonde is a popular hair color in many cultures. This sentence should be deleted.

PRACTICE 2

A. Directions: Cross out the irrelevant detail in each paragraph.

1. Why do people blame themselves when things go terribly wrong? Some psychologists believe that by blaming themselves, people find a reason for the upsetting event. Getting very ill is one bad thing that could happen. Finding a reason is more comforting than believing that the event took place for no reason at all.

2. It's almost time for the back-to-school rush. This year, come to Carter's to make sure that your child is outfitted with all the things that he or she needs. We have school supplies at rock-bottom prices. Adult students can also use school supplies. Check out our backpacks and lunch boxes in colors your kids will love. At Carter's, we have everything your kids will ever need!

3. Tenants: On Friday, April 23, the boiler in this building will be fixed. This job will be extremely expensive! There will be no water from 8 A.M. to 5 P.M. Please plan in advance, and draw out water the night before to be used the next day. We apologize for the inconvenience.

B. Questions 4 through 6 refer to the following cover letter.

(A)

Dear Mr. Soros:

(1) Thank you very much for taking the time to speak with me about the carpentry position. (2) It was a pleasure to meet you and to learn about your organization. (3) I enjoyed meeting you and learning about your organization.

(B)

(4) As you will see from the enclosed resume, I recently completed a program in carpentry at Dade Community College. (5) I have also worked in the carpentry field. (6) In addition, I held a secretarial job.

(C)

(7) With my education and experience, I believe that I could make a valuable contribution to your company. (8) Thank you for considering me for this position. (9) I look forward to hearing from you soon. (10) I would be honored to take the job if it were offered to me.

Sincerely,

Sandra Barnes

4. Which revision would improve the effectiveness of paragraph A?
   A. remove sentence 1
   B. move sentence 1 to follow sentence 2
   C. move sentence 2 to the beginning of paragraph B
   D. remove sentence 3

5. Sentence 6: In addition, I held a secretarial job.

   Which revision should be made to the placement of sentence 6?
   A. move sentence 6 to follow sentence 4
   B. move sentence 6 to follow sentence 8
   C. move sentence 6 to follow sentence 10
   D. remove sentence 6

6. Sentence 10: I would be honored to take the job if it were offered to me.

   Which revision should be made to the placement of sentence 10?
   A. move sentence 10 to follow sentence 2
   B. move sentence 10 to follow sentence 4
   C. move sentence 10 to follow sentence 5
   D. move sentence 10 to follow sentence 8

Answers and explanations start on page 190.

LESSON

3

CONNECTING IDEAS

Relate Sentences and Paragraphs

Good writing flows smoothly and logically from one sentence to the next and from one paragraph to the next. To make your writing flow, use **transitions** to show how ideas are related. Here are some common transitions and their uses.

Transitional Word or Phrase	Use it to . . .
for example, for instance	give an example
also, furthermore, in addition, in the same way, likewise, moreover, similarly	compare ideas or add to an idea
however, nevertheless, on the other hand, in contrast	contrast ideas
first, second, then, next, after that, later, at last, finally, in conclusion	show steps in a process or time order
because	show a cause
as a result, consequently	show a result
therefore, thus	draw a conclusion

You can link two sentences using transitions in the following ways:

EXAMPLES

Begin the second sentence with a transition followed by a comma: Raquel has many hobbies. For example, she paints furniture and sews clothes.

Put the transition within the second sentence and set it off with commas: Raquel has many hobbies. She paints furniture, for example, and sews clothes.

Combine the two sentences into one. Put a semicolon before the transition and a comma after it: Raquel has many hobbies; for example, she paints furniture and sews clothes.

Transitions can also be used to link one paragraph to another, highlighting the relationship between the two paragraphs.

EXAMPLE

Top performance in sports depends on "mental economy." Mental economy involves focusing the mind on the task at hand. When athletes think too much about what they're doing or worry about the outcome, they interfere with the communication between the brain and the muscles.

In addition, athletes must strive for "physical economy." Although athletes put forth a tremendous amount of effort, they must take care to pace themselves in order to conserve energy for the end of the event.

To decide which transition to use, see how the paragraph is organized and what you are trying to accomplish. For example, are you comparing two things? If so, you will want to use transitions that compare ideas. Similarly, when choosing transitions to introduce paragraphs, consider the organization of the entire essay.

Key Ideas

- Use transitions to help your writing flow from sentence to sentence and from paragraph to paragraph.
- Choose the transition that expresses the correct relationship between ideas.

GED® TEST TIP

When you use a transition at the beginning of a sentence, be sure you put a comma after the transition.

Practice 3

A. Directions: Rewrite each pair of sentences using a transition from the chart on page 110. Change the punctuation if necessary. Write your answers on a separate sheet of paper.

Example: We have worked very hard this year. Sales are at an all-time high.
We have worked very hard this year. As a result, sales are at an all-time high.

1. Our marketing efforts need to be enhanced. We will soon begin another marketing initiative.
2. Sales representatives say their jobs are extremely demanding. The salary is attractive.
3. The marketing director has instructed sales representatives to try some new ideas. Sales representatives can give away free samples.
4. A new ad campaign will be launched in just a few weeks. We expect sales to increase.

B. Questions 5 through 7 refer to the following paragraphs.

Library Cafés

Until very recently, eating was not something that most people associated with libraries. A patron would likely be chased out for munching on a sandwich in a corner. [Select...] and a croissant in some public libraries.

Following the lead of successful bookstores, libraries across the country are installing cafés. Some library cafés have menus that offer just as much variety as a regular [Select...], one of them offers 20 varieties of coffee, hot cider, and muffins. These refreshments make going to the library more pleasant and may therefore increase library patronage.

[Select...] may benefit a library financially. The income from the café adds to library revenues. Also, as more people enjoy coming to the library, they may be more likely to approve tax increases for it.

5. [Select...] and a croissant in some public libraries.
   A. Times however are changing, and these days patrons can even buy coffee
   B. Times are changing, however, and these days patrons can even buy coffee
   C. Times are changing, and these days, however patrons can even buy coffee
   D. Times are changing, and these days patrons can even buy coffee, however

6. Some library cafés have menus that offer just as much variety as those of a regular [Select...] one of them offers 20 varieties of coffee, hot cider, and muffins.
   A. restaurant, in addition,
   B. restaurant. For example,
   C. restaurant. Nevertheless,
   D. restaurant. Thus,

7. [Select...] may benefit a library financially.
   A. In addition, having a café
   B. On the other hand, having a café
   C. A café, by benefiting a library,
   D. Financially a café

Answers and explanations start on page 190.

Connecting Ideas Practice Questions

Questions 1 through 5 refer to the following paragraphs.

The Effects of Lack of Sleep

(A)

(1) Research shows that about 70 million North Americans have experienced the problem of sleep disruption. (2) Losing sleep is more than just an annoyance. (3) In some cases, it can have catastrophic results. (4) In the United States, sleepy drivers are responsible for at least 100,000 car crashes each year. (5) Most people need at least eight hours of shut-eye a night but get only six or seven. (6) Their fast-paced lives leave them little time for sleep. (7) Another factor is poor bedtime habits. (8) Family stresses may also cause sleep loss.

(B)

(9) A study of high school students showed that students with low grades went to bed 40 minutes later and got 25 minutes less sleep than students with high [Select... ▾] another study shows that when one gets fewer than six to eight hours of sleep, it is harder to learn new skills.

(C)

(11) If you have trouble sleeping, avoid caffeine and alcohol. (12) Get regular exercise during the day, when it won't make you too energized to sleep. (13) Exercise can also help you lose weight.

(D)

(14) Set times for going to bed and getting up each day, and stick to them. (15) Don't watch TV or use a computer late at night, since these stimulate visual response and interfere with sleep. (16) If you find you still can't sleep, get up and do something.

1. Which revision would improve the effectiveness of the article?

   Begin a new paragraph with

   A. sentence 3
   B. sentence 4
   C. sentence 5
   D. sentence 6

2. Which sentence would be most effective if inserted at the beginning of paragraph B?

   A. Some high school students get better grades than others.
   B. High-achieving students get more sleep.
   C. Lack of sleep interferes with mathematical ability.
   D. People need more sleep than they used to.

3. A study of high school students showed that students with low grades went to bed 40 minutes later and got 25 minutes less sleep than students with high [Select... ▾] another study shows that when one gets fewer than six to eight hours of sleep, it is harder to learn new skills.

   A. grades. Similarly,
   B. grades, likewise,
   C. grades. As a result,
   D. grades. Therefore,

4. Exercise can also help you lose weight.

   Which revision should be made to the placement of sentence 13?

   A. move sentence 13 to follow sentence 11
   B. move sentence 13 to follow sentence 14
   C. move sentence 13 to follow sentence 15
   D. remove sentence 13

5. Which revision would improve the effectiveness of the article?

   A. join paragraphs B and C
   B. move sentence 11 to the end of paragraph B
   C. remove sentence 14
   D. join paragraphs C and D

Questions 6 through 10 refer to the following paragraphs.

Getting Out Those Troublesome Stains

(A)

(1) Have you ever ruined a nice piece of clothing by staining it? (2) If so, the following information on stain removal may interest you. (3) By learning a few simple rules and keeping some household cleaners on hand, you can preserve your clothing. (4) First of all, the faster you act, the better. (5) With time, the stain will set. (6) Be sure to blot the stain rather than scrubbing it. (7) Scrubbing can actually drive the stain into the fabric.

(B)

(8) Use hot water on a grease stain such as salad dressing and cold water on a water-based stain such as wine, pasta sauce, or blood. (9) If you don't know what the stain is or where it came from, use room-temperature water. (10) Otherwise you might set the stain.

(C)

(11) Sometimes other liquids are more effective than water. (12) Lemon [Select...] ink, rust, and iodine. (13) White vinegar takes out alcohol, coffee, deodorants, and glue. (14) Liquid shampoo can be used on oil, tar, and grease. (15) Not surprisingly, it works the same way on an oil stain as it does on oil in your hair. (16) Rubbing alcohol removes stains from grass and soft drinks.

(D)

(17) If you find that a stain is not going away or is getting worse, stop and take your clothes to a dry cleaner. (18) Professionals know best. (19) Home remedies may not work on every stain.

6. Which revision would improve the effectiveness of the article?

   Begin a new paragraph with

   A. sentence 3
   B. sentence 4
   C. sentence 5
   D. sentence 6

7. Which sentence would be most effective if inserted at the beginning of paragraph B?

   A. Hot and cold water have many uses.
   B. Choose the right water temperature for cleaning each stain.
   C. Hot water takes out tough stains.
   D. The second step is to determine the proper use of hot water.

8. Lemon [Select...] ink, rust, and iodine.

   A. juice, for example removes
   B. juice, for example. Removes
   C. juice for example removes
   D. juice, for example, removes

9. Which revision would improve the effectiveness of paragraph C?

   A. move sentence 11 to follow sentence 12
   B. move sentence 12 to follow sentence 14
   C. remove sentence 14
   D. remove sentence 15

10. Home remedies may not work on every stain.

    Which revision should be made to the placement of sentence 19?

    A. move sentence 19 to the beginning of paragraph C
    B. move sentence 19 to follow sentence 13
    C. move sentence 19 to the beginning of paragraph D
    D. move sentence 19 to follow sentence 17

Questions 11 through 14 refer to the following memo.

To: All Employees
From: Denise Ellis, Benefits Manager

(A)

(1) Starting on January 1, Allcity will no longer be our insurance carrier. (2) Instead, you will have a choice of two other insurance carriers: HealthPlan and Rainbow Insurance Company.

(B)

(3) HealthPlan is an HMO. (4) You will not have to pay any money to doctors in advance with this plan, but you must go to doctors listed with the insurance company. (5) HMOs are becoming increasingly popular. (6) With Rainbow Insurance, you may choose any doctor you wish. (7) [Select...] you receive the service. (8) Afterwards, you submit the receipts to Rainbow Insurance. (9) Representatives of both companies will be here on December 2 to discuss the details of their plans. (10) Please sign up for an informa-tional session on that day. (11) The sign-up sheet is on the door of the conference room, where the meetings will take place.

(C)

(12) At the meeting, you will receive a card on which you must indicate your choice of company. (13) Please mark your choice in the appropriate box and submit it to me by December 5.

(D)

(14) If you do not submit your card in time, you may not be insured for the month of January. (15) If you are not able to attend any of the informational sessions, please let me know right away. (16) Feel free to contact me at ext. 2453 with any questions you may have about this process.

11. Which revision would improve the effectiveness of paragraph B?

A. remove sentence 3
B. move sentence 5 to the beginning of paragraph B
C. remove sentence 5
D. remove sentence 10

12. [Select...] you receive the service.

A. However, you must pay the health providers when
B. However you must pay, the health providers when
C. However you must pay the health providers when,
D. However you must pay the health providers, when

13. Which revision would improve the effectiveness of the memo?

Begin a new paragraph with

A. sentence 7
B. sentence 8
C. sentence 9
D. sentence 10

14. If you do not submit your card on time, you may not be insured for the month of January.

Which revision should be made to the placement of sentence 14?

A. move sentence 14 to the end of paragraph C
B. move sentence 14 to follow sentence 15
C. move sentence 14 to follow sentence 16
D. remove sentence 14

Questions 15 through 19 refer to the following paragraphs.

Repairing a Flat Bicycle Tire

(A)

(1) The first step in fixing a flat bicycle tire is to remove the wheel. (2) Next, release the brake. (3) Before you begin, let out any air in the tire. (4) If you are removing the back wheel, put the derailleur in high gear. (5) Then take off the axle nuts by unscrewing counterclockwise. (6) If your bike has safety washers, remove these also. (7) Then remove the wheel.

(B)

(8) Remove the tire, and mark the valve stem position on it. (9) If possible, remove the tire without using tools, because the inner tube punctures easily. (10) Use tire levers or the backs of forks and spoons if necessary. (11) When you find the leak, scrape the spot with sandpaper. (12) Remove the inner tube and inflate it, listening and feeling for air leaks. (13) Then apply cement to the tube, and let it dry completely before putting the patch on.

(C)

(14) First, inflate the tube and make sure the leak has been fixed. (15) Next, slip the inner tube back into the tire, and put the tire back on the rim. (16) Then inflate the tube to the correct pressure. (17) The pressure is right when there is enough air to steady the tire but not so much air that the tire cannot be squeezed between the brake pads.

(D)

(18) Put the bike back on its wheels, and then tighten the wheel nuts. (19) Select... ready to ride!

15. Which revision would improve the effectiveness of paragraph A?

    A. move sentence 2 to follow sentence 3
    B. begin a new paragraph with sentence 5
    C. move sentence 5 to follow sentence 7
    D. remove sentence 6

16. Which revision would improve the effectiveness of paragraph B?

    A. move sentence 11 to follow sentence 8
    B. move sentence 11 to follow sentence 9
    C. move sentence 11 to follow sentence 12
    D. move sentence 11 to follow sentence 13

17. Which sentence would be most effective if inserted at the beginning of paragraph C?

    A. All you have to do now is take care of the tire pressure.
    B. Fixing a flat tire is a long process that requires a lot of patience.
    C. The next step is to put the tire and tube back onto the rim.
    D. Patching the leak properly is also very important.

18. Which sentence would be most effective if inserted at the beginning of paragraph D?

    A. The final step is to reinstall the wheel.
    B. Fixing a flat tire requires careful planning.
    C. Whether you are an experienced cyclist or just a beginner, you can fix a flat tire.
    D. Try not to use sharp tools to fix a flat tire.

19. Select... ready to ride!

    A. Then readjust the tire pressure, and you're
    B. Moreover, readjust the tire pressure, and you're
    C. Moreover, readjusting the tire pressure, you're
    D. Also, having readjusted the tire pressure, you will be

Answers and explanations start on page 191.

LESSON

1

Unpack the Writing Prompt

Key Ideas

- The Extended Response will require reading one or two passages and writing a response to a prompt.
- To draft an acceptable response to the text, the first step is to "unpack" the prompt—to focus on the specific question you need to address.
- Your response must be evidence based, which means that it needs to be grounded in facts, details, and examples from the text.

GED® TEST TIP

It is advisable to read the prompt before you read the passages. That will help you to focus on the argument and the supporting evidence in the passage or passages.

The writing activity on the GED® *Reasoning Through Language Arts Test* is called an **Extended Response**. This task involves reading one passage or two paired passages and producing a piece of writing in a word-processing box on the computer screen. Page 28 shows how the reading and writing formats will look on the computer.

To master this assignment, you need to understand the purpose of **evidence-based writing**. This type of writing requires that you develop an argument by using evidence from the text(s) to support your claim.

On pages 56–59, you looked at writers' **arguments** as a reading activity alone. On the Extended Response activity, you will look at them in order to develop your *own* argument and supporting text in response to the writing **prompt**, or assignment.

Below are two arguments that you read on page 62. On the facing page is a writing prompt based on them. While these readings are much shorter than the ones on the *Reasoning Through Language Arts Test,* they give a good starting point for understanding how to **unpack the writing prompt**.

What does it mean to "unpack" a prompt? When you unpack a suitcase, you take things out and think about what you are going to do with them—wash them, fold them, hang them up, or put them in a drawer. Similarly, with a writing prompt, you will take it apart in your mind and plan how you are going to accomplish the task.

Reread the selections and the writing prompt on the facing page. Then practice unpacking the writing prompt by answering the questions numbered 1–6 and reading the explanation below.

Passage A

Coal, the source of half the energy in the United States, has been the dirtiest of all fossil fuels because it creates harmful emissions when burned. Help is on the way with the development of new "clean coal" technologies that reduce coal's environmental impact. These new technologies that purify exhaust gases as coal burns (wet scrubbers) and prevent the formation of harmful emissions in the first place (low-NO*x* burners). There is even gasification, which avoids burning coal altogether.

Passage B

"Clean coal" amounts to just an advertising slogan. Don't be fooled by claims about new technologies making coal a clean-burning fuel. The hazards to our environment start well before that. Coal mining wastes huge amounts of water—70 to 260 million gallons daily. Today's mining companies now use mountaintop removal, instead of traditional mining, to extract coal. Forty-nine states have issued fish intake advisories due to high mercury concentration in water, much of it due to coal-fired power plants.

Coal Writing Prompt

While the writer of Passage A proposes the benefits of clean coal, the writer of Passage B identifies drawbacks to this position.

In your response, analyze both selections to determine which position is better supported.

Use relevant and specific information from both selections to support your response.

Type your response in the box. This task will take 45 minutes to complete.

Unpacking the Writing Prompt

1. What is the writing assignment about?
2. What does the prompt ask you to do? Turn it into a question.
3. What are you being asked to include in your response?
4. Are you being asked for your opinion on the topic?
5. Are you being asked to take a position about the writers' arguments?
6. Where are you writing? How long do you have?

1. The writing assignment is about **the two selections that take different positions on clean coal.**
2. The prompt asks me: **Which of the positions about clean coal is better supported?**
3. The prompt states that I have to use **both relevant and specific information from the passage.**
4. No. I am **not being asked for my opinion about clean coal**.
5. Yes. I am being asked to take a position about **which writer I think made a stronger case**.
6. I am to **type in the box on the computer screen**. I will have **45 minutes** for the entire writing task.

PRACTICE 1

Questions 1 through 4 refer to the following writing prompt. (For this practice, there are no passages.)

Writing Prompt

Passage A cites Federal Communications Commission determinations and scientific studies that have concluded that radiation from cell phones has no adverse effects. However, Passage B cites studies that raise questions about traffic safety issues and the long-term health effects of cell phone use.

In your response, compare and analyze both selections to determine whether you agree with the writer of Passage A or Passage B. Use relevant and specific information from both selections to support your response.

Unpacking the Writing Prompt

1. What is the topic of the writing prompt?

   ____

2. What does the prompt ask you to do? (Put this in the form of a question.)

   ____

3. What are you asked to include in your response?

   ____

4. Are you being asked for your opinion on the topic or to take a position on the writers' arguments?

   ____

Answers and explanations start on page 191.

LESSON

2

WRITING ABOUT TEXT

Identify a Writer's Arguments and Assumptions

On the Reasoning Through Language Arts Test, you will be writing a response based on one or two passages. On page 56 you read that a written **argument** consists of the following:

- A statement, which is a **conclusion** about something
- The **evidence**, which is support that is given for the argument
- The **premises**, or the **assumptions**, behind the argument

Read a short passage. Identify the writer's conclusion about the topic and the assumptions behind it.

Secondhand smoke is the smoke that comes either from the lighted end of a cigarette, pipe, or cigar or from the exhalation of a smoker. Most people consider secondhand smoke to be less dangerous than the nicotine that a cigarette user intakes. However, the particles that come from the smoke of the lighted end of a cigarette, called sidestream smoke, contain higher concentrations of carcinogens, which are chemicals that cause cancer. These particles can be breathed in easily by people around smokers, especially in enclosed areas. Therefore, all restaurants should ban smoking inside.

1. What is the writer's topic?
   (1) Secondhand smoke and its effects
   (2) The most common carcinogens

2. What is the writer's conclusion about the topic?
   (1) Sidestream smoke contains high concentrations of carcinogens.
   (2) Smoking should be banned inside restaurants.

3. Which of the following is the writer's unstated assumption?
   (1) Carcinogens only come from sidestream smoke.
   (2) Restaurants should take steps to protect the health of their patrons.

In question 1, choice **(1)** is correct. The writer focuses on secondhand smoke throughout. In question 2, choice **(2)** is correct. The writer uses the information about secondhand smoke as support for the claim that smoking should be banned inside restaurants. In question 3, choice **(2)** is correct. The writer mentions that cancer-causing carcinogens can be breathed in easily in enclosed areas as the premise for how smoking indoors can be dangerous to others.

Key Ideas

- Your response to the writing assignment will be based on identifying a writer's argument.
- A writer's argument is a conclusion, which is supported by facts, details, and other evidence.
- While a writer may not directly state them, he or she has assumptions about the topic.

GED® TEST TIP

When you are reading the passages for the extended-response questions, ask yourself: What is the writer's conclusion?

PRACTICE 2

Directions: For each passage, answer the questions about topic, conclusions, and assumptions.

Passage 1

Some U.S. representatives advocate a bill requiring all young people to perform two years of military service by the age of 25. Proponents of the bill argue that this will not only prepare the U.S. military for any potential threat from other nations but will also build a greater spirit of patriotism among U.S. citizens. Citizens will be able to appreciate the service of the military and acquire a deeper respect toward honoring their country. However, making service a requirement for all citizens will have the opposite effect; people will feel burdened and resentful toward their government. Instead of focusing on increasing participation in the military, the government should more heavily promote volunteer programs to encourage citizens to help the poor or marginalized within their communities.

1. What is the writer's topic?

____

____

2. The writer's conclusion about the topic is

____

____

____

3. What is the writer's unstated assumption about the topic?

____

____

____

Passage 2

To best protect children from being subjected to portrayals of violence, we must reduce the amount of violence that is present in video games. Numerous studies done by various groups show a positive correlation between video game usage and violence.

Many people consider violence in video games a recent trend, but one of the earliest and most controversial video games was Death Race, released in 1976. In this game, the players controlled cars that ran over gremlins. The game was later pulled from stores due to public outcry. With the successful protest against Death Race as a model, we should be as proactive now to reduce or eliminate violence in video games.

4. What is the writer's topic?

____

5. What is the writer's conclusion about the topic?

____

____

____

6. What is the writer's unstated assumption about the topic?

____

____

Answers and explanations start on page 191.

LESSON

3

WRITING ABOUT TEXT

Develop a Thesis Statement

Key Ideas

- A thesis statement makes a claim and indicates that the passage will support the claim with specific and relevant information.
- A thesis statement differs from an opinion, which is a feeling or belief about the topic of the passage.
- A thesis statement is strengthened if it confronts any problems in a passage.

GED® TEST TIP

Although writers have different approaches, it is best to introduce your extended response with your thesis statement. This will let a reader know your position right away. Also, come back to your thesis statement as you write. This will keep you on track.

You have been reading and analyzing writers' arguments. Now it is your turn to develop a response to what writers have to say.

Once you have unpacked the prompt and read the reading passages, you will construct a **thesis statement** for your writing. This is your central argument. It differs from an **opinion** because it makes a claim that you will defend with evidence from the text.

A thesis statement does the following:

- makes your argument clear
- provides the reader with a road map of what you will be discussing

► Compare these two statements about the clean coal selections from page 116. Label the thesis statement with *TS* and the opinion with *O*.

____ I think that Passage A is better than Passage B because it does a good job of explaining the new technologies and reminds us that coal is responsible for half of our electricity.

____ I think that Passage B makes a better argument because it backs up its conclusion with information about overuse of water, mountaintop removal, and potential mercury poisoning.

The first statement should have ***O*** for opinion next to it because it is an assertion without any support. It is **subjective**—in that it tells what the reader likes, not what ideas the passage presents. It also repeats the **irrelevant** point—that half of our electricity depends on coal. While that may be factually true, it is **off-topic** when discussing whether or not coal can be a clean source of energy.

The second statement should have ***TS*** next to it because it meets the criteria for a thesis statement: it makes a claim and demonstrates that the writing that follows will discuss **specific** and **relevant** support for the claim.

Keep in mind that your conclusion may need to recognize a limitation or a problem. That problem may be contained in the passage writer's **unstated assumption**. For Passage B on page 116, the writer has already decided that the notion of clean coal is deceptive. You may strengthen your thesis statement by acknowledging and dealing with a problem.

Even though the writer of Passage B is biased against the idea of clean coal, I believe that he makes the stronger argument. He backs up his conclusions with specific information about the environmental impact of today's coal-mining processes.

PRACTICE 3

Directions: Read each paragraph. Write a thesis statement for a possible response to each.

ADVERTISING FOR PRESCRIPTION DRUGS ON TV

Sit down to enjoy any television show today, and you'll find that almost every other commercial seems to be pushing a prescription drug. Although this form of direct-to-consumer (DTC) advertising of prescription medication has become commonplace in American programming, it remains a relatively new development in the medical world. In fact, the practice is currently legal in only two countries, the United States and New Zealand. Patient advocates and those who wish to maintain high standards of healthcare argue that DTC advertising should be eliminated altogether. Advertising prescription medications on television creates a popular demand for the drugs, and it may lead individuals to pressure their health-care providers for treatments that are inappropriate or even dangerous. At the same time, because prescription commercials must name all potential side effects of a certain medication, the ads may frighten other individuals away from using drugs that are both safe and effective for the general public. While such DTC advertisements serve to increase the profits of drug companies, they do little to ensure that the public is better educated about its health-care choices.

1. What is the writer's argument about prescription drug advertising on TV?____________________

2. Write a thesis statement in response to the argument. State your position and indicate how you will support it.

MANY AMERICANS DON'T SPEAK A SECOND LANGUAGE

In an era in which people from different continents can connect in seconds by phone, email, or videochat, there is a growing demand for individuals who can speak multiple languages. Additionally, rapid immigration, particularly (in recent years) from Spanish- and Chinese-speaking countries, has ensured that America's population becomes more multilingual every day. Despite this, the majority of Americans are still fluent in American English only and know just a few key phrases of another language for polite but limited exchanges. With almost 18 percent of the country's population citing languages other than English as their primary tongues, many Americans recognize that their inability to speak a foreign language fluently places them at a disadvantage. Particularly in the fields of technology, business, education, and medicine, those who can competently communicate in the native languages of their peers, clients, students, or patients, respectively, will be better equipped to find common ground, work collaboratively, make advances, and build deeper relationships. To remain competitive both at home and internationally, Americans must make foreign language fluency the keystone of a well-rounded education.

3. What is the writer's argument about Americans not knowing a second language?

4. Write a thesis statement in response to the argument. State your position and indicate how you will support it.

Answers and sample thesis statements start on page 191.

LESSON

4

WRITING ABOUT TEXT

Collect Supporting Evidence

Once you have formulated your thesis statement, you need to use **evidence** from the passage or passages to support your claim. You should preview the **prompt** before you read the passage or passages. That benefit of this strategy is that you can:

- formulate your thesis statement while you are reading
- gather specific and relevant evidence to support your thesis

How can you gather information while you are reading? The computer-based GED® Test provides you with two essential tools for gathering evidence:

- an online **highlighter** that you can use to mark specific facts and examples to use in your response
- an offline **write-on board and erasable marker** that you can use to write your thesis statement and to take notes as you read

Thesis statement: Family time is a thing of the past because too many distractions interfere with conversation and other interactions.

Practice gathering evidence with the passage below. Circle specific pieces of evidence that support the thesis statement above.

> I know it sounds corny, but I miss the way my family was together when I was growing up. Even though Mom and Dad worked, we usually had breakfast together. Now, I work the night shift and sleep in the morning, while my husband is too harried with getting the kids to eat and making their lunches to get a preview of their day.
>
> After school, our kids have part-time jobs, and everyone gets home at different times. Even though I have dinner ready before I leave at 8:00 p.m., someone is doing homework, someone is on the Internet, and someone is texting friends that he or she saw an hour before. I can't remember the last time we all ate together and had a conversation. Even when I try to organize a movie night, it seems that one of us has social or work obligations. We all love each other, but it is hard to have what we can call family time. Thank goodness for holidays and vacations when we can slow down and enjoy each other.

Evidence statements that support the thesis statement:

- Breakfast time is hectic and one parent is asleep.
- After school, people are working or engaged in distractions.
- Family members don't eat dinner together.
- Not everyone is available for common activities, like movie night.

Key Ideas

- Formulate your thesis statement and collect supporting evidence while you read by using the tools provided.
- Gather supporting evidence that is specific and ties back to your thesis statement.
- Avoid facts that are interesting but not relevant to your central argument.

GED® TEST TIP

When you cite the writer's evidence, use phrases such as "The passage stated . . ."; "In the text . . ."; and "One example from the text is . . ."

PRACTICE 4

Directions: Read the prompt, the reading selection, and the writer's conclusion. List three pieces of supporting evidence from the passage that you could use in a response to the prompt. Add one piece of supporting evidence from your own experience or observations. <u>You will not be writing a response to this prompt</u>.

> **Drinking Age Prompt**
>
> The writer of this passage has a position on keeping the minimum legal drinking age at 21. Take a position in response to the writer's argument, using relevant and specific information from the selection to support your response.

The Case for Keeping the Minimum Drinking Age at 21

We owe it to young adults, teens, and children to keep the minimum drinking age right where it is: at 21. The dangers of alcohol are often overlooked due to the fact that it is not a prohibited substance, but make no mistake: it is eminently dangerous, particularly to our youth.

In larger doses—consistent with binge drinking—alcohol wreaks havoc on the sensitive chemistry of the brain. The feast-and-famine pattern of drinking that is typical of teenage drinkers can lead to permanent damage to the prefrontal cortex, the part of the brain responsible for planning and decisions. Since this portion of the brain continues to develop later in life, younger brains are particularly vulnerable to the effects of alcohol. Even in moderate doses, it causes long-term damage to the heart, the liver, and the stomach.

Proponents of a lower drinking age maintain that the allure of the taboo of alcohol encourages abuse among youth. The United Kingdom, however, has a long history of social drinking, and the legal drinking age is 18 in bars and 16 in restaurants; despite this, alcohol-related deaths had doubled in the U.K. in the decade before 2008. Indeed, a 2008 BBC documentary ranked alcohol as the fifth most dangerous drug in the U.K., ahead of speed, LSD, ecstasy, and cannabis.

As a nation, we recognized the dangers that alcohol represented to our citizens and communities when we united to pass a constitutional amendment against it a century ago. That experiment was abandoned only due to challenges of enforcement, but Al Capone could never have built a crime empire on the dimes of 18- to 20-year-olds alone. We owe it to our youth—and the future of our nation—to protect their brains and their lives.

Writer's Conclusion

The conclusion is that despite some reasons for lowering the legal drinking age, it should remain at 21.

1. Three pieces of evidence used in the passage to support this conclusion are . . .
   a. The passage states that ____________________
   ____
   ____

   b. Another fact from the passage is
   ____
   ____

   c. In support of this position, the text further says that ____________________
   ____
   ____

2. I (agree/disagree) with the position of this piece.

3. One piece of personal evidence I would use to support my position is ____________________
   ____
   ____
   ____
   ____

Answers begin on page 192.

LESSON

5

WRITING ABOUT TEXT

Plan Your Response

Key Ideas

- Take ten minutes to unpack the prompt, read the passage(s), and plan your response.
- As you read the passages, develop your thesis statement and collect supporting evidence with the online highlighter or by taking notes.
- Plan your response by either outlining or mapping the key ideas that you will use in the response.

GED® TEST TIP

Follow through on all of the planning steps before you write. You will have plenty of time to execute your plan, and your score will be higher if you have thought your response through and mapped it out.

You will have 45 minutes to complete the Extended-Response activity. An online clock at the top of your screen will let you know how much time you have left. Check it as you work through your response. You want to use that time wisely, and the best thing you can do is to take 10 minutes for **prewriting**, or planning, what you are going to write.

Successful test takers do this type of planning. It ensures that you understand the prompt, write a thesis statement, gather the relevant evidence, and have your ideas in place before you begin to write.

Extended-Response Strategy

This **Extended-Response Strategy** will maximize your ability to use the 45 minutes efficiently and effectively. As you work through the rest of this unit, practice managing each stage of the strategy.

Plan: 10 minutes

- Preview the writing prompt.
- Read the passage(s), highlighting or making notes of key details on the write-on board.
- Use the write-on board to write your thesis statement and plan your response with either an outline or an idea map

Draft: 25 minutes

- Write a thesis statement as the introduction to your response.
- Use your plan, citing specific evidence from the text to support your ideas.
- Provide other relevant information based on your own knowledge and perspective.
- Write a closing that summarizes your position or restates the thesis statement in another way.

Revise: 10 minutes

- Reread your thesis statement and review your response to make sure your response stayed focused on the prompt.
- Use the **Revision Questions** on page 134 to improve the response.
- Use the **Editing Questions** on page 136 to correct errors.

Prewriting Strategies

Two of the most useful prewriting strategies for any kind of writing, including evidence-based writing, are outlining and mapping. Look at both methods of grouping ideas based on the same thesis statement.

> **Thesis statement:** *People need both close friends and acquaintances because they meet our social needs in different ways.*

An **outline** depicts each main topic by using a system of numbers and letters stressing a logical progression of ideas. Here is an outline based on the thesis statement above.

I. Benefits of close friends
   a. Will always be there for you
   b. Can always be yourself with them
   c. Can have intimate conversations that are satisfying but confidential
   d. Stand the test of time

II. Benefits of acquaintances
   a. Add variety to your life
   b. Expand your world

III. Acquaintances fulfill some special needs
   a. Social needs—if you can't see closest friends every day
   b. Networking needs—when you need to search for a job, find a new day care provider, etc.
   c. Can make a party or other social event more interesting

An **idea map** uses a drawing to visually group ideas. To make a map, write your main idea in the center. Then draw lines from there to your main topics. From there, you attach the supporting ideas.

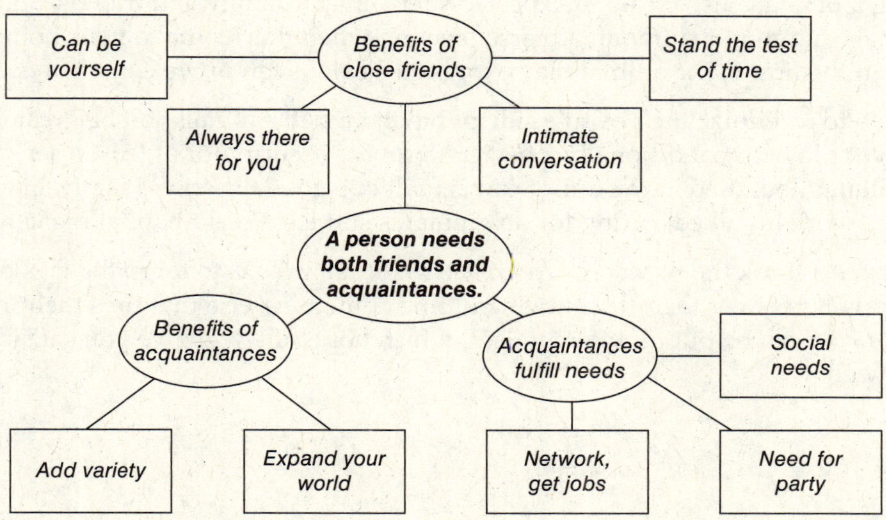

PRACTICE 5

Directions: Follow these steps to plan a response. You should allow 10 minutes for this task.

- Read the writing prompt to understand your task.
- Read the passage. Think about your thesis statement. Underline and take notes on key points that you will want to summarize or respond to.
- Write a thesis statement based on responding to the prompt and the passage.
- Make an outline and an idea map based on the selection.

Family Pets Writing Prompt

The writer of this passage explains the reasons a family should not own a pet. Read the selection and take a stand for or against the author's viewpoint, using relevant and specific information from the selection to support your response.

When you are trying to decide whether or not to buy a household pet, you need to weigh the pros and cons of doing so. Your children will make heartfelt pleas for an animal and will make wild claims about what they will do to help. However, the negative reasons outweigh the positive ones in terms of time, money, and inconvenience.

One major disadvantage is that you simply will have more household chores. You will need to take the pet on walks or clean out a box, cage, or fish bowl. Trust me. I've done them all. You will have to buy food regularly, sometimes even specialty food for particular pets or aging or sick animals. Finally, ongoing cleanup is needed for animals that shed fur, feathers, or skin.

There are other inconveniences as well for you and your family. You need specialized knowledge to care properly for the pet's health and safety. You will make more trips to the vet than you do to the doctor's office. This gets expensive. It can be time-consuming and expensive to go away for a weekend or a vacation, unless you have a cousin or a friend who owes you a favor.

Owning a pet may also create unexpected problems for family and friends. Some people are allergic to animals and might suffer an adverse reaction when they come to your home. Also, if a new baby arrives in the house, the animal may express its jealousy in unwelcome ways.

I do have to recognize the positive side of having a pet. Animals can be great companions and return your love unconditionally. They can provide security (or at least a sense of security). Also, that walking I belittled at the outset can actually be good exercise. Finally, I have to admit that with all of the work involved, caring for an animal is still less work than taking care of a child.

On balance, I think the wisest course of action for a family is to forgo the joys of pet ownership. The children will get over their discontent and find something else that fires their interest. The time and money saved can be put to different uses, which hopefully will give you satisfaction and companionship as well.

1. **Thesis Statement** According to the prompt, you are to take a position in agreement or disagreement with the writer of "Family Pets." Decide what you think and write your thesis statement below.

   I. I think that the writer's position on owning a family pet is ______________________

   because ____

   ____

   Then, on Test Day, either write an outline or make an idea map. Practice both approaches on this page.

2. **Outline** Write an outline, using this as a model. **Keep your outline; you will use it in Lesson 6.**

Also address related reasoning issues, either by stating and contradicting the **counterargument** (main argument against your position) and/or by addressing the writer's **faulty reasoning** (if any). .

I. Thesis statement
II. Main supporting reason related to the text
III. Another supporting reason related to the text
IV. Another supporting reason related to the text
V. Related arguments
   A. Counterargument
      i. Argument against my position
      ii. My rejection of the counterargument, with example
   B. Writer's faulty reasoning (if any)
      i. Why the writer's reasoning is faulty
      ii. Supporting example

3. **Idea Map** Make a map of your response to the passage. Use facts and evidence from the passage as well as your own ideas. Draw it on a sheet of paper. **Keep your map; you will use it in Lesson 6.**

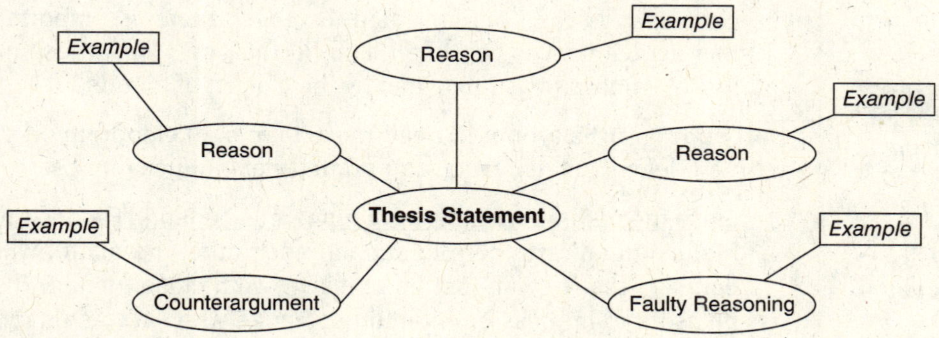

4. **Reflect** Which way worked better for you—outline or map? Practice both until you find the method that will work best for you on the test.

Sample responses start on page 192.

LESSON

6

WRITING ABOUT TEXT

Draft Your Response

Key Ideas

- Take 25 minutes to draft your response.
- Use your thesis statement to begin your introductory paragraph and to keep you focused as you write.
- Write several body paragraphs based on the facts, details, and evidence in your outline or idea map.
- Wrap up the response with a concluding paragraph that reinforces your thesis.

GED® TEST TIP

One key to a good score on the Extended Response is to cite specific evidence from the reading passage(s). This is called an "evidence-based" writing activity because you are expected to base your response on evidence from the texts.

You have practiced the first part of the **Extended-Response Strategy: Planning**. Once you have planned your writing, the next stage is to **draft** your response. You should take about 25 minutes to do the following:

- Use your thesis statement to **introduce** your argument and how you intend to support it.
- Use your plan to write the **body** of your response, **citing specific evidence from the text** to support your ideas.
- Provide **additional relevant information** based on your own knowledge and perspective.
- Consistently **check back** with your thesis statement to make sure that you are staying on track.
- Write a **closing** that summarizes your position or restates the thesis statement in another way.

Review the planning on page 125 for writing on the topic of close friends and acquaintances. See how that planning was used to draft the writing below. (Note that an underlined **topic sentence** introduces each paragraph.)

An **introduction** lays out your argument and how you will support it:

> <u>People need both close friends and acquaintances because they meet our social needs in different ways.</u> The special bond a person has with close friends can't be replicated. However, there are important needs that acquaintances can fulfill, and, in their own way, these needs are just as important as those met by the closest of friends.

Body paragraphs (you will need more than one) elaborate on your support with evidence, details, facts, and related personal examples.

> <u>Close friendships certainly have numerous benefits.</u> For one thing, loyal friends are always there to support each other, no matter what. A big bonus is that we can just be ourselves with close friends. There is no pressure to impress or entertain someone who accepts us for who we are. Some friendships last years, becoming deeper and more meaningful with time. For example, even though I am now 35, my best friend from high school and I are still in touch, sharing stories about our two-year-old boys.

A **closing paragraph** restates your main point to reinforce it.

> <u>So while it is important to have close friends, it is really rewarding to have a wide circle of acquaintances as well.</u> Even though the quality of the relationship may not be as deep, these people broaden our lives, experiences, and networks to enrich our experiences and help us to grow.

PRACTICE 6.1

Part A: Introduction

Directions: Practice writing an introduction based on the prompt and passage from page 126 and your planning from page 127. Write your introduction on a computer if possible. Save the file as *Family Pets Introduction.* If it is not possible to write it on a computer, compose your introduction neatly on paper so that you can revise it later.

> **Family Pets Writing Prompt**
>
> The writer of this passage explains the reasons a family should not own a pet. Read the selection and take a stand for or against the author's position, using relevant and specific information from the selection to support your response.

- Begin with a topic sentence that summarizes your thesis statement from page 127.
- Support your topic sentence with either
  - a preview of the main points you will be covering based on your outline or idea map; or
  - an example, description, or personal story—tied to the thesis statement—that will interest the reader.

Part B: Concluding Statement

Directions: Practice writing a concluding statement based on the prompt above and your planning from page 127. Write your conclusion on a computer if possible. Save the file as *Family Pets Conclusion.* If writing it on a computer is not possible, compose the concluding statement neatly on paper.

- Restate your thesis statement from page 127 in different words. (Don't just repeat what your reader has already read.)
- Make a statement that answers the question "So what?" Give your reader a reason to care about your argument.
- Don't introduce new arguments but leave the reader with something to think about that wraps up the paper.

Sample responses start on page 193.

PRACTICE 6.2

Directions: Plan and draft an extended response to the prompt below and the passage on the facing page. Write your response on a computer if possible. If you cannot, write neatly on paper so that you can revise it later.

Step 1—Plan: Take 10 minutes to read the prompt and the passage. Under the prompt, make an outline *or* draw an idea map to organize the following:

- your thesis statement
- your main points and supporting evidence from the passage
- counterarguments and your response *or* faulty reasoning in the passage

Step 2—Draft: Take 25 minutes to draft your response, which will include the following:

- an introductory statement with your thesis statement as the topic sentence
- body paragraphs, with your reasons accompanied by supporting evidence from the text
  - use phrases such as "As the writer says . . . ," "The information in the passage states . . . ," "This is supported in the passage by . . ."
- a concluding statement wrapping up the piece

It would be best to write the response on a computer. If that is not possible, write it out on a piece of paper. **Save your response, since you will be revising and editing it in Lesson 7.**

Cell Phone Writing Prompt

The passage addresses controversy about cell phone use. The Federal Communications Commission has determined that radiation from cell phones has no adverse effects. However, some studies raise questions about traffic safety issues and the long-term health effects of cell phone use.

In your response, compare the arguments in the reading selection and take a position on cell phone safety. Use relevant and specific information to support your response.

Cell Phones: Risky or Safe?

1 The Federal Communications Commission has determined that there is not enough evidence to link cell phones to cancer. But that does not mean cell phones are 100 percent safe. Many risks and unknowns are connected to the use of mobile phones. You should be aware of those risks and take steps to protect yourself.

2 Cell phones emit types of radiation that can penetrate several inches into the brain. These types of radiation are not normally associated with cancer, and most scientific studies show that frequent cell phone users do not have an increased risk of tumors. But a few scientists claim to have found a connection between mobile phones and a type of brain cancer known as glioma. Even a small chance of brain cancer should make you very nervous.

3 Also, that chance of cancer may increase in time. Mobile phones were very rare before the late 1990s. If the risk of phone-related disease increases sharply after 20 or 30 years of constant use, we might only find out after millions of people get sick. It's true that there is no increased illness observed among people who have worked at radio towers for 30 years or more, but cell phones are held much closer to the body than radio equipment is.

4 Finally, people who think their cell phones are completely safe may use them even when doing so is not wise. Being able to contact emergency services from anywhere is a major advantage of modern technology, but being distracted by that technology can cause accidents. Calling or texting while driving or operating machinery is dangerous, no matter how "safe" a piece of equipment your phone may be.

5 Be cautious with your cell phone. You may find that you need it to function in today's modern society, but your health and well-being are too important to risk through careless use of this technology. Do not assume that today's science proves that your phone is completely free of danger.

The *Extended Response Evaluation Guide* appears on page 225.

Practice 6.3

Directions: Plan and draft an extended response to the prompt and the paired passages on the facing page. Write your response on a computer, if possible. If you cannot, write neatly on a sheet of paper so that you can revise it later.

Step 1—Plan: Take 10 minutes to read the prompt below and the passages. Take notes as you read, or underline evidence that you will want to use. Make an outline *or* an idea map to organize:

- your thesis statement
- your main points and supporting evidence from the passages
- counterarguments and your response *or* faulty reasoning in either of the passages

Step 2—Draft: Take 25 minutes to draft your response with:

- an introductory statement with your thesis statement as the topic sentence
- body paragraphs, with your reasons accompanied by supporting evidence from the text
- a concluding statement wrapping up the piece

It would be best to write the response on a computer. If that is not possible, write it out on paper. **Save your response, since you will be revising and editing it on pages 145 and 147.**

Gettysburg Address Writing Prompt

Abraham Lincoln's Gettysburg Address is renowned as one of the most significant speeches of all time. Delivered in the midst of a brutal civil war, this address places that war in the context of U.S. history—past, present, and future. However, it was not universally acclaimed at the time, as shown by the excerpt from the *Chicago Times* newspaper.

Read both of the passages closely. Take a stand on which passage does a better job of explaining the significance of the Battle of Gettysburg's casualties. There were a total of more than 45,000 casualties on both sides, Union and Confederacy.

Use relevant and specific information from both passages to support your response.

Abraham Lincoln's Gettysburg Address

Fourscore and seven years ago our fathers brought forth on this continent a new nation, conceived in liberty and dedicated to the proposition that all men are created equal. Now we are engaged in a great civil war, testing whether that nation or any nation so conceived and so dedicated can long endure. But in a larger sense, we cannot dedicate, we cannot consecrate, we cannot hallow this ground. The brave men, living and dead who struggled here have consecrated it far above our poor power to add or detract. The world will little note nor long remember what we say here, but it can never forget what they did here. It is for us the living rather to be dedicated here to the unfinished work which they who fought here have thus far so nobly advanced. It is rather for us to be here dedicated to the great task remaining before us—that from these honored dead we take increased devotion to that cause for which they gave the last full measure of devotion—that we here highly resolve that these dead shall not have died in vain, that this nation under God shall have a new birth of freedom, and that government of the people, by the people, for the people shall not perish from the earth.

—Abraham Lincoln, November 19, 1863

Critical Review of the Gettysburg Address

. . . The President's exhibition . . . was an insult at least to the memories of a part of the dead, whom he was there professedly to honor—in its misstatement of the cause for which they died, it was a perversion of history so flagrant that the most extended charity cannot regard it as otherwise than willful. As a refutation. . . . we copy certain clauses in the Federal constitution:

"Representatives and direct taxes shall be apportioned among the several States which may be included in this Union, according to their respective numbers, which shall be determined by adding to the whole number of free persons, including those bound to service for a term of years, and excluding Indians not taxed, three-fifths of all other persons.

"The migration or importation of such persons as any of the States now existing shall think proper to admit shall not be prohibited by the Congress prior to the year 1808, but a tax or duty may be imposed on such importation, not exceeding ten dollars for each person. . . . No amendment to the constitution, made prior to 1808, shall affect the preceding clause.

"No person held to service or labor in one State under the laws thereof, escaping into another, shall, in consequence of any law or regulation therein, be discharged from such service or labor, but shall be delivered up on claim of the party to whom such service or labor may be due."

Do these provisions in the constitution dedicate the nation to "the proposition that all men are created equal"? Mr. Lincoln occupies his present position by virtue of this constitution, and is sworn to the maintenance and enforcement of these provisions. It was to uphold this constitution, and the Union created by it, that our officers and soldiers gave their lives at Gettysburg. How dared he, then, standing on their graves, misstate the cause for which they died, and libel the statesmen who founded the government?

Excerpted from the *Chicago Times*,
November 23, 1863

Evaluation criteria begins on page 225.

LESSON 7

Writing About Text

Revise and Edit Your Response

Key Ideas

- Take ten minutes to revise and edit your response.
- Reread the response to improve the clarity of your arguments; sufficiency of evidence from the text; and organization of sentences, paragraphs, and the entire piece.
- Use the delete, copy, and paste features on the computer to make these revisions.

GED® TEST TIP

When you practice revising before you take the test, read your drafts out loud. This will help you to "hear" weaknesses in your organization, sentence structure, and word choice.

Revising Your Work

Once you have completed your draft, you need to **revise**. You should take about five of the ten remaining minutes to read over your response and make improvements by using the copy, delete, and paste functions on the computer. Ask yourself:

- Does the introductory paragraph contain the **thesis statement** and lay out the main point of my response?
- Does each paragraph have **one main idea**, begin with a **topic sentence**, and support the thesis statement?
- Is there **specific and relevant supporting evidence from the text** for each main idea?
- Have I assessed the **validity** of the arguments in the passages?
- Is there a **clear flow of ideas** from one paragraph to the next, using transitional words, phrases, and ideas?
- Are there any **irrelevant ideas or sentences** that can be removed?
- Are there any **short, choppy sentences** that could be combined?
- Can I improve my **word choice** to be more specific or interesting?
- Is there a concluding paragraph that **restates and reinforces** the thesis?

Read the writing sample below and review the revisions that were made by hand to improve the draft. Think about why each change was made.

A job is much more pleasant when you like and admire your supervisor. A good supervisor must have excellent communication skills and must make it a priority to help workers get ahead.

^Communication is a key part of management.^ Supervisors need to give clear directions to spare the workers many hours of frustration. In addition, supervisors should be confident^and decisive.^ ~~They should also be decisive.~~ Finally, supervisors should be as honest as possible. Once they make a decision, they should stick to it, so^that^ everyone knows what the policy is.

Good bosses want to see their workers progress. Therefore, supervisors should give lots of encouragement and reward workers who display initiative and problem-solving abilities. ^Also,^ Supervisors should offer opportunities for workers to improve their skills^and education^.

PRACTICE 7.1

A. Directions: Read the response below, and revise the problems in sentence structure and organization. Try to complete your revisions in five minutes, but use more time if needed.

Most of us are aware of the consequences of speeding, which range from receiving a speeding ticket to getting into an accident. A quick survey of any highway will show that many drivers exceed the speed limit. Why do people speed? One common reason is that people do not think they will suffer any consequences. If they have never been stopped by the police or crashed their car, they don't see any reason to worry.

People simply need to get somewhere in a hurry. They realize that they are speeding but they have such a need to arrive on time that they don't care. They've got ants in their pants. A final reason is lack of respect for other drivers, one driver who is speeding makes road conditions less safe for everyone. Drivers who act as though they are in the Indy 500 they have no regard for the safety of others.

We know that people speed because of impatience and they don't fear the consequences. Another reason is no respect. Let's figure out what will make them stop.

B. Directions: Revise the response that you wrote on the topic below on page 130. Time yourself. Try to complete the revision in ten minutes. Save your work. You will use the response again.

Cell Phone Writing Prompt

The passage addresses controversy about cell phone use. The Federal Communications Commission has determined that radiation from cell phones has no adverse effects. However, some studies raise questions about traffic safety issues and the long-term health effects of cell phone use.

In your response, compare the arguments in the reading selection and take a position on cell phone safety. Use relevant and specific information to support your response.

C. Directions: After you check your answers to the exercise above, complete the strategy box below. If you need more practice with specific skills and concepts, review "Connecting Ideas" on pages 104–115 and "Polishing Your Writing" on pages 142–151.

MY TEST-TAKING STRATEGY

I need to pay special attention to these areas of revising. (Check all that apply.)

- ❏ Writing introductory paragraphs
- ❏ Writing concluding paragraphs
- ❏ Writing topic sentences
- ❏ Adding support to body paragraphs
- ❏ Putting sentences in logical places
- ❏ Putting in paragraph breaks
- ❏ Remembering to use transitions
- ❏ Deleting irrelevant details
- ❏ Combining short, choppy sentences
- ❏ Making sure each sentence makes sense

Answers and explanations start on page 193.

Key Ideas

- Edit your work to make sure there are no errors in sentence structure, grammar, usage, or mechanics.
- An editing checklist can help you find errors as you practice for the Reasoning Through Language Arts test.

ON THE GED® TEST

There are no "spell check" or "grammar check" features on the GED® test. If you can, turn them off on your computer while you practice writing your response. Then turn the features back on when you review your work.

Editing Your Work

Once you're satisfied with the organization and clarity of your essay, check for other errors in sentence structure, as well as errors in grammar, usage, and mechanics. To edit your response, take another five minutes to reread your response, and ask yourself these questions:

- Are all the sentences complete?
- Are there any run-ons or comma splices that should be corrected?
- Are all lists parallel in structure?
- Are nouns and pronouns used correctly?
- Are verb forms and tenses used correctly?
- Does the subject of each sentence match the verb?
- Is the punctuation correct?
- Is capitalization used correctly?
- Are all words correctly spelled?
- Are there any inappropriate word choices?

► Read the paragraph below, and notice how the errors were corrected.

A job is much more pleasant when you like and admire your supervisor. A good supervisor must have excellent communication skills, and must make it a priority to help workers get ahead. In addition, a supervisor should be a fair and moral person.

Clear communication is a key part of Management. Supervisors need to give clear directions. To spare the workers many hours of frustration. In addition, supervisors should be confident and decisive. Once they made a decision, they should stick to it so everyone knows what the policy is. Finally, supervisors should be as honest as possible.

Good bosses want to see their workers progress. Therefore, supervisors should ~~give lots of~~ encourage~~ment~~ and reward workers who display initiative, and problem-solving abilities. Also, supervisors should offer opportunities for workers to improve their skills, and education.

Top-notch supervisors ~~has~~ have a high level of moral character. They reward honesty and fire workers who have lied or cheated. Some bosses keep employees who lie if ~~his~~ their skills are valuable to the Company, but I feel that this is an example of poor management.

Knowing the qualities of a good supervisor is important for both bosses and workers. The next time you apply for a job, think about whether ~~you're~~ your prospective boss is a moral person and a clear communicator who wants you to succeed.

PRACTICE 7.2

A. **Directions: Read the body of the writing sample. Correct errors in sentence structure, grammar, usage, mechanics, and word choice. Try to finish editing in five minutes, but use more time if needed.**

One common reason for speeding is that people don't think they will suffer any consequences. If they have never been stopped by the Police or crashed there car they don't see any reason too worry.

Another reason is that people simply are needing to get somewhere in a hurry. They realize that they are speeding, but they have such a need to arrive on time that they dont care. There impatience get the better of them.

A final reason is lack of respect for other drivers, one driver who is speeding make road conditions less safe for everyone. Drivers who act as though they are in the indy 500 got no regard for the safety of others.

B. **Directions: Edit the response that you wrote on the topic below, which you saw on page 130. Time yourself and try to complete the edit in five minutes.**

Cell Phone Writing Prompt

The passage addresses controversy about cell phone use. The Federal Communications Commission has determined that radiation from cell phones has no adverse effects. However, some studies raise questions about traffic safety issues and the long-term health effects of cell phone use.

In your response, compare the arguments in the reading selection and take a position on cell phone safety. Use relevant and specific information to support your response.

C. **Directions: After you check your answers to the exercise above, complete the strategy box below. If you need more practice with specific skills and concepts, review the sections in the book that correspond to these skills.**

MY TEST-TAKING STRATEGY

I need to pay special attention to these areas of editing. (Check all that apply.)

- ❑ Making sure my sentences are complete
- ❑ Correcting run-ons and comma splices
- ❑ Using parallel structure
- ❑ Using nouns and pronouns correctly
- ❑ Using verb forms and tenses correctly
- ❑ Matching subjects and verbs
- ❑ Making sure punctuation is correct
- ❑ Using capitalization correctly
- ❑ Making sure words are spelled correctly
- ❑ Choosing appropriate words

Answers and explanations start on page 193.

WRITING ABOUT TEXT PRACTICE

Part A

Directions: Plan and draft an extended response to the prompt below and the passage on the facing page. Write your response on a computer if possible. If you cannot, write neatly on paper so that you can revise it later.

Step 1—Plan: Take 10 minutes to read the prompt and the passage. Under the prompt, make an outline *or* draw an idea map to organize:

- your thesis statement
- your main points and supporting evidence from the passage
- counterarguments and your response *or* faulty reasoning in the passage

Step 2—Draft: Take 25 minutes to draft your response, which will include the following:

- an introduction, with your thesis statement as the topic sentence
- body paragraphs, with your reasons accompanied by supporting evidence from the text
  - use phrases such as "As the writer says . . . ," "The information in the passage states . . . ," "This is supported in the passage by . . ."
- a concluding statement wrapping up the piece

Step 3—Revise and Edit: Take 10 minutes to reread your response to:

- revise to improve organization, cohesion, and clarity of sentences, paragraphs, and the entire piece
- edit to correct errors in sentence structure, grammar, punctuation, capitalization, and spelling

Social Networking on the Internet—Positive or Negative?

The passage addresses the serious impact that the explosion of social networking has had on our lives. In recent years, social relations have developed online that allow us to connect with friends or create communities around common interests. Supporters feel that these networks create greater interaction and increased information. Critics say that this trend actually limits social interactions and creates short- and long-term risks for the users.

In your response, compare the arguments in the reading selection and take a position favoring either the benefits or the drawbacks of social networking. Use relevant and specific information to support your response.

"Social Networking on the Internet—Positive or Negative?"

In a hundred years, humanity will look back and try to pinpoint the moment in its history when it overcame the clumsy limits of flesh-and-blood existence. When it does, Internet social networking will stand out as an important change, not just in the ways in which we communicate with each other but also, and perhaps more importantly, in the ways in which we perceive ourselves.

At this primitive moment, our contacts on social networks are still people we have met in person, for the most part. And there was a time when this was natural: you have to choose your friends from the selection available to you. But the menu has changed. The great promise of Internet socialization is that congregation is no longer at the mercy of geography. If I join an online community of checkers enthusiasts whose members are scattered across four continents, our interactions will be little different than if we all lived in the United States. Our shared interest, rather than where our bodies happen to live, is what brings us together.

As our online friendships increasingly supplant our in-person friendships, our online personalities begin to replace our old selves, too. What happens when two-thirds of my acquaintances know me by an invented username rather than by my real name, or by an animated icon of a dancing stickman rather than by my face? The answer: I learn that I can essentially define myself for this group of people. I can be exactly who I want to be.

With time, we will all come to shift to interest-based interactions almost exclusively. If you've always felt alone because you've never been able to find anyone who shares your greatest passion—and that passion happens to be watching macramé competitions—then the Internet opens up a new world of like-minded individuals to you. You'll share experiences, pictures, and tips and live as you never could have 30 years ago, when you would have been forced to endure your isolation.

At the same time, we must ask ourselves: Is this something we want to encourage? One of the great protective mechanisms of the flesh-and-blood version of human communities is shame. As unfair as it may sound to ridicule our poor macramé enthusiast, social disapproval is an important tool for discouraging destructive behavior and extremism. When online communities offer a meeting place for outcasts, the shunning of these tendencies loses its force. It is no coincidence that online communities are the single most fertile recruiting ground for terrorism. And isn't accepting differences in others—rather than surrounding ourselves with homogeneous communities of like-minded friends—an important part of the human experience?

For children of the 20th century, there is something else very alarming in the idea of channeling so many of our interactions through the Internet. In the heyday of the Soviet Union, a video camera in every home was presented as the greatest tool a totalitarian state could wish for. If all my interactions pass through the Internet, won't the government be watching me? Regardless of whether it will or won't, it certainly seems now to have that option.

We also must wonder what will become of our most cherished traits as we transition to an existence of ones and zeroes. As biological beings, we have emotional needs tied to touch and warmth. None of my online friends can give my dancing stickman a hug!

Ultimately, the new possibilities that the online world opens up to us are irresistible and herald a new era of finely tuned communities with unprecedented potential. The challenge will lie in making the most of this new world without losing the vital elements of our nonelectronic human experience.

Evaluation criteria begins on page 225.

Part B

Directions: Develop an extended response to the prompt below and the paired passages on the facing page. Write your response on a computer if possible. If you cannot, write neatly on paper so that you can revise it later.

Step 1—Plan: Take 10 minutes to read the prompt and the passages. Under the prompt, make an outline *or* draw an idea map to organize:

- your thesis statement
- your main points and supporting evidence from the passage
- counterarguments and your response *or* faulty reasoning in the passage

Step 2—Draft: Take 25 minutes to draft your response, which will include the following:

- an introductory statement, with your thesis statement as the topic sentence
- body paragraphs, with your reasons accompanied by supporting evidence from the text
  - use phrases such as "As the writer says . . . ," "The information in the passage states . . . ," "This is supported in the passage by . . ."
- a concluding statement wrapping up the piece

Step 3—Revise and Edit: Take 10 minutes to reread your response and do the following:

- revise to improve organization, cohesion, and clarity of sentences, paragraphs, and the entire piece
- edit to correct errors in sentence structure, grammar, punctuation, capitalization, and spelling

Health and Safety on the Job

The first passage presents regulations of the U.S. Occupational Safety and Health Administration (OSHA). The second passage is a newspaper article about workers who successfully sued their employer, claiming that they were fired because they had reported injuries on the job.

Read both the OSHA regulations and the news report carefully. Take a position on whether or not you think that the court decision was correct based on the OSHA guidelines.

Use relevant and specific information from both passages to support your response.

OSHA Standards and Worker Protection

OSHA standards are rules that describe the methods that employers must use to protect their employees from hazards. There are OSHA standards for Construction work, Agriculture, Maritime operations, and General Industry, which are the standards that apply to most worksites. These standards limit the amount of hazardous chemicals workers can be exposed to, require the use of certain safe practices and equipment, and require employers to monitor hazards and keep records of workplace injuries and illnesses. Examples of OSHA standards include requirements to: provide fall protection, prevent trenching cave ins, prevent some infectious diseases, assure that workers safely enter confined spaces, prevent exposure to harmful substances like asbestos, put guards on machines, provide respirators or other safety equipment, and provide training for certain dangerous jobs.

You Cannot Be Punished or Discriminated Against for Using Your OSHA Rights

The OSHA Act protects workers who complain to their employer, OSHA or other government agencies about unsafe or unhealthful working conditions in the workplace or environmental problems. You cannot be transferred, denied a raise, have your hours reduced, be fired, or punished in any other way because you used any right given to you under the OSHA Act. Help is available from OSHA for whistleblowers.

If you have been punished or discriminated against for using your rights, you must file a complaint with OSHA within 30 days of the alleged reprisal for most complaints.

Source: U.S. Occupational Safety and Health Administration

OSHA fines Norfolk Southern $802K for firing workers

The U.S. Occupational Safety and Health Administration announced Monday that it was fining a Norfolk Southern Corp. subsidiary more than $800,000 for firing three workers who had reported injuries on the job.

OSHA, a division of the U.S. Department of Labor, ordered Norfolk Southern Railway Co. to pay the former workers a total of $802,169 in damages. The agency also said the railroad company must clear the workers' disciplinary records and post workplace notices and offer training on whistleblower rights.

"OSHA's investigations have found that the company continues to retaliate against employees for reporting work-related injuries and has effectively created a chilling effect in the railroad industry," the Labor Department said in a news release.

Norfolk Southern spokesman Robin Chapman said the company would appeal the decisions on all three workers before an administrative law judge at the Labor Department.

Two of the three incidents occurred in 2010, according to the agency's release. An engineer in Louisville, Ky., and a conductor in Harrisburg, Pa., were fired after reporting injuries from falls in or near company bathrooms.

Norfolk Southern accused the employees of falsifying their injuries, the agency said. The company also accused the conductor of failing to promptly report the injury. "The day before the injury, the employee had been lauded for excellent performance, highlighted by no lost work time due to injuries in his 35-year career," according to the Labor Department release.

OSHA found that the company hearings for both workers were "flawed." In the case of the engineer, the hearing "was orchestrated to intentionally support the decision to terminate the employee," the release said.

In the third incident, an employee in Greenville, S.C., was fired after he reported being hit by a company truck. Norfolk Southern accused him of "improper performance of duties." The agency found he was treated "disparately in comparison to four other employees involved in the incident," none of whom had reported injuries.

"Firing workers for reporting an injury is not only illegal, it also endangers all workers," David Michaels, an assistant U.S. secretary of labor, said in a statement. "To prevent more injuries, railroad workers must be able to report an injury without fear of retaliation."

The *Extended Response Evaluation Guide* appears on page 225.

LESSON

1

POLISHING YOUR WRITING

Strengthen Sentences

Key Ideas

- Read your work as a whole to make sure that it is clear and logical.
- Imagine that you are reading your work for the first time.
- Correct any sentences that have errors in structure or punctuation.

GED® TEST TIP

To prepare for the Extended Response, practice prewriting, drafting, and revising often. Frequent practice will help you feel more comfortable and confident as a writer.

Revising Unclear and Incorrect Sentences

When you write your response, your first step is to get your ideas down. To do this, you follow a prewriting and drafting plan like the ones on pages 116–133. When you are finished drafting, go back and reread what you have written. As you read each sentence, ask yourself:

- Do the ideas in the sentence make sense? If not, how can I make the sentence clearer? Add some words? Drop or move a confusing word or phrase? Insert or delete punctuation? Change the words?
- Is the sentence structure correct? If not, how can I correct it?

Read the paragraph below, and think about how you would revise the errors in clarity and sentence structure. Then compare it with the revised paragraph.

Paragraph with unclear and incorrect sentences:

Working outdoors has many advantages over working indoors. When you are outside you are in contact with nature. You can enjoy the sunshine on your face, hear the birds, and to smell the flowers. You don't have to consult the weather forecast on TV. In contrast, sitting in a climate-controlled cubicle, it is not known whether the sky is sunny or cloudy. Also, most outdoor jobs require you to use your body, that can be a huge advantage. Finally, if you work indoors, you might be sitting down at a desk, and typing all day long. After work, instead of relaxing. You'll probably have to go to the gym to work out.

Paragraph with revised sentence structure:

Working outdoors has many advantages over working indoors. When you are <u>outside, you</u> are in contact with nature. You can enjoy the sunshine on your face, hear the birds, and <u>smell</u> the flowers. You don't have to consult the weather forecast on TV. In contrast, <u>when you sit in a climate-controlled cubicle, you don't know</u> whether the sky is sunny or cloudy. Also, most outdoor jobs require you to use your <u>body, and that</u> can be a huge advantage. Finally, if you work indoors, you might be sitting down at a <u>desk and typing</u> all day long. After work, instead of <u>relaxing, you'll</u> probably have to go to the gym to work out.

Use these **revision marks** when you revise your sentences on paper:

- To delete a word or punctuation mark, cross it out.
- To add a word or punctuation mark, insert a caret (^) in the line where you want it to go, and then write it in above the line.
- To change a word, cross it out and write the new word above it.
- To move a word or phrase, circle it and draw an arrow to its new position.
- To capitalize a letter, draw three lines under it.

PRACTICE 1

A. Directions: Read and revise the sentences. Correct these problems by using revision marks.

☑ fragments, run-ons, and comma splices
☑ incorrect coordination and subordination
☑ misplaced or dangling modifiers
☑ problems in parallel structure

EXAMPLE: It's fun to do a family tree, you can learn a lot.

1. First, write down what you know about your family then interview relatives.
2. Videotaping or to record the interviews is a good idea.
3. Ask relatives to provide exact names, dates, and give other details.
4. Making copies of documents such as birth certificates and marriage licenses.
5. Interviewing older family members, they'll often tell you stories you never heard.
6. Record all the information you get and put it in a three-ring binder carefully.
7. Some people use their computers to do genealogy searches, they get very good results.
8. However, one must have the time, the patience, and know-how to use the Internet.
9. If you decide to learn more about your roots don't be surprised to find yourself at a huge family reunion.
10. The whole process of putting together a family tree and contacting long-lost family members.

B. Directions: Read the paragraphs below. Use revision marks to correct problems with sentences.

It was a beautiful day, the blue ocean sparkled in the sunlight. A perfect day for going to the beach. Looking across the sand, two little girls were building a sandcastle and made a moat next to it. Renelle spread out her towel she anchored it with her shoes and beach bag and began to read a magazine. Suddenly she heard a voice. "Are you going to get in the water, or are you just going to lie there?" Renelle looked up, and saw her friend Terry. She laughed softly and she got up and she greeted Terry. Putting on her sandals, the two of them walked across the burning sand to the water's edge.

Renelle loved going to the beach. Going to the beach relaxed her. Going to the beach helped her forget about her problems. It didn't cost money like most other forms of entertainment. Most of Renelle's friends also spent a lot of time at the beach so that was another incentive.

Answers and explanations start on page 193.

LESSON

2

POLISHING YOUR WRITING

Improve Organization

Key Ideas

- Revise your response so that the organization is clear to the reader.
- Make sure that paragraph breaks fall in the right places.
- Check for faulty transitions and irrelevant details.

GED® TEST TIP

When you write a draft on paper, leave wide margins and space between lines so that you can more easily use the revision marks. On a computer, you can use the cut, copy, and paste functions to revise.

Revising Problems in Organization

When you reread your response, you may also need to make changes in organization to make the response clearer to the reader. As you read, ask yourself:

- Is my main idea clear?
- Are there a clear introduction, body of support, and conclusion?
- Is the paragraphing correct? Does each paragraph relate to only one main idea? Should any paragraphs be split into two? Should any be combined?
- Does each paragraph have a topic sentence that tells the main idea? Are any of the other sentences in a place that doesn't make sense? Are there any irrelevant details that should be removed?
- Does the writing flow smoothly from sentence to sentence and from paragraph to paragraph? If not, where can I add transitions?

Read the sample paragraph below. Think about how you would correct the errors in organization. Then compare it with the revised paragraph.

Paragraph with problems in organization:

(1) Many people believe that changes in technology have improved our communication with others. (2) I believe that the opposite is true. (3) So-called technological improvements have led to a marked decline in the quality of interpersonal communication. (4) In the old days, when you called someone, the person was likely to pick up the phone to find out who was calling. (5) Nowadays, screening devices make that unnecessary. (6) By listening to your voice on the answering machine or by seeing your phone number pop up on his caller identification box, the other person can decide that he doesn't care to speak to you. (7) This encourages long games of "phone tag." (8) Television is another example—you can barely get a word out of someone who is glued to the tube.

Paragraphs with revised organization:

(1) Many people believe that changes in technology have improved our communication with others. (2) However, I believe that the opposite is true. (3) So-called technological improvements have led to a marked decline in the quality of interpersonal communication.

(*) Phone use is one area in which communication has suffered. (4) In the old days, when you called someone, the person was likely to pick up the phone to find out who was calling. (5) Nowadays, screening devices make that unnecessary. (6) By listening to your voice on the answering machine or by seeing your phone number pop up on his caller identification box, the other person can decide that he doesn't care to speak to you. (7) This encourages long games of "phone tag."

In the revised paragraphs, the transition *however* was added to sentence 2. The piece was divided into two paragraphs—an introductory paragraph and a body paragraph about phone use. A topic sentence (marked with *) was added. Sentence 8 of the original, which was not related to telephones, was deleted.

Use these symbols to revise essay organization:

- To change whole sentences, use the same marks you used to change words.
- To start a new paragraph, use the paragraph symbol (¶).

PRACTICE 2

A. Directions: Using the revision marks, revise the paragraphs below. One revision has been made for you.

We've all heard countless advertising campaigns warning us not to litter. Yet some people still think nothing of throwing a soda can out of their car window onto the highway or dropping a candy wrapper on the sidewalk. Most of us realize that we are upsetting a delicate ecological balance when we don't dispose of our trash properly. ¶ Why do people continue to litter? One reason people litter is that they just don't care about others. It doesn't bother them to leave their trash in front of someone else's apartment building, forcing another person to deal with the problem.

This inconsiderate attitude is also reflected in the refusal to recycle plastic, glass, and newspapers. People figure that they won't be around in the future when the landfills are used up, so who cares? Another possible reason for littering is low self-esteem. If people don't feel good about themselves, they won't be motivated to keep their environment looking attractive. Low self-esteem can cause many other problems, including depression and lack of self-confidence. People who have high self-esteem believe that it's important to keep their home, the planet Earth, clean and beautiful.

B. Directions: Revise the response that you wrote to the Gettysburg Address writing prompt on page 132.

Be sure to check for:

- ☑ clear main idea
- ☑ introduction, body, and conclusion
- ☑ correct paragraphing
- ☑ topic sentences
- ☑ logical placement of sentences
- ☑ irrelevant details that should be removed
- ☑ clear transitions

Save your work. You will use it in the next step of the writing process, editing.

Answers and explanations start on page 194.

LESSON 3

POLISHING YOUR WRITING

Word Choice

Key Ideas

- Use precise words instead of vague ones.
- Express your ideas in as few words as possible.
- When writing a response, use formal language instead of slang.

GED® TEST TIP

When you read your draft, focus on the specific words and ask yourself, "Can I make this clearer or more concise?" If so, revise accordingly to improve your score on the response.

After you have written and revised your response, you will need to edit it. In the editing stage of the writing process, you check for correct grammar, usage, and word choice. You may already have made some organizational changes. The kinds of changes you make when you are editing will be smaller—more like fine-tuning.

Word choice is an important aspect of writing. There are several aspects of word choice to look at when you are editing: using precise words, avoiding wordiness, and avoiding slang.

People often use vague terms when they are speaking. They say things like, "It was a great party!" or "The weather is nice today." General words like *great* and *nice* are okay in conversation because the listener can ask questions such as, "What was so great about the party?" In writing, however, you should try to write specific words that create a clear picture for the reader.

With vague words: Tim took a long hike in the beautiful mountains.
With precise words: Tim took a 12-mile hike in the rocky, snowy mountains.

With vague words: He walked through a forest where the ground was covered with pine needles.
With precise words: He meandered through a forest where the ground was carpeted with pine needles.

It's also helpful to your reader if you write concisely and avoid wordiness. Being brief helps the reader focus on your message. If you notice that you have said the same thing twice, cut out the extra words.

Too wordy: Tim's dream and the thing he hopes for most of all is to make a home for himself and live in a cabin in the woods.
More concise: Tim's most cherished dream is to live in a cabin in the woods.

Too wordy: The only thing getting in the way of his having this dream come true is that his wife isn't so sure that it's such a fantastic idea.
More concise: The only obstacle to realizing his dream is his wife's resistance.

Finally, avoid using slang when writing your essay. Though people sometimes use informal language when speaking, essay writing calls for more formal language. Take care to express yourself appropriately.

With slang: Tim is going to hit the road at seven tonight.
With more formal language: Tim is going to leave town at seven tonight.

With slang: He needs a better map because he's totally clueless about directions.
With more formal language: He needs a better map because he has difficulty understanding directions.

PRACTICE 3

A. Directions: Replace each of the underlined words or phrases with more appropriate language. Write your answers on a separate sheet of paper.

1. Families International is a <u>nonprofit organization that does not make any money</u>.

2. We give aid to <u>many</u> children in the Third World every year.

3. These children must endure <u>lousy</u> living conditions.

4. Your donation, even if it is only five <u>bucks</u>, will help a child get food and clothing.

5. Please send your donation <u>as soon and as quickly as possible</u> to the following address.

B. Directions: Edit the paragraphs below for correct grammar and usage, paying special attention to nouns and pronouns, subject-verb agreement, and regular and irregular verbs.

If you ever order merchandise from a catalog, you should be aware of your rights. All companies, regardless of what state they are located in, is required to ship your order within 30 days unless they have advertise a different shipping time. If a company is unable to meet the shipping deadline, they must send you an "Option Notice." You can choose to wait longer or get a refund.

Some consumers complaining about receiving merchandise that they did not order. They were told that companies that engaged in this practice broken the law. If they send you a product you haven't order, it is yours to keep.

If you receive a package that been damaged, don't open it. Write "REFUSED" on the package, and return it to the seller. There's no need to add new postage as long as the package come by regular mail.

C. Directions: Revise the response you wrote to the Gettysburg Address writing prompt on page 132.

Be sure to check for:

- ☑ Correct use of nouns and pronouns
- ☑ Correct use of regular and irregular verbs
- ☑ Subject-verb agreement
- ☑ Word choice

Answers and explanations start on page 194.

POLISHING YOUR WRITING PRACTICE QUESTIONS

<u>Questions 1 through 5</u> refer to the following paragraphs.

Gardening for success

(A)

(1) Flowers, herbs, and shrubs can beautify both small and large spaces in your home or yard. (2) In addition, growing your own vegetables can be enjoyable and healthful. (3) If you want to be a successful Select... you follow some simple guidelines.

(B)

(4) First, determine whether you'll be gardening indoors or outdoors. (5) This might depend on what type of home you live in, or it might depend on the climate. (6) If you live in an apartment building and don't have access to a community garden, an indoor garden might be right for you. (7) An indoor garden is also an Select... for the plants that you'd like to grow.

(C)

(8) Indoors, you'll need to place your plants near a window where they'll get some sunlight each day. (9) Choose your growing space carefully, whether indoors or outdoors. (10) Outdoors, find a spot that doesn't have a lot of rocks or clay. (11) Likewise, you should choose your plants carefully.

(D)

(12) Investigate various Select... find out how much sunlight and water they need and what temperature they prefer. (13) You might be surprised to find, for instance, that you shouldn't try to grow basil in a shady side yard or impatiens in full sun. (14) A little extra effort up front will help you avoid common gardening pitfalls and enjoy your garden more.

1. If you want to be a successful Select... you follow some simple guidelines.

   A. gardener, importantly
   B. gardener, but it's important that
   C. gardener, it's important that
   D. gardener. And it's important that

2. An indoor garden is also an Select... for the plants that you'd like to grow.

   A. option if you live in a climate that is too extreme
   B. option if one lives in a climate that is not good
   C. option, if you live in a climate that is not good
   D. option if you live in a climate that is not good

3. Which revision would improve the effectiveness of paragraph C?

   A. move sentence 11 to the beginning of paragraph C
   B. move sentence 8 to follow sentence 9
   C. move sentence 8 to follow sentence 10
   D. move sentence 8 to follow sentence 11

4. Which revision would improve the effectiveness of the article?

   A. move sentence 12 to the end of paragraph C
   B. move sentence 3 to the beginning of paragraph B
   C. move sentence 7 to the beginning of paragraph C
   D. move sentence 11 to the beginning of paragraph D

5. Investigate various Select... find out how much sunlight and water they need and what temperature they prefer.

   A. plants, but
   B. plants or
   C. plants to
   D. plants, and then

<u>Questions 6 through 10</u> refer to the following paragraphs.

Rowing Across the Atlantic

When I was a child, my grandmother often told me stories about her father. He was born in [Select...] the United States when he was 2 years old. His trip to this country was a mystery to me.

"Dad always said he came over in a rowboat," Granny explained. I tried to imagine a 2-year-old boy rowing across the [Select...] seemed impossible that he could have done that. [Select...] Atlantic Ocean *in a rowboat*?

I had many questions for Granny. "Were his parents with him?" I asked. "No, I think he came by himself," she explained, laughing. Was she [Select...]? The stories always ended with Granny wiping tears from her eyes. She had several grandchildren. "Oh, how I wish you had known him," she cried.

6. He was born in [Select...] the United States when he was 2 years old.

   A. Wales and had come to
   B. Wales which coming to
   C. Wales which had come to
   D. Wales, which had come to

7. I tried to imagine a 2-year-old boy rowing across the [Select...] seemed impossible that he could have done that.

   A. ocean however it
   B. ocean, thus it
   C. ocean. Thus it
   D. ocean; it

8. [Select...] Atlantic Ocean *in a rowboat*?

   A. Could he had crossed to
   B. He could have crossed the really big
   C. Could he have crossed the vast
   D. Could he crossed the really big

9. Was she [Select...]?

   A. totally pulling my leg
   B. kidding me
   C. totally joking
   D. for real

10. Which sentence should be removed from the last paragraph?

    A. Sentence 10
    B. Sentence 11
    C. Sentence 12
    D. Sentence 13

Questions 11 through 14 refer to the following paragraphs.

Southern Gothic Writer

(A)

Flannery O'Connor was a gifted Southern writer. She wrote many short stories and two novels. She is known for writing in a Southern gothic style and exploring topics of religion, ethics, [Select...] explored the dark side of human nature.

(B)

One of O'Connor's most popular stories, "A Good Man is Hard to Find" was written in 1953 and focuses on a man called The Misfit. [Select...] her most shocking story. It raises important questions of good and evil, morality and immorality, and Southern historical issues.

(C)

When Flannery was just 26, she was diagnosed with lupus. The disease that had killed her father. To manage her health, she returned to her family's farm, Andalusia, in Milledgeville, Georgia. There, she lived with her mother Regina and wrote many of her most important works. She delighted in raising birds of all varieties, including peafowl.

(D)

During her time at Andalusia, [Select...]. Although she was only expected to live for five years after her lupus diagnosis, she managed to survive for fourteen.

11. She is known for writing in a Southern gothic style and exploring topics of religion, ethics, [Select...] explored the dark side of human nature.

   A. and morality she also frequently
   B. and morality she also, frequently
   C. and morality frequently
   D. and morality. She also frequently

12. [Select...] her most shocking story.

   A. Many figure this is
   B. Many consider this
   C. Many think it ought to be a
   D. Many reckon this ought to be her

13. When Flannery was just 26, she was diagnosed with lupus. The disease that had killed her father.

   Which is the best way to revise these two sentences?

   A. Switch the order of the two sentences.
   B. Insert the second sentence after the comma in the first sentence.
   C. Combine the two sentences by replacing the period with a comma.
   D. Remove the second sentence.

14. During her time at Andalusia, [Select...].

   A. Flannery maintained many fulfilling correspondences that gave her the insight into human behavior that is evident in her writing
   B. Flannery also maintained many correspondences with friends, family, and other writers, which is why she had a special insight into human behavior that is displayed in her writing
   C. Flannery also maintained many fulfilling correspondences with friends, family, and other writers which is why she is believed to have had a special insight into human behavior that is in her writing
   D. Flannery maintained many correspondences with friends, family, and other writers which is why she is believed to have had a special insight into human behavior

Questions 15 through 19 refer to the following paragraphs.

Notification of Utility Repairs

Universal Utilities will soon begin repairs of the underground lines in your neighborhood. This Select... to receive the exceptional service you have come to expect from us.

We will begin by installing a new pipeline under your street. Select... the smaller line that runs from the street to your home. Lastly we will install a new meter at your home.

This work will require our company's trucks to be in your neighborhood. We apologize for any inconvenience this may cause during peak travel Select... may experience a temporary disruption in your utility service. Select...

If you have any questions Select... . We can be reached by telephone, or you may visit our website. Thank you for allowing us to serve your utility needs.

15. This Select... to receive the exceptional service you have come to expect from us.

    A. will ensure you continue
    B. will ensure you always continue
    C. is ensuring you always continue
    D. will ensure they always continue

16. Select... the smaller line that runs from the street to your home.

    A. Than next we will replace
    B. Then we will replace
    C. Then next we will replace
    D. Then next we will have replaced

17. We apologize for any inconvenience this may cause during peak travel Select... may experience a temporary disruption in your utility service.

    A. times, you
    B. times but you
    C. times. You
    D. times, and so you

18. Select...

    A. However we will adjust your bill accordingly if your service is interrupts.
    B. However we will adjust your bill accordingly if your service is interrupted.
    C. However we will adjust your bill accordingly thus your service is interrupted.
    D. However, we will adjust your bill accordingly if your service is interrupted.

19. If you have any questions Select... .

    A. about the scheduled repairs. Please contact our office
    B. about the scheduled repairs, please contact our office
    C. about the scheduled repairs please contact our office
    D. , about the scheduled repairs. Please contact our office

Answers and explanations begin on page 194.

LESSON

1

USING GRAMMAR CORRECTLY

Noun and Pronoun Agreement

Key Ideas

- A noun names a person, place, thing, or idea.
- A pronoun takes the place of a noun.
- Use subject, object, and possessive pronouns in the proper places.

GED® TEST TIP

To choose the option with the correct pronoun in a compound like "They went to the party with James and I," take out "James and" and ask yourself whether the sentence still sounds correct.

Using Nouns and Pronouns

A **noun** names a person (such as *woman* or *Anne*), a place (such as *drugstore* or *Florida*), a thing (such as *car* or *Titanic*), or an idea (*truth* or *Buddhism*). A **proper noun** refers to a specific person, place, thing, or idea; a **common noun** is more general. For example, *Anne* is a proper noun; *woman* is a common noun.

A **pronoun** is a word that replaces a noun. The **antecedent** is the noun that is being replaced, as shown below:

EXAMPLE

Steven lost his address book. It held many important phone numbers.
antecedent (address book) pronoun (It)

There are three types of pronouns: subject, object, and possessive.

EXAMPLES

A **subject pronoun** replaces the subject of a sentence.

Steven called home. He was very worried.
subject (Steven) subject pronoun (He)

An **object pronoun** replaces the object of a verb or of a preposition.
His wife called Steven. She asked him what the problem was.
object pronoun (object of a verb) (him)

She and Steven looked for it.
object pronoun (object of a preposition) (it)

A **possessive pronoun** replaces a possessive noun.
Steven needed Kelly's number. He called 411 to get her number.
possessive noun (Kelly's) possessive pronoun (her)

Use this chart for help in remembering the three types of pronouns:

Subject Pronoun: replaces subject	Object Pronoun: replaces object	Possessive Pronoun: shows ownership
I	me	my, mine
you	you	your, yours
he	him	his
she	her	her, hers
it	it	its
we	us	ours
they	them	their, theirs

Avoid these mistakes with pronouns in compound subjects and objects:

Incorrect pronoun in compound subject: Linda and me went to the movies.
Correct: Linda and I went to the movies.

Incorrect pronoun in compound object: We saw Kareem and he at the theater.
Correct: We saw Kareem and him at the theater.

PRACTICE 1.1

A. Directions: Write the correct pronoun to replace each underlined noun.

1. Laurie and Paul just moved to California. ______________________

2. A neighbor told Laurie and Paul that saving water was important there. ______________

3. He said they should turn the water off when brushing their teeth. ________________

4. Laurie's sister suggested getting a special shower head that saves water. ______________

5. Laurie and Laurie's sister will go shopping for it on Sunday. ______________________

B. Questions 6 through 8 refer to the following letter.

To Whom It May Concern:

I am writing to recommend Bonetta Williams for the position of managerial assistant in your firm. I believe that she is highly qualfied for the position, and I urge you to strongly consider her candidacy.

[Select...] have worked together for three years. As my secretary, she has proven to be responsible and efficient. [Select...] her work done on time and looks for ways to help others. In addition, I find her extremely intelligent and likable. I will be sorry to see her go.

My supervisor, Walter Constantine, has also worked with Bonetta and would be happy to speak with you if necessary. Please contact [Select...] if you need any further information.

Sincerely,

Carol Rhodes

6. [Select...] have worked together for three years.

   A. Bonetta and me
   B. We (Bonetta and me)
   C. Bonetta and me,
   D. Bonetta and I

7. [Select...] her work done on time and looks for ways to help others.

   A. She always getting
   B. Her always getting
   C. Her always gets
   D. She always gets

8. Please contact [Select...] if you need any further information.

   A. Walter and I
   B. Walter or me
   C. him or I
   D. he or me

Answers and explanations start on page 195.

Key Ideas

- A pronoun should match its antecedent in person and number.
- Make sure it is clear which antecedent a pronoun refers to.
- If necessary, use a noun in place of a pronoun, or construct the sentence differently so that the antecedent is clear.

GED® TEST TIP

Take into account the whole passage when you are determining which pronoun is correct. A common error to watch for is when a paragraph begins with the third-person form one *and then shifts to the second-person form* you.

Pronoun-Antecedent Agreement

Pronouns should agree with their antecedents, or the nouns they refer to. For example, a pronoun and its antecedent must agree in number. If the antecedent is singular, the pronoun should be singular. If the antecedent is plural, the pronoun should be plural.

EXAMPLES

Andy's company is very progressive. It pays for his college classes.
(company: singular antecedent; It: singular pronoun)

Many employees want to learn more skills, so they take classes.
(employees: plural antecedent; they: plural pronoun)

Incorrect: Any employee who is interested should submit their application.
Correct: Any employee who is interested should submit his or her application.
Correct: Employees who are interested should submit their applications.

Note that for collective nouns (such as *company, jury, family, team, committee, union*), you generally use the singular pronoun *it*.

Incorrect: The committee announced that they will hold weekly meetings.
Correct: The committee announced that it will hold weekly meetings.

A pronoun and its antecedent must agree in person. To agree, they both must be first person (referring to the speaker), second person (the person spoken to), or third person (the person or thing spoken about).

First person	Second person	Third person
I, me, my mine	you, your, yours	he, him, his
we, us, our, ours		she, her, hers
		it, its
		they, them, their, theirs

The indefinite pronoun *one* is like a third-person personal pronoun. A common error in writing (and one that is tested on the Reasoning Through Language Arts Test) is an incorrect shift between the third-person *one* and the second-person *you.*

Incorrect shift: If one attends college classes, you can be reimbursed.
Correct: If one attends college classes, one can be reimbursed.
Correct: If one attends college classes, he or she can be reimbursed.
Correct: If you attend college classes, you can be reimbursed.

It must be clear which antecedent a pronoun refers to. If necessary, use a noun in place of the pronoun, or reconstruct the sentence.

Unclear: Carlos spoke to his boss, and he told him about the program.
Clear (noun replaces pronoun): Carlos spoke to his boss, and his boss told him about the program.
Clear (different construction): Carlos spoke to his boss, who told him about the program.

Unclear: Michelle helped Shania fill out the financial aid application that she had picked up.
Correct (different construction): After picking up a financial aid application for Shania, Michelle helped her fill it out.

PRACTICE 1.2

A. Directions: Correct any errors in pronoun use. If there are no errors, write *C*. You may also have to change some verbs.

EXAMPLE: People who live in small towns know ~~one has~~ they have access to fewer amenities than big-city dwellers.

___ **1.** Sally is moving to a small town. Her mother is concerned about the health-care options they offer.

___ **2.** Sally tried to reassure her mother, but it was hard for her to believe her.

___ **3.** Sally asked a friend who lives in the town for information about it's health-care facilities.

___ **4.** The town has a freestanding clinic where a person can go when they are sick.

___ **5.** There is also a nearby hospital, and they have a very good reputation.

___ **6.** If one is concerned about health care, you should sign up for a good insurance plan.

B. Questions 7 through 9 refer to the following paragraphs.

The Best Discipline

What should parents do when their children act up? Parents often like the idea of punishment, but punishment may not be the most effective solution. If the punishment results from the parent's anger, it won't work. Instead, children [Select...] parents angry.

One parenting expert feels that [Select...] should be clear about their expectations from the outset so that children will not unknowingly violate rules. They should respond to children's misbehavior in a calm and neutral fashion. It's also important to choose a consequence related to the action. If a child hits or bites in a play group, for example, it would be most appropriate not to allow [Select...] for a short time. He or she will begin to see the connection.

7. Instead, children [Select...] parents angry.

A. will learn only that they shouldn't make one's
B. will have learned only that they shouldn't make one's
C. will learn only that you shouldn't make one's
D. will learn only that they shouldn't make their

8. One parenting expert feels that [Select...] should be clear about their expectations from the outset so that children will not unknowingly violate rules.

A. he
B. we
C. one
D. parents

9. If a child hits or bites in a play group, for example, it would be most appropriate not to allow [Select...] for a short time.

A. the child to play with them
B. them to play with them
C. the child to play with the group
D. the child to plays with them

Answers and explanations start on page 195.

LESSON 2

USING GRAMMAR CORRECTLY

Verb Forms and Tenses

Key Ideas

- Each verb has four forms: present, present participle, past, and past participle.
- Verb forms are used to create different tenses, which show time relationships.
- Use clues in the sentence and paragraph to help decide which tense to use.

GED® TEST TIP

Some passages on the GED® Test have a verb-tense question based on the tense of the entire passage. Make sure you select verb forms that are consistent with the tense of the passage.

Regular Verbs

An important part of writing correctly is using the right verb forms. A **verb** is a word that indicates action or being. Each verb has a base form and four other forms. A **regular verb** follows a consistent pattern to create each verb form.

Base form: look

Tense	Verb form	How to write it
Present	look/looks	with *I, you, we, they:* use the base form
		with *he, she, it:* add *-s* to the base form
Present participle	looking	add *-ing*
Past	looked	add *-ed* (*-d* if verb ends with *e*)
Past participle	looked	add *-ed* (*-d* if verb ends with *e*)

The forms are used to create different **verb tenses**, or times. The table below shows how verb tense and form are related. Notice that when you use certain tenses, you must also use a **helping verb**—often a form of *be* or *have.*

Tense	Verb form	Use
Present	look/looks	a habitual action, general truth, or state of being: *I look at the newspaper every day.*
Past	looked	an action that has been completed: *I looked at it this morning.*
Future	will look	an action that has not yet happened: *I will look at it tonight, too.*
Present progressive	am/is/are looking	an action in progress: *I am looking at it right now.*
Present perfect	have/has looked	an action that began in the past and continues until now: *I have looked at it every day this week.*
Past perfect	had looked	an action that was completed before a specific time in the past: *I had looked at it before it got wet.*
Future perfect	will have looked	an action that will be completed by a specific time in the future: *I will have looked at it by the time I get home.*

Sentences often contain clues that tell you which tense to use. For instance, time words and phrases like *yesterday* or *last week* show that the past should be used, *tonight* and *next month* indicate the future, and *by tonight, since 2000,* and *for seven years* indicate the perfect tenses.

Other verbs in the sentence can be clues: *I look at the newspaper whenever I get the chance.* Finally, verbs in other sentences also can be clues. The verbs in a paragraph or passage are generally in the same tense.

PRACTICE 2.1

A. Directions: Rewrite each verb in its correct tense. Use clues in each sentence for help in choosing the tense.

EXAMPLE: Between 1892 and 1924, about 12 million immigrants *entered* (enter) the U.S. through Ellis Island in New York.

1. By the 1950s, Ellis Island ____________ (cease) to be an important immigration checkpoint.
2. The government ____________ (close) Ellis Island to immigration in 1954.
3. Now Ellis Island ____________ (function) as a national monument.
4. Since the island was reopened as a museum in 1990, many tourists ____________ (visit) it.
5. Soon, a genealogical center ____________ (open).
6. The island ____________ (look) different than it did originally because 24 acres of landfill have been added.
7. Now we ____________ (think) about taking a trip to Ellis Island next month.

B. Questions 8 through 10 refer to the following advertisement.

Don't Miss Your Chance!

The Express Lane credit card [Select...] a fantastic deal right now, for a limited time only. [Select...], you will receive a 20 percent discount on your first five purchases!

The Express Lane card carries no monthly charge. You'll pay a low $35 fee just once a year. Become an Express Lane member now. Your savings opportunities [Select...]!

8. The Express Lane credit card [Select...] a fantastic deal right now, for a limited time only.

   A. offered
   B. is offering
   C. offers
   D. will offer

9. [Select...], you will receive a 20 percent discount on your first five purchases!

   A. If you are signing up for Express Lane before April 9
   B. If you have signed up for Express Lane before April 9
   C. If you will sign up for Express Lane before April 9
   D. If you sign up for Express Lane before April 9

10. Your savings opportunities [Select...]!

   A. will have been amazing you
   B. would be amazing you
   C. will be amazing you
   D. will amaze you

Answers and explanations start on page 195.

Key Ideas

- Irregular verb forms do not follow a single pattern.
- Some irregular verbs follow an *i, a, u* pattern.

GED® TEST TIP

When you choose an answer that changes a verb, read the sentence again, with your choice in it. Doing so may help you "hear" whether the verb form is correct.

Irregular Verbs

Most verbs are regular verbs; their past and participle forms follow the same pattern. Some verbs, however, are **irregular verbs.** Although some irregular verbs follow a pattern, most do not.

A common error with irregular verbs is using the past participle in place of the past—for instance, *I been there* instead of *I was there.* Discover which irregular verb forms, if any, give you problems. Then learn the correct forms. Here are some tips for learning the forms of irregular verbs:

- If you find two verbs that rhyme in the present form (for example, *grow* and *throw*), check to see if they have the same forms in the past and past participles (*grew, grown; threw, thrown*). If so, learn them together.
- Learn which verbs follow the *i, a, u* pattern: *sing, sang, sung; drink, drank, drunk; sink, sank, sunk.* However, be aware that there are exceptions (*bring, brought, brought*).

Here is a list of common irregular verbs.

Present Form	Past Form	Past Participle Form
am, are, is	was, were	been
become	became	become
begin	began	begun
blow	blew	blown
break	broke	broken
bring	brought	brought
buy	bought	bought
choose	chose	chosen
come	came	come
do	did	done
drink	drank	drunk
eat	ate	eaten
fall	fell	fallen
fly	flew	flown
freeze	froze	frozen
get	got	gotten
give	gave	given
go	went	gone
grow	grew	grown
have, has	had	had
know	knew	known
leave	left	left
lose	lost	lost
ride	rode	ridden
run	ran	run
see	saw	seen
shake	shook	shaken
show	showed	shown
speak	spoke	spoken
steal	stole	stolen
take	took	taken
throw	threw	thrown
wear	wore	worn
write	wrote	written

PRACTICE 2.2

A. Directions: Write the correct form of the verb shown in parentheses.

EXAMPLE: Since November, the school's heating system ___*has broken*___ (break) down several times.

1. Yesterday the technician ______________ (come) to resolve the problem once and for all.
2. School employees ______________ (show) him the boiler.
3. The technician said, "If you ______________ (speak) to me about this sooner, it would have been easier to fix."
4. He ______________ (take) parts out of the heating system and replaced them with new ones.
5. He said, "I've never ______________ (see) such a poorly installed system."

B. Questions 6 through 8 refer to the following paragraphs.

TV Rating Systems

In 1996, television industry representatives announced that the industry had formed TV Parental Guidelines. This rating system, designed to give parents advance warning about the content of TV shows, [Select...] TV in 1997. The ratings system [Select...] down into six different categories, ranging from "All Children" to "Mature Audiences Only."

Six months later, after pressure from advocacy groups, the television industry agreed to include additional labels to advise viewers if a show they were about to view contained violence, sexual activity, coarse language, or sexually suggestive language. These labels [Select...] more specific and therefore more helpful information about an upcoming show.

6. This rating system, designed to give parents advance warning about the content of TV shows, [Select...] TV in 1997.

A. begun to appear on
B. began to appearing on
C. had begun to appear on
D. began to appear on

7. The ratings system [Select...] down into six different categories, ranging from "All Children" to "Mature Audiences Only."

A. broke itself
B. broke
C. was broken
D. had broken

8. These labels [Select...] more specific and therefore more helpful information about an upcoming show.

A. now given viewers
B. now give viewers
C. now will give viewers
D. now have given viewers

Answers and explanations start on page 195.

LESSON

3

USING GRAMMAR CORRECTLY

Subject-Verb Agreement

Key Ideas

- A verb must match its subject in number.
- Collective nouns are singular when they refer to a group as a single unit.
- Indefinite pronouns may be singular, plural, or both.

GED® TEST TIP

To check for correct subject-verb agreement, ask yourself: Does the verb agree with its subject? Is the verb in the right form? Is the verb in the right tense for both the sentence and the passage?

Agreement with a Simple Subject

In the present tense, subjects and verbs must agree in number. To understand the basics of subject-verb agreement, study the chart below. Notice that present tense verbs take an *-s* ending when they are used with the pronoun subjects *he, she,* and *it* or their noun equivalents.

Verb Forms for Singular Subjects	Verb Forms for Plural Subjects
I jump	*we* jump
you jump	*you* jump
he, she, it jumps	*they* jump

To master subject-verb agreement for the GED® Test, be aware of these special nouns and pronouns:

Collective nouns are usually singular, even though they may seem plural. A collective noun names a group, such as *army, crew, crowd, staff, family, herd,* or *flock.* If the group is considered to be a single unit, it is singular.

EXAMPLES

The army is a good place to learn discipline.
The church choir sings each Sunday.

Some nouns that end in *-s* may look plural, but in fact they are not.

EXAMPLE

Politics is an interesting topic.

Indefinite pronouns do not refer to a specific person. Some indefinite pronouns are singular, some are plural, and some may be either.

Singular	anyone, everyone, someone, no one, one, anybody, everybody, somebody, nobody, anything, everything, something, nothing, another, other, either, neither, each, much
Plural	many, several, few, both
Singular or plural	all, none, some, any, part, most

EXAMPLES

Singular: These days, it seems as if almost everyone is joining a health club.
Singular: Most of the equipment is easy to use.
Plural: Most of the exercise classes are fun
Plural: A few are advanced classes for those already in great shape.

PRACTICE 3.1

A. Directions: Underline the correct verb form to complete each sentence.

EXAMPLE: Every Monday, the National Orchestra (perform, performs) live on the radio.

1. The public (is, are) invited to listen free of charge.

2. Free tickets (becomes, become) available one hour before the performance.

3. The performance (is, are) usually held in Barnes Hall.

4. Many well-known musicians (has, have) played there.

5. Everyone (seem, seems) to enjoy these concerts very much.

6. The concert series (is, are) very popular.

B. Questions 7 through 9 refer to the following article.

The Speed of Sound

Most of us [Select...] airplane noise that is so loud it sounds like an explosion. [Select...] fly faster than the speed of sound. Listeners on the ground hear the noise, but it is not audible to passengers.

The speed of sound is 1,088 feet per second at 32°F at sea level. It is different at other temperatures and in other substances. For example, sound travels faster in water than in air. Sound takes about one second to move a mile under water, but five seconds to move a mile through air. It travels through ice cold vapor at 4,708 feet per second and through ice cold water at 4,938 feet per second. Surprisingly, [Select...] very well. For instance, sound travels through glass at speeds up to 19,690 feet per second.

7. Most of us [Select...] airplane noise that is so loud it sounds like an explosion.

A. were hearing
B. have heard
C. having heard
D. hears

8. [Select...] fly faster than the speed of sound.

A. That noise occurs when a plane start to
B. That noise occurred when a plane start to
C. That noise occurs when a plane starts to
D. That noise occur when a plane start to

9. Surprisingly, [Select...] very well.

A. some other materials conducts sound
B. some other materials conduct sound
C. some other materials conducted sound
D. any other material conducts sound

Answers and explanations start on page 195.

Key Ideas

- If a compound subject is joined by *and*, use a plural verb.
- If a compound subject is joined by *or*, *either . . . or*, or *neither . . . nor*, the verb should agree with the subject closer to it.
- When checking subject-verb agreement, ignore interrupting phrases and watch for inverted structure.

GED® TEST TIP

Read there's *as* there is *and* here's *as* here is.

Agreement with a Compound Subject

A compound subject is made up of two or more subjects joined by *and* or *or*. To make a verb agree with a compound subject, follow these guidelines:

When two or more subjects are joined by *and*, the compound subject is plural. Use the correct verb form for the plural.

EXAMPLE: Tricia and her sister are caring for their mother.

If two subjects are joined by *or*, the verb agrees with the subject closer to it:

EXAMPLE: A health aide or a nurse visits each day.

When subjects are joined by *either . . . or* or *neither . . . nor*, the verb agrees with the subject closer to it.

EXAMPLE: Neither the sisters nor their brother has medical training.

Interrupting Words

Sometimes a word or group of words comes between the subject and the verb. In that case, locate the subject by asking yourself, What is this sentence really about? Mentally cross out the interruptor. Then make the verb agree with the subject.

EXAMPLE: The medicine ~~prescribed by the doctors~~ is on a high shelf.
subject interruptor verb

Interrupting phrases often begin with prepositions, such as *of, in, on, from, with, to,* and *for.*

EXAMPLE: A pile ~~of medical supplies~~ rests in the front hallway.

Interrupting phrases may be set off by commas. Watch especially for phrases beginning with words like *along with, as well as, besides,* and *in addition to.*

EXAMPLES

Dr. Silva~~, who is one of the surgeons,~~ consults with the family.
The sisters~~, along with the medical team,~~ keep the patient comfortable.

Inverted Structure

Checking subject-verb agreement can be tricky when the sentence structure is **inverted**—that is, when the subject comes after the verb. Most questions and sentences that begin with *here* or *there* are inverted.

EXAMPLES

Does the pharmacy have enough medicine to fill the prescription?
Here are the hospital supplies that Tricia ordered.

Incorrect: What is Tricia and her family going to do?
Correct: What are Tricia and her family going to do?

Incorrect: Do Tricia want to send her mother to a hospital?
Correct: Does Tricia want to send her mother to a hospital?

Incorrect: There's the bandages. (Remember that *There's* is short for *There is.*)
Correct: There are the bandages.

Practice 3.2

A. Directions: If a sentence contains an interrupting phrase, cross out the interruptor. Then underline the correct verb to complete the sentence.

EXAMPLE: Brushing and flossing ~~with regularity~~ (is, are) key to good dental health.

1. Many toothpastes on the market (carry, carries) a seal of approval from the American Dental Association.
2. Products carrying the seal (are, is) tested to guarantee that they are safe and effective.
3. Fluoride, an important ingredient in many toothpastes, (strengthens, strengthen) teeth and (attacks, attack) bacteria that cause tooth decay.
4. There (is, are) toothpastes that claim to have special benefits, like tartar control or whitening.
5. Some pharmacies and supermarkets (offers, offer) store-brand toothpaste at a low price.
6. Any toothpaste with fluoride and good flavor (is, are) fine to use, even if it's not a brand-name toothpaste.

B. Questions 7 through 9 refer to the following paragraphs.

Unemployment Insurance

Unemployment insurance provides workers who have lost their jobs with partial replacement of their salaries. Each state [Select...] its own laws. [Select...] the amount received. When the unemployment rate rises above a certain level, states are required to extend the benefits. The state and federal governments share the cost of the additional benefits.

In most states, employer contributions pay for this program. Unemployed workers who wish to [Select...] public employment office to learn about job openings.

7. Each state [Select...] its own laws.

   A. administers its own program and have
   B. administer its own program and have
   C. administers its own program and has
   D. administers it's own program and have

8. [Select...] the amount received.

   A. Wage level and the length of employment determine
   B. Wage level and the length of employment determines
   C. Wage level and the length of employment would be determined by
   D. Wage level and the length of employment will then determine

9. Unemployed workers who wish to [Select...] public employment office to learn about job openings.

   A. draw benefits reports regularly to their
   B. draw benefits, reports regularly to their
   C. draw benefits report regularly to their
   D. draw benefits reports regularly to there

Answers and explanations start on page 195.

USING GRAMMAR CORRECTLY PRACTICE QUESTIONS

Questions 1 through 5 refer to the following paragraphs.

Unorthodox Tennis Stars

Venus and Serena Williams are not your typical tennis stars. For one thing, they are African Americans in a game that few African Americans have become famous for playing; those who preceded them were Althea Gibson, Arthur Ashe, and Zina Garrison. For another, Venus and Serena are sisters.

Tennis players often receive hours of instruction from Select... that way for Venus and Serena. Instead, their father, the former owner of a security-services business, taught them how to play on public courts, after teaching himself through books and films. The family lived in a rough neighborhood, and gang members watched over the girls while Select... practiced.

The practice paid off. Venus had won 63 tournaments by the time she turned 12, and she became a professional at 14. In just a few years, she Select... millions of dollars in endorsements and prizes. Serena, turning professional a year after Venus, had a slower start. However, some experts think she may now be better than her sister.

The two sisters, Select... . Though they sometimes face each other on the court, Select... .

1. Tennis players often receive hours of instruction from Select... that way for Venus and Serena.

   A. highly paid coaches, but it doesn't happen
   B. highly paid coaches but it doesn't happen
   C. highly paid coaches, but it didn't happen
   D. highly paid coach, but it doesn't happen

2. The family lived in a rough neighborhood, and gang members watched over the girls while Select... practiced.

   A. they
   B. the girls
   C. each
   D. them

3. In just a few years, she Select... millions of dollars in endorsements and prizes.

   A. is earning
   B. earned
   C. earn
   D. will earn

4. The two sisters, Select... .

   A. who live in Palm Beach Gardens, Florida, is best friends
   B. who lives in Palm Beach Gardens, Florida, is best friends
   C. who live in Palm Beach Gardens, Florida is best friends
   D. who live in Palm Beach Gardens, Florida, are best friends

5. Though they sometimes face each other on the court, Select... .

   A. there been no trace of sibling rivalry
   B. there had not been a trace of sibling rivalry
   C. there will be no trace of sibling rivalry
   D. there is no trace of sibling rivalry

Questions 6 through 10 refer to the following paragraphs.

Getting the Best Service for Your Car

Have you had trouble finding a good mechanic? By following these tips, you can improve your chances of getting quality service.

Even before your car breaks down, look for a shop you like and trust. Ask Select... good service at a reasonable price. Don't Select... to home, for another shop may have a better deal. Be wary of ads that offer rock-bottom prices. Specials like Select... .

Be as specific as possible when you describe your car's problem to the mechanic. If the technician must spend time trying to determine Select... cost more. You also need to request information about both estimates and guarantees before the repair work starts. Ask for a price range rather than an exact estimate. Find out how long the guarantee lasts and whether Select... any time or mileage limits.

If you don't understand a repair explanation, ask for clarification right away. In addition, keep records of all repairs and billing in case of a dispute.

6. Ask Select... good service at a reasonable price.

   A. people where they will receive
   B. people where they have received
   C. people where they receiving
   D. them where they will receive

7. Don't Select... to home, for another shop may have a better deal.

   A. have picked a shop just because it's close
   B. be picking a shop just because it's close
   C. have picked a shop just because its close
   D. pick a shop just because it's close

8. Specials like Select... .

   A. these often comes with restrictions attached
   B. this often comes with restrictions attached
   C. these often came with restrictions attached
   D. these often come with restrictions attached

9. If the technician must spend time trying to determine Select... cost more.

   A. what's wrong, it will
   B. what are wrong, it will
   C. what's wrong it will
   D. what's wrong, the repair job will

10. Find out how long the guarantee lasts and whether Select... any time or mileage limits.

    A. there is
    B. there be
    C. there are
    D. there were

<u>Questions 11</u> through 15 refer to the following letter.

Taxpayer Notification

We have received your tax return and have noted some inconsistencies in it. We are therefore proposing a number of changes to your return. These [Select...] on your refund are outlined below.

First, the amount you claimed for self-employed income differs from our records. If you wish to contest this change, please [Select...]. Second, you have made an error in your calculations. Please review [Select...].

Because of these changes to your return, the amount of taxes you owe [Select...]. Your refund has therefore been reduced accordingly.

Contact us if you have any questions about these specific problems or about the documents you must send to contest the changes. Be sure to send the last page of this letter when replying by mail. If we determine that your return was correct as filed, we [Select...] your account.

11. These [Select...] on your refund are outlined below.

A. changes and its effect
B. changes and their effect
C. changes, and its effect
D. changes and it's effect

12. If you wish to contest this change, please [Select...].

A. send photocopies of one's records
B. to send photocopies of one's records
C. send photocopies of your records
D. send photocopies of their records

13. Please review [Select...].

A. our calculations, which is appended to this letter
B. are calculations, which is appended (to this letter)
C. our calculations which is appended to this letter
D. our calculations, which are appended to this letter

14. Because of these changes to your return, the amount of taxes you owe [Select...].

A. has increased
B. have increased
C. is increasing
D. are increasing

15. If we determine that your return was correct as filed, we [Select...] your account.

A. are crediting
B. will credit
C. will have credited
D. had credited

<u>Questions 16 through 20</u> refer to the following paragraphs.

Disability Etiquette

Many of us [Select...] know how to act when meeting someone who has a disability. The main thing to remember [Select...] just like everyone else. They want to be treated with respect and dignity. Beyond that, try the following tips.

When you meet a person with a disability, speak and act with [Select...] as you would with anyone else. Use your usual tone of voice. A person who has trouble hearing you will let you know. Don't talk down to the person or stare. Refrain from using a term like *handicap,* which focuses on the disability rather than on the person. Instead, use a term such as *physically disabled* or say, "He uses a wheelchair."

Any assistive equipment, [Select...]. Unless you have the person's express permission, you should not touch it. Also, don't pet a blind person's guide dog because distracting [Select...] could put the owner in danger.

Finally, if you have a child with you, don't prevent him or her from talking to the person or asking questions. Children are often more accepting than adults.

16. Many of us [Select...] know how to act when meeting someone who has a disability.

    A. does not
    B. don't
    C. didn't
    D. never does

17. The main thing to remember [Select...] just like everyone else.

    A. is that people with disabilities has feelings
    B. are that people with disabilities has feelings
    C. is that people with disabilities have feelings
    D. is that those with disabilities has feelings

18. When you meet a person with a disability, speak and act with [Select...] as you would with anyone else.

    A. he or her
    B. him or her
    C. him or she
    D. them

19. Any assistive equipment, [Select...].

    A. such as a wheelchair, cane or communication board, is the person's property
    B. such as a wheelchair, cane, or communication board, is the person's property
    C. such as wheelchair, cane, or communication board, are the person's property
    D. such as a wheelchair, such as a cane, or a communication board, are the person's property

20. Also, don't pet a blind person's guide dog because distracting [Select...] could put the owner in danger.

    A. a blind person's guide dog
    B. it
    C. her
    D. them

Answers and explanations start on page 196.

LESSON

1

USING WRITING MECHANICS

Comma Use

Key Ideas

- In a compound sentence, use a comma before the coordinating conjunction.
- Be careful not to use a comma between two words or phrases joined by *and*.
- Insert a comma after an introductory word, phrase, or clause.

GED® TEST TIP

Read a sentence out loud to see if you hear a pause. Before you insert a comma, be sure that you can base your decision on a comma rule.

As a general rule, **commas** indicate where readers would pause in a sentence if they were reading it aloud. Below are specific guidelines for using commas.

Commas in Compound Sentences

In a compound sentence, place a comma immediately before the coordinating conjunction.

EXAMPLES

Some people are insecure about hosting a party, but others are relaxed and confident.

Many hosts have years of practice, and they have some organizational tips.

Watch out, though, for sentences that appear to be compound but are not. Some sentences have one main clause but have a compound subject or a compound predicate. If a sentence does not have two independent clauses, a comma is not needed before the coordinating conjunction.

Incorrect: Planning, and list making are two key organizational techniques.
Correct: Planning and list making are two key organizational techniques.

Incorrect: Making a list reduces disorganization, and helps you feel in control.
Correct: Making a list reduces disorganization and helps you feel in control.

Commas after Introductory Elements

In general, a comma should follow an introductory word, phrase, or clause to separate the introductory element from the main part of the sentence.

EXAMPLES

Introductory words:
Yes, listing your ideas can be very helpful.
However, making a list is only the first step.

Introductory phrases:
Giving it some thought, carefully draw up a guest list.
For a casual feel, have an open house.
On the day of the party, do as much as you can first thing in the morning.
By party time, you should be able to relax.

Introductory clauses:
Before you make a list, decide what kind of party you will have.
If you are a good cook, you might choose to have a dinner party.

Remember that only a subordinate clause at the beginning of a sentence requires a comma after it. A subordinate clause at the end of the sentence generally does not.

No comma: Decide what kind of party you will have before you make a list.

PRACTICE 1.1

A. Directions: Insert commas where needed in the sentences below. If no commas are required, write *NC*.

_____ **1.** Train travel is more pleasant than riding a bus but it can be more expensive.

_____ **2.** When you're on a train you can stand up and stretch if you need to.

_____ **3.** Most trains have club cars where passengers can get snacks and sometimes even sit at tables.

_____ **4.** Unlike buses trains sometimes have seats that face each other.

_____ **5.** Traveling through a scenic area you may find that your train has a double-decker car that offers a better view.

_____ **6.** Lowered airfares and many people's unwillingness to spend long hours in a train have contributed to the declining popularity of rail travel.

B. <u>Questions 7 through 9</u> refer to the following paragraphs.

Low-Fat Cooking

To have a more healthful diet, try cooking with less fat. It's not as hard as you think! [Select...] such as steaming, poaching, or baking. When you do include oil in the preparation of your dish, use less of it. Vinegar can be used without oil in salad [Select...] the flavor can be enhanced with fresh herbs.

Another tactic is to cut down on dairy fat. Avoid regular milk, cream, and sour cream. Add low-fat dairy products or another liquid to your dish instead. Many dairy foods come in a [Select...] to the palate, some are.

7. [Select...] such as steaming, poaching, or baking.

A. For starters, use cooking methods that require little or no oil or butter,
B. For starters use cooking methods that require little or no oil or butter
C. For starters use cooking methods that require little or no oil or butter,
D. For starters use cooking methods that require little, or no oil or butter,

8. Vinegar can be used without oil in salad [Select...] the flavor can be enhanced with fresh herbs.

A. dressing, and
B. dressing and,
C. dressing, or
D. dressing, for example

9. Many dairy foods come in a [Select...] to the palate, some are.

A. low-fat version and though, not all of them may be pleasing
B. low-fat version, and though, not all of them may be pleasing,
C. low-fat version, and though, not all of them may be pleasing
D. low-fat version, and though not all of them may be pleasing

Answers and explanations start on page 196.

Key Ideas

- Separate the items in a series with commas.
- Put commas around an appositive only if it gives nonessential details about a noun.
- Don't put a comma between a subject and a verb.
- Don't use a comma between two items joined by *and* or *or*.

GED® TEST TIP

When an option involves removing a comma, see if you can apply a specific rule for using a comma in that place. If you cannot, the comma should probably be removed.

Commas in a Series

When three or more items are listed in a series, place commas *between* the items:

EXAMPLES

Keith, Darnelle, Marisol, and Doug are ready to take the GED® Test.
They have taken a class, studied together, and prepared well.

The comma before the final *and* or *or* is optional (for example, *March 7, March 14, or March 21*). Placing a comma there is not tested on the *Reasoning Through Language Arts Test*, but using one there will help you place commas correctly in the series. To use commas between the items in a series, count the number of items listed and subtract one. That is the number of commas you should use.

Commas with Appositives

An **appositive** is a word or group of words that gives more information about a noun by renaming it.

EXAMPLES

Marisol, an experienced writer, feels confident about the essay.
Doug's only sister, Gina, was the first in the family to receive a high school equivalency degree.

To decide whether to set off an appositive with commas, mentally cross out the appositive. Then ask, *"Can I still identify the person, place, or thing described in the sentence?"* If you can, use commas around the appositive.

EXAMPLES

Mann College, a local community college, offers GED® test courses.
Keith, who attended GED® test classes for a year, has done well there.

Here you can identify the noun without the appositive. Each appositive adds more information, but it is not essential to your understanding. Usually when an appositive is renaming a proper noun, it is not essential.

On the other hand, if you cannot identify the person, place, or thing without the appositive, do not set off the appositive with commas.

EXAMPLES

Keith and his friend Antoine plan to work in construction.
Students who study faithfully usually do well on the test.

In these examples, you cannot identify the nouns without the appositives. You would ask, *"Which friend?"* and *"Which students?"* The appositives are essential to your understanding and should not be set off by commas.

Comma Errors to Avoid

It is easy to overuse commas. Avoid this error by following these guidelines:

Do not use a comma between the subject and the verb.

Incorrect: Park College, is the school Doug hopes to attend.

Do not use a comma between two subjects, two verbs, or two other items joined by *and* or *or*.

Incorrect: Science, and math are hard subjects for Keith.
Incorrect: Darnell writes practice essays, and reads.
Incorrect: They will review his application, and transcript.

PRACTICE 1.2

A. Directions: Insert commas where needed in the sentences below. If no commas are required, write *NC*.

_____ **1.** Kwanzaa is a week-long African American holiday that celebrates culture community and family.

_____ **2.** Kwanzaa a wintertime holiday is based on an ancient African harvest celebration.

_____ **3.** It was developed in modern times by scholar Maulana Karenga.

_____ **4.** Kwanzaa celebrations include rituals such as singing dancing drumming and poetry reading.

_____ **5.** The family lights one candle every day for each of seven principles: unity self-determination responsibility cooperative economics purpose creativity and faith.

_____ **6.** A day during which people consider their moral worthiness marks the end of Kwanzaa.

B. Questions 7 through 9 refer to the following paragraphs.

Childproofing Your Home

If you have small children, you no doubt appreciate the need to make your home as safe as possible. It is a fact that [Select...]. Taking a few simple measures might reduce the number of times you take your kids to the emergency room.

Start by putting childproof locks on all cupboards in which [Select...]. To keep babies and toddlers from entering dangerous areas, put baby gates in doorways and install sleeves on doorknobs. Install safety locks on doors and windows. Make sure that older [Select...] can open them in an emergency. To prevent burns in the bathtub, keep the water temperature below 120°F. Cover unused outlets with outlet plugs.

7. It is a fact that [Select...].

A. home accidents are responsible for more children's injuries than all childhood diseases combined
B. home accidents, is responsible for more children's injuries than all childhood diseases combined
C. home accidents, are responsible for more children's injuries, than all childhood diseases combined
D. home accidents, being responsible for more children's injuries than all childhood diseases combined

8. Start by putting childproof locks on all cupboards in which [Select...].

A. medicines poisons, or fragile objects are stored
B. medicines, poisons, or fragile objects are stored
C. medicines poisons, or fragile objects, are stored
D. medicines poisons, or fragile objects is stored

9. Make sure that older [Select...] can open them in an emergency.

A. children those ten and up
B. children, those ten, and up,
C. children, those ten and up,
D. children those ten and up,

Answers and explanations start on page 196.

LESSON **2**

Using Writing Mechanics

Capitalization

Key Ideas

- Capitalize proper nouns and adjectives.
- Capitalize days of the week, months, and names of holidays but not seasons.
- Capitalize titles if they come before a person's name or are used to address the person.

GED® TEST TIP

Use the "proper noun" test to determine if a word should be capitalized. To capitalize, make sure the word or phrase is the name of a person, place or thing: "my uncle" is fine, and so is "Uncle Leo."

To recognize capitalization errors on the Reasoning Through Language Arts test and to use capital letters correctly in your response, follow these guidelines.

Capitalize proper nouns. A **proper noun** is the name of a specific person, place, thing, or idea. If a proper noun has two or more words, capitalize each word.

EXAMPLES

Claude Normand is a major contributor to Portland Community Hospital.
The hospital is located on Camden Road in Portland, Maine.
The hospital and charities such as the American Cancer Society rely on contributions from citizens.
All major religions, from Islam to Christianity, support giving to charity.

Note that the key words in addresses are proper nouns and are capitalized. The key words include the names of streets, cities, states, and countries.

Do not capitalize common nouns, which do not refer to a specific person, place, or thing.

EXAMPLE

Incorrect: Many Doctors volunteer at Clinics in the City.
Correct: Many doctors volunteer at clinics in the city.

Capitalize the names of proper adjectives. A **proper adjective** is formed from a proper noun.

EXAMPLE

Mr. Normand has a French Canadian heritage.

Capitalize a title before a person's name. Do not capitalize a title when it appears without a person's name unless it is used in direct address.

EXAMPLES

Title before name: Mr. Normand met recently with Dr. Halverson and Mayor Maresky.
Title without name: The doctor and mayor were very receptive to his ideas.
Direct address: He said, "Thank you, Mayor, for listening to my proposal."

Capitalize names of holidays, days of the week, and months. Do not capitalize the names of seasons.

EXAMPLES

Memorial Day is always the last Monday in May and is a paid holiday.
The project will be completed by the end of spring.

Capitalize names of specific school courses and all languages.

EXAMPLE

I am taking Introduction to Computers 101, English, and math.

PRACTICE 2

A. Directions: Correct the capitalization errors in the sentences below.

EXAMPLE:

I am writing to thank the ~~S~~(s)taff of the Waterside Physical Therapy ~~c~~(C)enter.

1. Last Spring, I broke my arm in a car accident.
2. My internist, doctor claudia McNally, referred me to Waterside.
3. The center's Director, Ilana Harris, assigned me a physical therapist named Ellie Royce.
4. Ellie studied physical therapy in her native London and used british methods of treatment that relieved my pain quite effectively.
5. She also did therapy with me in the pool at Rainbow health club.
6. I finished my treatments just before labor day, and I feel 100 percent better, thanks to Ellie.

B. <u>Questions 7 through 9</u> refer to the following paragraphs.

An Unusual Breed

The Akita is a Japanese dog breed that dates to ancient times. The breed has a special spiritual meaning for many. For example, when a child is born, well-wishers give the family small statues of Akitas to express hopes for future happiness and health. In the past, [Select...] allowed to own his breed.

Akitas are massive, powerful dogs, used for hunting game and guarding. Starting in the 17th century, [Select...]. In 1937, Akitas were brought to [Select...].

7. In the past, [Select...] allowed to own this breed.

A. only Emperors and nobles were
B. only emperors and nobles were
C. only Emperors and Nobles were
D. only Emperors and nobles are

8. Starting in the 17th century, [Select...].

A. they were trained to hunt game and waterfowl in the Mountains of Japan
B. they were trained to hunt game and waterfowl, in the Mountains of Japan
C. they were trained to hunt game and waterfowl in the mountains of Japan
D. they were trained to hunt game, and waterfowl in the Mountains of Japan

9. In 1937, Akitas were brought to [Select...].

A. america by author Helen Keller
B. America by author Helen Keller
C. america by Author Helen Keller
D. america by author helen keller

Answers and explanations start on page 196.

LESSON 3

USING WRITING MECHANICS

Possessives and Contractions

Key Ideas

- Use apostrophes with possessive nouns but not with possessive pronouns.
- Use an apostrophe to replace the missing letters in a contraction.
- To decide whether to use a possessive or contraction, test to see whether the full form of the contraction makes sense in the sentence.

GED® TEST TIP

Contractions are acceptable in informal speech and writing. However, try to avoid them in more formal writing situations, such as the GED® Extended Response.

Some of the most common spelling errors involve possessives and contractions. Follow these guidelines when spelling these words:

A **possessive** shows ownership. Use apostrophes with possessive nouns. Do not use apostrophes with possessive pronouns.

EXAMPLES

Possessive nouns: friend's car Marta's map the dogs' leashes
Possessive pronouns: his, hers, ours, yours, theirs, its
Correct: The car's tires are new. The map is hers.

If a noun is singular or if it is plural but does not end in *s*, add an apostrophe + *s* to form the possessive.

Singular possessive: cat's boss's women's

If a noun is plural and ends in *s*, add an apostrophe after the final *s*.

Plural possessive: workers' ladies'

A singular possessive often sounds like a plural noun. Use an apostrophe only with the possessive.

Correct: My company's benefits (possessive) make it one of the best companies (plural) to work for.

A **contraction** shortens two words by combining the second word with the first and leaving out one or more letters. An apostrophe takes the place of the missing letters. Some contractions combine pronouns with verbs.

EXAMPLES

here is → here's there is → there's I am → I'm

Other contractions combine verbs with the word not.

EXAMPLES

have not → haven't do not → don't will not → won't

Be careful to use the apostrophe in place of the missing letter or letters. Notice that the correct position is not necessarily the point at which the two words come together.

Incorrect: You do'nt have to come with us tonight. (*do'nt* should be *don't*)

Some possessives and contractions sound the same (*your* and *you're, its* and *it's, their* and *they're*). To determine whether to use a possessive or a contraction, substitute the two words that make up the contraction. If the substitution makes sense, the contraction is correct. If not, use a possessive.

PRACTICE 3

A. Directions: Underline the correct word or words to complete each sentence.

EXAMPLE: I'm (your, you're) downstairs neighbor, and (I've, Iv'e) been having trouble sleeping lately because of noise late at night.

1. (Theirs, There's) a noise that sounds like the thumping beat of rock music.

2. I (ca'nt, can't) be sure (who's, whose) responsible, but (its, it's) coming from your apartment.

3. My roommates and I have discussed this, and (were, we're) running out of patience.

4. You should talk to your children if the stereo is (theirs, there's).

5. Please be considerate of your neighbors just as we are considerate of (our's, ours).

B. Questions 6 through 8 refer to the paragraphs that follow.

Sales Trainees Wanted

Do you have a warm smile? Do people feel comfortable with you? Do you have a friendly phone manner? Do you have good organizational skills? Are you good at solving problems? If you've answered yes to these [Select...] skills at Macro Software.

Macro Software is one of the industry leaders in software distribution. [Select...] to offer a mail order service that was the first of its kind. We pride ourselves on our high-quality products, quick delivery times, and excellent customer service.

We are currently hiring sales trainees for our Miami office. Interested [Select...] to Jim Burns, Macro Software, 904 Ocean Drive, Miami, Florida.

6. If you've answered yes to these [Select...] skills at Macro Software.

A. questions, we need you're
B. questions we need you're
C. questions, we needs you're
D. questions, we need your

7. [Select...] to offer a mail order service that was the first of its kind.

A. In addition to hour chain of stores, we're proud
B. In addition to our chain of stores, we're proud
C. In addition to our chain of stores, were proud
D. In addition, to our chain of stores, were proud

8. Interested [Select...] to Jim Burns, Macro Software, 904 Ocean Drive, Miami, Florida.

A. party's should send they're resumes
B. parties should send their resumes
C. parties should send they're resume's
D. parties should send they're resumes

Answers and explanations start on page 197.

LESSON

4

USING WRITING MECHANICS

Homonyms

Key Ideas

Homonyms are words that sound the same but have different spellings and different meanings.

GED® TEST TIP

Possessives, contractions, and homonyms are the kinds of spelling items that appear on the GED® Test. Study the ones that give you problems.

Homonyms are words that sound alike but are spelled differently and have different meanings. The following chart lists homonyms and other commonly confused words that people often misspell.

Word	Meaning	Word in Sentence
accept	to receive willingly	I accept responsibility for my actions.
except	excluding	Everyone went except Molly.
affect	to have an impact	Did the medicine affect you?
effect	a result	The effects will wear off soon.
board	a piece of wood	Nail that board to the other one.
bored	not interested	Rami was bored in wood shop class.
brake	to stop; something that stops	Put your foot on the brake!
break	to shatter in pieces	Be careful, or you'll break your arm.
close	to shut	Please close that bag.
clothes	something to wear	I'm going to return those clothes.
desert	to leave behind; arid land	Don't desert a friend in need.
dessert	sweet food served after dinner	They offer dessert to their guests.
fare	money paid by a passenger	The subway fare was just raised.
fair	just, right	A lot of people think it's not fair.
forth	forward	Let's go forth!
fourth	in the 4th position	It is our fourth trip in three days.
grate	to shred	We need to grate some potatoes.
great	fantastic; of large size	It's going to be a great casserole.
hole	opening	There's a hole in the sweater.
whole	entire	Soon the whole thing will fall apart.
know	to understand	I don't know what's wrong with him.
no	opposite of *yes*	He has no sense.
led	past of the verb *lead;* brought	He led the worker to the supply room.
lead	a material in pencils	They gave her some lead pencils.
lessen	to decrease	Will you lessen the sugar in the recipe?
lesson	something you learn; moral	That will teach him a lesson.
male	a boy or man	There are both females and males in the Army.
mail	to send a message through the post office; a message sent	Send the letter through the mail.
passed	went by	Have you passed the post office?
past	opposite of *future*	Yes, in the past.
peace	opposite of *war*	When will there be world peace?
piece	a part	That's only a piece of the problem.
principal	head of a school	The principal has called a meeting.
principle	a guiding rule; a moral	He has no principles.
than	compared with	I used to have more money than you.
then	after that; at that time	Then I spent most of mine.
there	at that place	The car is over there.
their	belonging to them	It is their car.
they're	they are	They're going to sell it.
to	indicates a direction	Go to the grocery store.
too	also, in addition	Sharmaine will go, too.
two	the number 2	Buy me two loaves of bread.

PRACTICE 4

A. Directions: Underline the correct word or words to complete each sentence.

EXAMPLE: The chairman of the (board, bored) has called this meeting.

1. This is our (fourth, forth) meeting on the topic of funding.

2. We don't (no, know) any other sources of funding.

3. The director of the organization brought up this (whole, hole) issue.

4. Next (weak, week), we plan to submit a proposal.

5. We worry that a request for funding may (affect, effect) our nonprofit status.

6. In the (past, passed), we could rely on government funding.

B. Questions 6 through 8 refer to the paragraphs that follow.

Equal Pay for Equal Work?

In 1963, women earned only 59 percent of the wages men earned. In 1997, the figure was still just 74 percent. Women [Select...]?

One explanation is that the statistics include older women. [Select...] prevail. In contrast, women under the age of 25 earn about 92 percent of what men earn. However, upon closer examination, this theory falls flat. Women in entry-level jobs have always earned salaries similar to those of their male peers. The problem is that women don't receive the same raises and promotions that men get. [Select...]

7. Women [Select...]?

A. have logged grate achievements in the workforce, so why don't they receive fair pay
B. has logged great achievements in the workforce, so why don't they receive fair pay
C. have logged great achievements in the workforce, so why don't they receive fair pay
D. have logged great achievements in the workforce, so why don't they receive fare pay

8. [Select...] prevail.

A. In principle, the age gap could account for the wage gap because older women still work in jobs in which attitudes and conditions of the past
B. In principal, the age gap could account for the wage gap because older women still working in jobs in which attitudes and conditions of the past
C. In principal, the age gap could account for the wage gap because older women still work in jobs in which attitudes and conditions of the passed
D. In principal, the age gap could account four the wage gap because older women still work in jobs in which attitudes and conditions of the past

9. [Select...]

A. The effect is that, as women get older, the gap between men's and women's salaries becomes greater.
B. The affect is that, as women get older, the gap between men's and women's salaries become greater.
C. The affect is that, as women get older, the gap between men's and women's salaries becomes grater.
D. The affect is that as women get older, the gap between men's and women's salaries becomes greater.

Answers and explanations start on page 197.

USING WRITING MECHANICS PRACTICE QUESTIONS

Questions 1 through 5 refer to the following paragraphs.

Single Parents and Relationships

Children of single parents don't exactly cheer their parents on at the start of a new relationship. [Select...] and generally try to ruin their parents' chances. If you are a parent in this situation, you need to [Select...] your children that you love them. However, also let [Select...] doing the right thing.

Your children may become quickly attached to a new date, even within the course of an evening. Alternatively, they may fear that you plan to marry each potential partner you bring home. For these reasons, it makes sense not to introduce all your dates to your children. Try to see your dates at times when [Select...].

Once you become committed to a particular person, it's important to include your partner in family events gradually. Don't be surprised if your children have a negative reaction to your new partner. This time may be difficult for your kids. They're not used to seeing you with a new partner, and they may be realizing that a reconciliation with your ex-spouse is impossible. If communication breaks [Select...] family counseling. Children may be more willing to share their worries and complaints in that setting.

1. [Select...] and generally try to ruin their parents' chances.

   A. Instead children may have tantrums erase phone messages,
   B. Instead, children may have tantrums, erase phone messages,
   C. Instead, children may have tantrums, erase phone messages,
   D. Instead children, may has tantrums, erase phone messages,

2. If you are a parent in this situation, you need to [Select...] your children that you love them.

   A. understand, and showing
   B. understand. And show
   C. understand and show
   D. understand, and you show

3. However, also let [Select...] doing the right thing.

   A. you're kids know that you feel your
   B. you're kids know that you feel you're
   C. your kids know that you feel your
   D. your kids know that you feel you're

4. Try to see your dates at times when [Select...].

   A. you're children are'nt at home
   B. your children are'nt at home
   C. your children aren't at home
   D. your children isn't at home

5. If communication breaks [Select...] family counseling.

   A. down will consider
   B. down, consider
   C. down. Consider
   D. down, and consider

Questions 6 through 10 refer to the following paragraphs.

The History of Daylight Saving Time

We set our clocks forward every spring and back every fall, but few of us stop to think about why we do this. One of the main reasons for daylight saving [Select...]. In the evening, we use lights, TVs, and electrical appliances. Daylight saving time makes the period between sunset and bedtime one hour shorter, and therefore less electricity is used.

With daylight saving time, each time zone changes [Select...]. Time zones were introduced by the railroads to make schedules standard across the country. In 1918, [Select...] the rail time zones official. That same year, a second law put the country on daylight saving time for the rest of World War I. The law was unpopular, however, and it was repealed seven months later. Daylight saving time was also in force during most of World War II.

From 1945 to 1966, each state and town could decide whether to observe daylight saving time. The resulting inconsistencies created a great deal of confusion. [Select...] to put out new schedules every time a state started or ended daylight saving time. Then came the Uniform Time Act of 1966, which established starting and [Select...]. This law was amended in 1986, when the starting date was moved almost a month earlier to save energy.

6. One of the main reasons for daylight saving [Select...].

   A. time, is to save energy
   B. time is to save energy
   C. time, are to save energy
   D. times, is to save energy

7. With daylight saving time, each time zone changes [Select...].

   A. it's standard time by an hour
   B. its standard time by an hour
   C. it's standard time by an our
   D. it's standard time, by an hour

8. In 1918, [Select...] the rail time zones official.

   A. congress passed a law making
   B. Congress passed a law making
   C. congress past a law making
   D. congress passed a law made

9. [Select...] to put out new schedules every time a state started or ended daylight saving time.

   A. For example, radio and TV stations had
   B. For example radio and TV stations have
   C. For example radio and TV stations had
   D. For example radio and TV stations, had

10. Then came the Uniform Time Act of 1966, which established starting and [Select...].

    A. ending dates for daylight savings time, in the spring and fall
    B. ending date's for daylight savings time, in the spring and fall
    C. ending dates for daylight savings time in the spring and fall
    D. ending dates for daylight savings time, in the Spring and Fall

Questions 11 through 15 refer to the following paragraphs.

Rules and Regulations

Thank you [Select...]. Before using our facility, please read these rules and regulations carefully.

[Select...] When you enter the pool or exercise room, a security guard will request to see your card and will deny you entrance without it.

Guests are welcome to use the pool and exercise room, but only when accompanied by members. The guest fee is $10 per day. When bringing guests, please have them sign in at the desk in the lobby. They will be given a guest card for the day.

Pool safety is very important. [Select...] and other flotation devices are available for your use. Do not hesitate to ask lifeguards for help. Children under the age of 12 must swim in the [Select...] by an adult. Swimming classes are available to help both children and adults improve their skills.

You must [Select...] for any class you wish to take. Members receive a significant discount. Registration may be limited to a certain number of participants.

11. Thank you [Select...].

   A. for joining Spring Valley Community center
   B. for joining Spring Valley community center
   C. for joining Spring Valley Community Center
   D. for joining, Spring Valley Community center

12. [Select...]

   A. Please have your membership card with you at all times when your in the building.
   B. Please have you're membership card with you at all times when you're in the building.
   C. Please have your membership card with you at all times' when your in the building.
   D. Please have your membership card with you at all times when you're in the building.

13. [Select...] and other flotation devices are available for your use.

   A. If you are a weak swimmer, life jackets
   B. If you are a week swimmer life jackets
   C. If you are a week swimmer, life jackets
   D. If you are a week swimmer, live jackets

14. Children under the age of 12 must swim in the [Select...] by an adult.

   A. children's pool, unless they're supervised
   B. childrens' pool, unless they're supervised
   C. children's pool, unless their supervised
   D. children's pool unless they're supervised

15. You must [Select...] for any class you wish to take.

   A. register, pay
   B. register and pay
   C. register. And pay
   D. register. Pay

Questions 16 through 20 refer to the following paragraphs.

Racial Profiling

African American and Hispanic motorists are much more likely to be stopped by police Select... no apparent reason. What's their offense? It may be that these individuals have been targeted because of their race.

Blacks and Hispanics, who some police officers believe are more likely to commit crimes, have been systematically targeted by police. Police statistics Select... occurs in every geographic location. Motorists, pedestrians, and airline passengers have been searched. The police do not make class Select... of every station in life have been victims of this practice.

The statistical evidence shows a clear pattern. On one Maryland highway, 73 percent of those stopped by police were African American, even though blacks represented only 17 percent of all drivers. Hispanics make up only 8 percent of the population in Select... of drivers stopped there are Hispanic. Select... dispute the studies that document racial profiling. They maintain that the problem has been confined to a small number of officers and can be remedied easily.

16. African American and Hispanic motorists are much more likely to be stopped by police Select... no apparent reason.

    A. then their white counterparts, often for
    B. then, their white counterparts, often for
    C. than their white counterparts, often for
    D. then their white counterparts, often four

17. Police statistics Select... occurs in every geographic location.

    A. from 23 States show that this policy, called racial profiling
    B. from 23 states, show that this policy, called racial profiling
    C. from 23 states show that this policy, called racial profiling,
    D. from 23 states show that this policy, called racial profiling

18. The police do not make class Select... of every station in life have been victims of this practice.

    A. distinctions. For nonwhites
    B. distinctions, for nonwhites
    C. distinctions moreover nonwhites
    D. distinctions nonwhites

19. Hispanics make up only 8 percent of the population in Select... of drivers stopped there are Hispanic.

    A. illinois, yet 30 percent
    B. Illinois, yet 30 percent
    C. illinois yet 30 percent
    D. illinois, and 30 percent

20. Select... dispute the studies that document racial profiling.

    A. However police superintendents chiefs of police, and other law enforcement officials
    B. However, police superintendents, chiefs of police, and other law enforcement officials
    C. However, police superintendents chiefs of police, and other law enforcement officials,
    D. However, police superintendents chiefs of police and other law enforcement officials

Answers and explanations start on page 197.

Practice Questions Answers and Explanations

Interpreting Nonfiction and Informational Text

Lesson 1: Main Ideas and Details

Practice 1, page 31

1. **A. searching for a place to call home** The author states this feeling directly in the first two lines and in the last paragraph.
2. **D. the gods** The second sentence in the second paragraph says, "It was ordained by the deities."
3. **D. It was simply part of their beliefs to follow the pole.** The meaning of the pole is explained beginning with the fourth sentence of the second paragraph. The last sentence explains that the Chickasaws lacked sorrow because they trusted the pole's command.
4. **C. understands that her tendency to search is part of her Chickasaw heritage** The details about the author's search for a home, combined with the information that "the search for a homeland is part of the Chickasaw migration legend," helps you understand this main idea.
5. **D. accepts that she is Chickasaw** You can see that the writer is saying that her Chickasaw heritage is an inescapable part of who she is.

Lesson 2: Restatement and Summary

Practice 2, page 33

1. **C. lack of proper paperwork** As the writer discusses the problems, he states that he wants an "itemized list" and "a proper bill of sale." He does mention the premium price, choice (D), but that price is the reason he expects proper paperwork and is not a complaint in and of itself.
2. **B. the car to be repaired free of charge if the cause of the problem is discovered** This expectation is stated in the fifth paragraph of the letter.
3. **C. The service and warranty on the customer's car have been unacceptable.** The letter is a detailed list of the customer's complaints. They can be summed up by saying that both the service and the warranty have not been as promised.

Lesson 3: Application of Ideas

Practice 3, page 35

1. **A. overcoming a bad habit** The writer advises those trying to break free of credit card debt: "Stick with it until you're free again."
2. **B. never use the credit cards** The last paragraph implies that the author approves of using credit cards only once you have already gotten out of debt, and then only for convenience. Thus, if you are in debt, you should stop using your credit cards.
3. **C. losing weight by avoiding all-you-can-eat buffets** Basically, the advice is that you gradually lose your debt by not adding anything to it. This is similar to helping yourself lose weight by not adding to it with portions of food you don't need.
4. **C. "Live within your means."** This statement can be inferred from the advice "don't borrow any more," and "what I'm against is buying more on your credit cards than you can pay for at the end of the month."

Lesson 4: Cause and Effect

Practice 4, page 37

1. **C. It affected nearly everyone.** This answer summarizes the meaning of the first two sentences of the passage.
2. **A. Many people lost the mortgages on their homes.** This answer is stated in the first paragraph: "men and women who saw their mortgages foreclosed." Choices (B) and (D) are both mentioned as causes, not effects, of the depression.
3. **B. low worker incomes** The second paragraph states, "but the actual cause of the collapse was an unhealthy economy. . . . Most laborers . . . could not afford to buy the automobiles . . . because their incomes were too low."
4. **B. They had little effect.** The writer tells what Herbert Hoover did as president to curb the depression ("loans to businesses and banks") but then states that "his efforts proved to be too little and too late."
5. **D. The depression left people emotionally scarred.** The first paragraph states, "No one who lived through those years . . . could ever completely forget." The statement about eating mustard that is provided in the question addresses this emotional effect rather than issues related to farmers, workers, the economy, or the number of individuals affected.

Lesson 5: Compare and Contrast

Practice 5, page 39

1. **D. leave some of his possessions behind** This answer is found in the seventh and eighth lines of paragraph 1.
2. **C. They provided milk and pulled wagons.** The selection states that "cows . . . gave milk all the way to the sink of the Humboldt where they died, having acted as draught animals for several weeks after the oxen had perished."
3. **A. the provisions of each group of travelers** Each paragraph talks about a different group and what it had to offer the wagon train. For example, "Much in contrast to these men were four batchelors . . . who had a wagon drawn by four oxen . . . cows following behind."
4. **A. be happy to have people who could cook and sew** The writer was interested in assessing how self-sufficient the group could be and what each group could offer the entire wagon train. For example, she writes, "but as he was a wagon maker and his companion a blacksmith by trade and both were accommodating

there were always ready hands to 'pry the wheel out of mire.'"

5. **A. They must cooperate and work together.** Throughout the excerpt is evidence that all the travelers depended on each other for animals, food, and physical help, such as pulling wagons out of the mud.

Lesson 6: Conclusions and Generalizations

Practice 6.1, page 41

1. **A. It is rewarding and one of life's joys.** The passage states that "my teacher's genius . . . made the first years of my education so beautiful." She also delights in observing and learning from the tadpole.
2. **D. insightful and grateful** The writer has insight about the connection between herself and the tadpole: "Thus I learned from life itself. At the beginning I was only a little mass of possibilities." The writer is also grateful to her teacher: "nor has she ceased trying . . . to make my life sweet and useful."
3. **C. show Helen how addition is used in everyday life** You can apply what you learn in the diary entry: "Thus I learned from life itself. . . . She has never since let pass an opportunity to point out the beauty that is in everything. . . ." The teacher would therefore probably use everyday life situations to teach.
4. **D. as an anecdote followed by a generalization based on the anecdote** The writer tells the story of the tadpoles (an anecdote) and relates it to her attitude toward life and learning.
5. **D. Their development is not entirely smooth.** The writer describes the tadpole having difficulty after leaping out of the bowl. This is similar to the quotation about "the stony course" of a child's education.

Practice 6.2, page 43

1. **C. On the whole, temperatures are not rising.** The writer states that rising temperatures are "quite simply not what is happening," based on the cold temperatures of the day before.
2. **A. Shady Hollow was hit with a record cold temperature yesterday.** This one piece of information is the example the author uses to support the generalization that temperatures, generally speaking, are not rising.
3. **D. nationwide data tables of temperatures from the 1980s through today** The author's generalization suffers from being based on one temperature reading. His generalization would be more likely to be valid if informed by many temperature readings over time.

Lesson 7: Word Choice

Practice 7, page 45

1. **D. the CoolForter blanket** The first sentence of paragraph 2 tells you two things about the CoolForter blanket: that "it works like an electric blanket," and that "it feels like a dream."
2. **B. to show that the blanket is a pleasant indulgence** To "coddle" is to treat gently or take care of a person. Choice (B) describes this idea.
3. **A. fluid** Many people associate the word *chemical* with toxicity or harm. A more neutral word to describe the cooling substance without inaccurate specificity is *fluid*.
4. **C. bland** The word *bland* indicates a lack of interesting features. Unlike the word *neutral,* which also indicates a lack of characteristic features, the word *bland* can carry a negative connotation.
5. **D. It allows the consumer to compare the CoolForter's energy usage to that of a familiar item.** The author's choice of a light bulb, an item with which most readers are probably familiar, emphasizes that the CoolForter blanket will not use excessive amounts of energy.

Lesson 8: Writer's Tone and Point of View

Practice 8, page 47

1. **C. the Internet writers** The writer mentions "Internet sass" and then goes on to say that "you gotta love it" because it keeps writers "off the street and out of trouble."
2. **A. The Internet reviews were much more interesting than the TV show.** The review states, "They [Internet writers] were taking hours and hours of primetime dross and turning it into decadent, amoral, sharp, electronic gold."
3. **A. The show was boring.** The reviewer's main opinion of the show is that it was bad and boring ("non-goings-on of the non-people in the non-house"). Someone yawning supports the idea of boredom.
4. **C. informal and hip** Phrases such as "the dude" and "you gotta love it" contribute to an informal and modern, or hip, tone.
5. **C. someone knowledgeable about the media** The reviewer talks knowledgeably about both television and the Internet.

Lesson 9: Text Structure

Practice 9, page 49

1. **B. exposure to the cowpox disease** As seen in the text, James's recovery from cowpox followed his exposure to it. Note that choice (D) refers to Jenner exposing James to smallpox, not cowpox.
2. **C. "After being exposed to the disease"** The transition word *After* tells the reader that James's exposure came before his catching cowpox and recovery from it. Thus, it gives the reader explicit information about the order of the steps in the process.
3. **B. A number of factors can damage a garden.** As discussed in the passage, factors such as weather, pests, and diseases can affect plants and cause damage, undoing the time and work that have been invested.

Interpreting Nonfiction and Informational Text Practice Questions, pages 50–53

1. **D. hit a boy in the arm to get his attention** The writer talks about breaking a ruler over the head of a boy she likes; you can therefore conclude that she

would hit a boy in the arm to get his attention. She responds physically and without much thought to consequences.

2. **B. She was just pretending she didn't want to go to the principal's office.** The circumstances of Brer Rabbit pretending he was afraid to go into the briar patch where he was born and raised are similar to the speaker pretending to be afraid to go to the principal's office.
3. **C. unusual** From the different examples of how Frank Doleman behaved (allowing a young girl to play chess in his office and not punishing boys sent to his office), you conclude that he was an unusual principal.
4. **A. confident** The additional information you get from the new quotation and the examples of her behavior, plus the overall tone of the excerpt, suggest a confident young girl.
5. **C. concerned but hopeful** The author is worried about the health impact of soda consumption on teenagers. But she is also hopeful; in the last sentence, she states that more can be done to reduce the consumption of sugary beverages.
6. **D. Young people will choose healthier beverages if they are better educated about the dangers of regular soda consumption.** The last paragraph supports this choice. Choice (A) is unsupported by the passage: even though the author does not condemn the legal measures mentioned in paragraph 2, you do not know whether she would support an overall ban. Choice (B) is unsupported also; the author never mentions diet soda.
7. **C. Young people who drink these beverages regularly will eventually suffer from the same ailments as those who drink soda regularly.** The author points out that, even though juice and energy drinks have somewhat less sugar than soda, regular consumption of those products "is likely to be just as damaging in the long term."
8. **B. effective to some extent** After describing the measures, the author begins paragraph 3 by stating, "These efforts appear to be paying off" but goes on to explain why they may not fully solve the problem of sugar consumption among teenagers.
9. **C. Reducing excessive consumption of soda.** The author is referring to the efforts described in paragraph 2, all of which attempted to reduce soda consumption.
10. **C. The cost of mandated coverage will lessen the ability of NATS to hire and supply temporary workers.** This question is basically answered in paragraph 2: "the cost of mandates could weaken the ability of the temporary help industry to act as a 'jobs bridge.'"
11. **A. Many workers are losing their jobs and need temporary jobs until they find permanent work again.** The third paragraph explains this reason.
12. **D. to raise awareness of one side of an issue** The whole passage—plus knowledge of who Edward A. Lenz is—helps you see that its purpose is to explain the position of the NATS.
13. **B. Women will not resort to wearing pants or other restrictive men's clothing.** This statement and the lines that follow it help you see that Stanton is saying men can wear their restrictive clothing; women want no part of it.
14. **D. a cloth worn around the neck** By looking at the context clues—or words around the word *stock*—you can see that it is something worn around the neck.
15. **B. speak up about current events** This very direct speech of Stanton's indicates her straight-to-the-point personality. She is not interested in criticism for its own sake but rather speaks up about issues she strongly believes in.
16. **A. Women are fighting for the right to vote.** The phrase "over the horns of bigotry" helps you see that women are fighting for something. The last paragraph of the excerpt helps you see that they are fighting for the right to vote.

Analyzing Nonfiction and Informational Text

Lesson 1: Purpose of Text

Practice 1, page 55

1. **B. tell how creative engineers saved astronauts** This passage is a narrative about the process of saving the lives of the Apollo 13 astronauts, including in particular the role of engineers. Choices (A), (C), and (D) are all far too broad.
2. **B. supports the writer's main recommendation** The writer recommends that the state cut sales taxes on new vehicles. Preventing deaths with the modern safety features on new cars is one of the reasons for this recommendation.
3. **D. inform about the historical importance of silk** The passage begins by discussing the "historical importance" of silk, and continues throughout to introduce new points about this topic.
4. **C. It provides examples of silk's historical importance in trade and culture.** Nomads traveling to China for silk and the creation of the "Silk Road" are examples of silk's importance.

Lesson 2: Effectiveness of Argument

Practice 2, page 57

1. **B. The federal government should automatically raise the minimum wage to match price increases.** The author states that "[s]everal states have taken the sensible step of automatically raising their minimum wage to adjust for inflation and consumer price increases." Later, she also states that "the federal government should follow the lead of the states." Thus, the author is recommending that the federal government should adjust the minimum wage for price increases. The rest of the passage serves to support this recommendation.

2. **D. Those states have systems superior to the federal system of manual increases.** The author's main point is that the federal government should adopt automatic minimum wage increases, as some states currently have done. Thus, she believes that the states' systems are better than the current federal system.
3. **C. Over the past 40 years, the federal minimum wage has not kept pace with inflation.** Choice (C) is a historical fact provided in the second paragraph as evidence to support the writer's argument.
4. **B. Ensuring sustainable incomes for hardworking citizens is a responsibility of lawmakers.** The author states that lawmakers must ensure stability for workers but does not justify why they must do so. She assumes that this is part of the job lawmakers should do.

Lesson 3: Validity of Arguments

Practice 3, page 59

1. **C. DRE systems offer more security and accuracy than other voting systems.** The writer introduces DRE voting, describes several voting systems, and concludes by suggesting that DRE prevents the problems associated with these systems and is therefore better.
2. **B. DRE voting avoids problems associated with other voting systems.** The writer supports the assertion that DRE voting is the most accurate and secure voting system by listing problems that might be encountered with other voting systems and then stating that DRE voting avoids such problems.
3. **A. Each voter's choices are recorded in the DRE voting system.** This is one of the facts that the writer cites in support of the assertion that DRE is secure and accurate. The other three answer choices cite facts that are included in the passage, but those facts are all background information and do not give direct support to the writer's main point.
4. **C. The writer fails to consider that even if DRE voting addresses all the flaws of previous systems, it may introduce unique flaws of its own.** The writer's conclusion is based solely on the fact that DRE voting avoids problems that have been associated with the other systems mentioned in the passage. Because no information is given about possible flaws of DRE voting, the reader has no way to verify the writer's claim that DRE voting is the most accurate and secure system.

Lesson 4: Text Related by Theme or Topic

Practice 4, page 61

1. **C. online piracy of music files** Both passages are focused on reasons why online piracy is harmful and the need to take further action.
2. **B. additional action to combat online piracy is warranted because piracy causes financial loses to the music industry.** The first passage concludes that more must be done to prevent online piracy. The main factual information the writer uses to support this thesis is information about the financial damage that piracy causes.
3. **A. Fear of piracy makes it difficult for new, experimental acts to get signed.** Both passages reach the same conclusion: more must be done to prevent piracy of music files. Choice (A) is the only answer choice that provides direct support for the conclusion of Passage 2, and, therefore, also for that of Passage 1.
4. **A. Online piracy of digital files has a harmful effect on the music industry.** Both authors provide different reasons as to why piracy is potentially harmful, but both agree that it has a negative effect on the industry.

Lesson 5: Text with Opposing Arguments

Practice 5, page 63

1. **C. the MPAA movie rating system** Each writer is making an argument about the relevance and trustworthiness of the MPAA rating system.
2. **B. The MPAA rating system is a useful tool for parents.** The writer of the Argument in Passage 1 uses information about the MPAA rating system to support her argument that the system helps parents to make sound decisions.
3. **D. The MPAA rating system should not be trusted.** In the second sentence, the writer indicates that the MPAA rating system is not a useful guide, and concludes by recommending that parents use a different source of advice.
4. **A. She largely approves of the MPAA rating system as a guideline for parents.** The passage provides no information about the writer's own child-rearing decisions, choice (B), or about her opinion of the effect of the Hays Code on the movie industry, choice (D). Also, her statements about the rating system are uniformly positive, making choice (C) incorrect.

Lesson 6: Texts with Related Graphic Information

Practice 6, page 65

1. **D. Governing parties can use their power to shape electoral districts to their advantage.** The passage and the figures focus on demonstrating how gerrymandering works. Choices (A) and (B) are not supported at all by the passage, and choice (C) is far too extreme.
2. **B. Through gerrymandering, a governing party can be elected to a greater number of seats than its voter support might otherwise allow.** The second paragraph describes how the second grid figure shows one party winning 75 percent of the seats from 60 percent of the vote, rather than the 50 percent of seats shown in the first grid figure.
3. **A. They illustrate the advantages a party can obtain through gerrymandering.** As discussed in the passage's second paragraph, the figures show how a party can benefit from the process.

While choices (C) and (D) may or may not be true statements, they do not describe how the figures support the passage.

Analyzing Nonfiction and Informational Text Practice Questions, pages 66–69

1. **D. to discuss whether communication technology helps or hurts relationships** This answer choice reflects the scope of the article introduced at the end of the first paragraph.
2. **B. how technology affects interpersonal connections** The question at the end of paragraph 1 introduces this topic. Paragraph 2 discusses positive effects of communication technology while paragraph 3 discusses a negative effect.
3. **D. The caption reveals that the woman's friends will use their phones during their visit.** The caption is similar to a scenario described in the first paragraph of the passage. In both cases, people are choosing to use technology rather than to enjoy the company of those with whom they have an established relationship.
4. **B. New communication technologies may adversely impact important human relationships.** The author's concluding paragraph discusses how communication technology can connect us with so many people that we have less time and energy to spend on relationships with friends and family, and the caption of the image reveals that the visiting friends plan to spend time on their phones rather than in conversing with one another.
5. **B. the giant squid is the world's longest cephalopod** The author's introduction and conclusion both raise this point, and the evidence in the paragraph supports this thesis.
6. **D. The giant squid is longer than the colossal squid.** The author provides scientific evidence about the colossal squid to support the passage's main idea about the giant squid.
7. **C. The length of the longest known colossal squid specimen is ten meters.** This factual evidence supports the author's main idea.
8. **A. The longest known colossal squid is ten meters long, so there is no colossal squid longer than the longest giant squid.** According to paragraph 2, there are very few samples of colossal squid, and all of them have been juveniles. It is improper to draw a conclusion about the entire colossal squid species on the basis of such limited evidence.
9. **B. mercury dental amalgam** Though the authors have somewhat different opinions on the subject, both passages are centrally about mercury dental amalgam.
10. **C. Mercury amalgam fillings should be banned because they are unhealthy and bad for the environment.** The first sentence of Passage 1 states that mercury amalgam should be banned for use in dental fillings. The first paragraph cites health reasons for this opinion. The second paragraph cites environmental reasons. Choice (D) is mentioned in Passage 1, but it serves as support for the author's main point.
11. **D. It is a convincing statistic from a reliable source.** The statement that 40–50 percent of mercury in wastewater is from an easily preventable source is a convincing statistic. The EPA is a large non-political government agency and so is likely to provide reliable information.
12. **A. Consumers have no other reason, such as cost or durability, to prefer mercury amalgam to composite fillings.** The author of Passage 1 states that "banning mercury amalgam would draw no consumer backlash" because resin composite fillings are better for cosmetic reasons. The author assumes that there is no other reason to prefer mercury amalgam.
13. **B. Resin composite fillings look better than mercury amalgam fillings when each is used on visible tooth surfaces.** The author of Passage 2 states that amalgam is preferable to resin composite whenever there is no cosmetic need for a tooth-colored filling. Thus, you can infer that he believes that resin composite fillings look more like natural teeth than mercury amalgam.
14. **A. Passage 1, because it cites no sources for the study or the statistic it cites** The author of passage 1 says that "it has been estimated" that 4 percent of the mercury in Lake Superior comes from dental amalgam, but the author cites no source. The author also gives no source for the 2001 study that is cited in the first paragraph.
15. **D. Mercury that accumulates in body tissues causes a variety of health problems.** The study cited in the first paragraph of Passage 1 found a correlation between mercury amalgam fillings and a number of health conditions. A correlation does not prove causation, but the author of Passage 1 states that "this accumulated mercury causes a variety of health problems."

Interpreting Fiction

Lesson 1: Plot Elements

Practice 1, page 71

1. **B. swearing that he was telling the truth** The following statement in the excerpt gives the context and meaning: "It is nevertheless God's own truth, the sacred truth. I repeat it on my soul and my salvation."
2. **D. confronted him and then asked to be searched** According to the excerpt, when the harness-maker comes in and repeats his story, the two "abused each other for an hour. At his own request, Maître Hauchecorne was searched."
3. **C. A peasant is accused of taking a pocketbook.** As you read the excerpt, you understand that a harness-maker has accused a peasant of taking a pocketbook, and the mayor of the town believes the harness-maker.

4. **The elements go in this order:**

3	The peasant and the harness-maker argue.
2	The peasant explains that he picked up a piece of string, not a pocketbook.
4	The mayor issues a warning to the peasant.
1	The mayor states that the harness-maker witnessed the peasant stealing the pocketbook.

Lesson 2: Inferences

Practice 2, page 73

1. **A. had always loved her** In the first paragraph, Josephine recalls her husband's face: "the face that had never looked save with love upon her." The term *save* means "except."
2. **C. spread her arms out in welcome** The first paragraph explains that although Josephine knew she would cry at the sight of her dead husband, "that bitter moment" would soon give way to years of freedom, which she welcomed.
3. **A. she was overcome and thrilled to see her husband** The doctors assumed that Josephine was so glad to learn her husband had not died in an accident that she was shocked and overjoyed to see him walk in the door.
4. **B. She was shocked that she would not be free.** Much of the excerpt is about Josephine looking forward to the freedom of being without her husband. When she learns that her husband is alive, she also learns that she will not be free.

Lesson 3: Character

Practice 3, page 75

1. **B. He is frightened about seeing the ghost of his wife.** The witch, supposedly speaking as Yaji's wife, says that she lies in her grave longing for Yaji to die and join her. She then asks, "Shall I come to meet you?" Throughout the passage, Yaji seems uncomfortable. At this moment you can infer that he is scared.
2. **C. untrustworthy** The witch is tricking Yaji. The witch has her own interests at heart when she pretends it is the wife requesting, "Give this witch plenty of money."
3. **D. neglectful** The information we are given about Yaji suggests that he treated his wife poorly when she was alive and now does not tend her grave.

Lesson 4: Theme

Practice 4, page 77

1. **B. finds a new explanation** After his father tells the boy he is dreaming, the boy states, "I decided that it was a magic horse and man that I'd seen."
2. **B. imaginative** The detailed description of the dream and the boy's insistence on believing in it are signs of his imaginative powers.
3. **A. He wants to reconcile what he saw with what his father told him.** Initially the boy seems to think that he saw a real, ordinary horse, but his father explains why this is unlikely. However, the boy does not accept the explanation that he was merely dreaming. Thus, he thinks of a new explanation.
4. **B. having enough money to pay some bills** The father is a practical man, a realist—"where were poor people like us going to find big gray stallions?" Because of the family's poverty, the father would probably enjoy having money to pay bills.
5. **D. Morning and youth are full of possibility.** The end of the excerpt states, "I believed that magic hides in the early morning . . . you might find something so beautiful . . . nothing else in life could ever be better."

Lesson 5: Style and Point of View

Practice 5, page 79

1. **B. He takes things in stride.** When Coach chides Bobby for having three malts, Bobby jokes with him and then pretends to hide them. Bobby is not angry or defensive in a way that could justify choice (D).
2. **C. the actions and speech of the characters** The narrator reports only what can be seen or heard by any observer. As a reader, you don't learn anyone's thoughts or feelings. You must infer them from their actions and speech.
3. **A. informal** Throughout the excerpt, people speak and act quite informally: Daphne washes up in a drinking fountain, Coach speaks with a spoon in his mouth, Bobby jokes with Coach, and so on.
4. **D. not entirely honest about his feelings** In his discussion with Daphne, Coach tries to explain his wife's need for an apartment of her own. Yet he sounds hostile and cuts his wife off when she speaks of her apartment. You can conclude he was hiding his real feelings from Daphne.

Lesson 6: Figurative Language

Practice 6, page 81

1. **B. rain clouds approaching** Lines 8–9 state,"patch of cloud spreads, darkening/Like a water-stain on silk." The following line mentions the coming rain: ". . . *quickly, before the rain!*"
2. **C. The rain caused their makeup to run.** The previous two lines mention "soaked by the shower" and "drenched." Immediately preceding the mention of "ruined faces" is a description of "streaked mascara." The girls' makeup is streaked because of the rain.
3. **B. the wind is so strong that it is blowing spray from the river into the boat** The figurative language helps you "see" the effects of the strong wind by painting a picture of curtains embroidered with white foamy water blown from the river.
4. **A. quick and easy** A knife cuts through a melon quickly and easily, and that is how cold, wet autumn weather has cut through the warm summer day.
5. **C. wry and observant** Throughout the poem, the speaker observes and comments on what is going on around him with a dryly humorous, or wry, attitude.

Interpreting Fiction Practice Questions, Pages 82–85

1. **C. self-concerned** Leroy's condition inspires Norma Jean to care for herself. She discusses herself and her body, and the passage gives no indication that any of the other answers fit her character.
2. **C. won't be driving his truck for a while** The passage tells us Leroy is injured and probably won't drive, so describing the truck as roosting, or sleeping, implies it will not be used.
3. **D. doesn't want to face what to do next** The passage says that Leroy is "not sure what to do next" and is making his crafts "in the meantime."
4. **A. It took some courage.** The fourth paragraph says the boy's "heart was in his mouth" and the sixth paragraph explains the boy was "scared as he looked down."
5. **B. alone** The boy has come to believe that you cannot rely on anyone but yourself. He is alone on the deck and sees the bird alone atop the mast. Even though it needs help, he is not going to help it at first.
6. **D. loneliness and sense of belonging** The sailor-boy begins the excerpt believing that everyone must look after himself. The final sentence of the excerpt states that his adventure leaves him with the belief that "the sky, the ship, the bird and himself were all one."
7. **D. triumphant** The mood of the piece rises as the boy climbs the mast to save the bird. At the top, he feels proud of what he has chosen to do and succeeded at doing and feels at one with everything.
8. **C. start singing again** A clue is given in the phrase "but his parched tongue clove to the roof of his mouth, he could not utter a stave." His mouth, dry from fear, could not utter a note of the song.
9. **A. panic** Reading those words both alone and in context gives you a sense of Ichabod's panic-stricken haste to get away.
10. **C. suspenseful** There is mystery and tension over whether the headless horseman will catch up with Ichabod and, if so, what he will do. The events that are happening and the way they are told create suspense.
11. **B. too scared to think rationally** When you realize that Ichabod mistakenly thought he saw a head when it was in reality a pumpkin, you can see that he was letting his fear get the better of his judgment.
12. **B. reading** Reading had always been a "gentle thing" to Henry. He is not pleased with the students he has taught and not interested in the politics and history they bring to interpretations of literature.
13. **C. a dime a dozen** Henry thinks of the younger students as "mass produced" undergraduates. In other words, they are all the same.
14. **A. dissect literature too much and ruin the meaning** Henry views reading as delicate, the meaning comes "whole, unbroken." This is in contrast to the older students, who overanalyze everything they read ("carve and quarter") and apply their own modern interpretations to it ("stuffed with their political-sexual agendas").
15. **C. disapproving** Henry is critical and dissatisfied with college students.
16. **D. disapproving** Henry is displeased with college students and with college offerings such as the humanities courses taught by his brother. You can conclude that in general he disapproves of the state of college education.

Writing Effective Sentences

Lesson 1: Simple Sentences

Practice 1, page 87

A. The revisions are samples. Your rewrites may differ.

1. **F** It drives his girlfriend crazy.
2. **F** As soon as he comes home from work, he starts talking on the telephone.
3. **C**
4. **F** Dave's sister and his best friend like to talk on the telephone, too.

B. 5. **C. call from** Choice (C) correctly forms a complete sentence and avoids creating a sentence fragment, as choices (A) and (B) do. "A conference calling" in Choice (D) is badly worded.

6. **C. if you're closing a deal, you can bring your lawyer into the conversation** Choice (C) includes a subject, thus creating a complete sentence. Choice (D) includes an incorrect verb form in *might could*.
7. **C. service can** Choice (C) uses the correct verb and avoids making a sentence fragment (as choice (D) does).

Lesson 2: Compound and Complex Sentences

Practice 2.1, page 89

A. 1. It was late, <u>and</u> I was walking home from work.

2. My co-worker, Judy, had offered to drive me, <u>but</u> I had refused.
3. It was a warm night, <u>so</u> I decided to get some fresh air.
4. It was really my choice. I could have taken a cab, <u>or</u> I could have walked.
5. I heard a loud noise, <u>so</u> I ran the last block to my house. Later, I learned that it was only a car backfiring.

B. 6. **B. An air courier carries shipping documents on an international flight and** A comma is required when two independent clauses are joined but not when two verbs are joined (*carries . . . gets*). All the incorrect choices have unnecessary commas.

7. **A. airlines, but** *But* is the most logical coordinating conjunction here. Most travelers on major airlines can check baggage. Because there are two clauses (*couriers . . . fly . . . they can't check*), a comma is needed.
8. **B. in advance, but they get their tickets on the day of the flight** A comma precedes a coordinating conjunction joining two independent clauses.

Practice 2.2, page 91

A. 1. Most fatal fires occur when a family is asleep.

2. Because a smoke alarm wakes you up, it can allow you to escape.

3. Try to replace the smoke detector's battery before it goes dead.
4. Although smoke detectors cost money, the expense is worth it.

B. 5. **B. are making a business call,** The subordinate clause should be followed by a comma. Choice (C) is incorrect because the present tense is needed for a statement that is generally true.
6. **A. After you identify yourself, ask** The introductory phrase should be followed by a comma. Choice (B) is incorrect because the word *Whenever* is not appropriate here.
7. **D. up, thank** Choice (D) correctly combines an introductory phrase and an independent clause to form a complex sentence.

Lesson 3: Run-Ons and Comma Splices

Practice 3, page 93

A. There are several possible correct answers. There may be other correct answers in addition to those listed.
1. Jeff just got his driver's license, and he's very excited. OR Jeff just got his driver's license. He's very excited.
2. He bought a car that has a lot of miles on it, so it wasn't very expensive. OR Because he bought a car that has a lot of miles on it, it wasn't very expensive.
3. He doesn't have a lot of free time, but he'd like to take a car trip. OR Although he doesn't have a lot of free time, he'd like to take a car trip.
4. He needs to find out about car insurance, get a good map, and join an auto club.

B. 5. **A. pictures if you just** Choice (A) correctly forms a complex sentence by adding a subordinating conjunction.
6. **B. Be patient and wait** Choice (B) correctly uses a coordinating conjunction. Don't be misled by the apparent lack of a subject; both clauses are commands, meaning the subject, *you*, is implied but unstated.
7. **C. the autofocus option, because most cameras** Choice (C) correctly forms a compound sentence with a subordinating conjunction and a comma.

Lesson 4: Subordinate Ideas

Practice 4, page 95

A. There are several possible answers for each question. Sample answers:
1. Tornadoes and earthquakes can cause a lot of damage.
2. Earthquakes are somewhat common in California, but many Californians do not seem to mind.
3. On May 20, 2013, a tornado in Oklahoma killed twenty-three people and injured almost 400.
4. Tornadoes can occur anywhere in the United States and at any time of year.

B. 5. **D. repaired up** Choice (D) avoids forming two short, choppy clauses and instead forms one smooth sentence. The other choices are run-ons, excessively wordy, or both.
6. **A. may be brought or mailed to the service center** Choice (A) forms a compound predicate and avoids expressing ideas in short, choppy sentences.
7. **D. due to accidents, mishandling, or** Choice (D) makes one smooth, detailed sentence by forming a compound predicate.

Lesson 5: Modify Ideas

Practice 5, page 97

A. There are several possible answers for each question. Sample answers:
1. Trent's sister, who is a health professional, encouraged him to become a nurse.
2. When he wakes up the patients to take their blood pressure, they get rather annoyed.
3. He carefully writes their temperature and blood pressure on their charts.
4. It is hard to make visitors who are talking with the patients leave at 9:00 pm.

B. 5. **B. a person who is not the birth child of the adopter the rights of a son or daughter** Only choice (C) displays correct modifier placement.
6. **C. An agency requires a "home study" to determine** All the wrong answer choices include misplaced modifiers.
7. **D. frequently handle these adoptions when parents ask them to** Choice (D) is the only answer choice that correctly places the modifier "frequently."

Lesson 6: Parallel Structure

Practice 6, page 99

A. There are several possible answers for each question. Sample answers:
1. Jenna has worked in a factory, in a store, and as a waitress.
2. She would like to put her kids in a better school and to get a better job.
3. She thinks the kids' father is irresponsible, lazy, and uncaring.
4. He doesn't have the time, the energy, or the money to give them what they deserve.

B. 5. **C. safer, more comfortable, and more pleasant** Choice (C) correctly makes all the adjectives into comparatives (*safer, more comfortable,* and *more pleasant*).
6. **D. computers, and** Choice (D) correctly forms a list in which all items display parallel construction.
7. **C. the secret code, press ON, and leave immediately** Only choice (C) makes all the verbs in the sentence (*punch, press,* and *leave*) parallel.

Writing Effective Sentences Practice Questions, pages 100–103

1. **B. Seal your windows so that cold air can't get through** When an independent clause comes before a subordinate clause in a complex sentence, there is no need to use a comma.
2. **B. day and 62° at night** Choice (B) is the only answer choice that avoids short, choppy sentences.
3. **D. sun, keep** Choice (D) is the only choice that correctly links the subordinate clause at the beginning of the sentence with the independent clause that starts with "keep."
4. **D. home. Do change** Choice (D) avoids making a comma splice or a run-on. It also is consistent with the theme of the paragraph as being a list of recommendations.

5. **A. will not cool down any faster when your air conditioner is on full blast** Only choice (A) correctly places the modifying phrase *any faster*.
6. **B. When I got the television home, I discovered** In this sentence, *When* begins a subordinate clause. A comma should be placed after a subordinate clause that begins a complex sentence.
7. **A. I returned to the store to see if the problem could** Only choice (A) correctly adds the subject "I" and uses the proper verb tenses.
8. **A. He claimed that because the TV had been used,** Only choice (A) correctly adds a subject, *He*, to make it clear who was claiming that the TV had been used.
9. **A. angry and frustrated about the treatment I received** Choice (A) makes a smooth complex predicate instead of a choppy run-on sentence, a run-on, or a comma splice.
10. **C. refund or get** Choice (C) puts both verbs in the same form. Choice (A) is grammatically correct but illogically suggests that Jeffrey will return *and* repair the TV.
11. **A. work productively if you feel alone** This choice correctly places *productively* close to the word it modifies (*work*) and avoids lengthy or wordy constructions.
12. **C. can make your day more pleasant and give you energy** A comma is not required before a coordinating conjunction that joins two verbs.
13. **B. Things get messy when the friendship unravels** A comma is not required in a complex sentence when the subordinate clause follows the independent clause. The verb form *get* is more appropriate than *are getting*, because the sentence does not refer to something that is necessarily happening right now.
14. **A. work or talk** Both verbs in the sentence should be in the same form. There is no need for a comma when a coordinating conjunction joins two verbs.
15. **B. may be hard, but it's worth the effort** A comma is required before the coordinating conjunction that joins the two independent clauses in a compound sentence.
16. **D. hoaxes designed** Choice (D) efficiently turns the second part of the sentence into a descriptive phrase while avoiding wordiness.
17. **B. check a claim like this by contacting the agency** Choice (B) efficiently turns the second part of the sentence into a modifying phrase while avoiding wordiness.
18. **C. know. This** Choice (C) expresses the ideas as two independent clauses. Choice (A) is missing the comma required when joining two independent clauses with a conjunction.
19. **D. keep your computer equipment safe and avoid spreading hysteria** Choice (D) joins the two ideas in a compound predicate. A comma is not needed in a compound predicate.

Connecting Ideas

Lesson 1: Organize Ideas into Paragraphs

Practice 1.1, page 105

A. 1. The pharmacist at the local drugstore is very helpful.
2. No MI
3. Every vote counts, so let your voice be heard and vote!
4. When you are traveling, it's a good idea to mark your luggage clearly.
5. Listening to music can benefit you in many ways.

B. 6. **C. sentence 4** Sentences 1–3 explain who gets colds and how frequently. Sentences 4–6 are about the causes and prevention of colds.
7. **D. join paragraphs B and C** Sentence 10 in paragraph C is related to the main idea of paragraph B, the prevention of colds.

Practice 1.2, page 107

A. Your topic sentences should be similar to these:
1. Satellites have many different functions in today's world.
2. All signs show that the economy is headed for a slump.
3. The library has adopted a new dress code for employees.

B. 4. **D. Repetitive strain injury is a painful condition resulting from repeated use of the hands.** The original topic sentence is too general. The other options don't tell the central point: what repetitive strain injury is.
5. **B. A number of factors contribute to repetitive strain injury.** This sentence covers the three causes of repetitive strain injury mentioned in the paragraph.

Lesson 2: Use Logical Order and Relevant Ideas

Practice 2, page 109

A. 1. Irrelevant detail: Getting very ill is one bad thing that could happen.
2. Irrelevant detail: Adult students can also use school supplies.
3. Irrelevant detail: This job will be extremely expensive!

B. 4. **D. remove sentence 3** This sentence adds no new information to what was given in the previous sentences.
5. **D. remove sentence 6** The information about the secretarial job is not relevant to getting a job in carpentry.
6. **D. move sentence 10 to follow sentence 8** It would be more logical to place sentence 9 at the end of the letter.

Lesson 3: Relate Sentences and Paragraphs

Practice 3, page 111

A. Your transitions should be similar to these:
1. Our marketing efforts need to be enhanced. Therefore, we will soon begin another marketing initiative.
2. Sales representatives say that their jobs are extremely demanding. However, the salary is attractive.
3. The marketing director has instructed sales representatives to try some new ideas. For example, sales representatives can give away free samples.
4. A new ad campaign will be launched in just a few weeks. As a result, we expect sales to increase.

B. 5. **B. Times are changing, however, and these days patrons can even buy coffee** This position is the most logical for the transition. Also, because it is in the middle of a sentence, it should be set off by commas.

6. **B. restaurant. For example,** The second sentence offers an example of the broad menu described in the first sentence.
7. **A. In addition, having a cafe** This option inserts a helpful transition to move the reader smoothly from paragraph B to paragraph C.

Connecting Ideas Practice Questions, page 112–115

1. **C. sentence 5** Sentences 1–4 are about the general problem of sleep disruption, whereas sentences 5–8 are about reasons why people don't get enough sleep.
2. **B. High-achieving students get more sleep.** Both studies relate to the impact of lack of sleep on learning.
3. **A. grades. Similarly,** The ideas on either side of the "Select" button are similar, so they can be connected this way.
4. **D. remove sentence 13** The paragraph is about sleep, not losing weight.
5. **D. join paragraphs (C) and (D)** Both paragraphs contain tips for getting more sleep.
6. **B. sentence 4** Sentences 1–3 introduce the purpose of the passage. Sentences 4–7 contain general rules for stain removal.
7. **B. Choose the right water temperature for cleaning each stain.** This sentence is appropriate since the paragraph discusses hot, cold, and room-temperature water.
8. **D. juice, for example, removes** When a transition is placed in the middle of a sentence, commas should both precede and follow it.
9. **D. remove sentence 15** Sentence 15 explains a minor detail and moves away from the main idea of the paragraph.
10. **C. move sentence 19 to the beginning of paragraph D** Putting sentence 19 at the beginning of the paragraph lets readers know in advance what point the paragraph will make.
11. **C. remove sentence 5** Sentence 5 is a general statement about HMOs. It is not relevant to the explanation of which insurance carriers are being made available.
12. **A. However, you must pay the health providers when** A comma should follow when a transition begins a sentence.
13. **C. sentence 9** Until sentence 9, paragraph B is about the differences between the two insurance plans. Sentence 9 introduces the idea of the informational sessions.
14. **A. move sentence 14 to the end of paragraph C** Sentence 14 refers to the card that was mentioned in paragraph C and so continues that idea.
15. **A. move sentence 2 to follow sentence 3** The description of removing the wheel should start with the initial step.
16. **C. move sentence 11 to follow sentence 12** Sentence 11 tells what to do with the spot where there is a leak, so it should follow the information on finding that spot.
17. **C. The next step is to put the tire and tube back onto the rim.** Paragraph C describes the process of putting the tire and tube back on the rim.
18. **A. The final step is to reinstall the wheel.** Paragraph D describes the final step in the process; putting the wheel back on the bike.
19. **A. Then readjust the tire pressure, and you're** Of the choices given, *then* is the most appropriate transition for describing steps in a process.

Writing About Text

Lesson 1: Unpack the Writing Prompt

Practice 1, page 117

1. The topic of the writing prompt is **a pair of passages that discuss the safety of cell phones.**
2. The writing prompt asks me: **Do I agree with the writer of Passage A or the writer of Passage B, and what information led me to that decision?**
3. I am asked to include **specific information from *both* passages to support my response.**
4. Yes, I am being asked for **my position on the topic.**

Lesson 2: Identify a Writer's Argument and Assumptions

Practice 2, page 119

Your answers should be similar to this, but your wording may vary.

1. Mandatory military service
2. We should promote participation in volunteer programs rather than require mandatory military service.
3. There are a couple of assumptions you might have identified. One is: the potential drawback of mandatory military service (that is, the resentment it might generate) outweighs its potential benefit (preparing the U.S. military to face foreign threats). Another is: it would be better to heavily promote volunteer programs than to leave things the way they are now.
4. violence in video games
5. People should protest violent video games to protect children from portrayals of excessive violence.
6. There are a couple of assumptions you might have identified. First: the studies mentioned in the first paragraph, which indicated a correlation between violent video games and violent behavior, actually indicate a causal relationship. Second: the strategies effective in 1976 will still be effective today.

Lesson 3: Develop a Thesis Statement

Practice 3, page 121

These answers are samples; your answers may vary.

1. Prescription drug advertising on TV is harmful because it can lead patients to request or refuse medication for reasons that are not medically sound.
2. The author's argument against direct-to-consumer advertisement of prescription medication is unconvincing because it does not provide any statistical data about how drug advertisements have actually affected consumer behavior.

   Alternatively, you might have written something like this: The author's argument against direct-to-consumer advertisement of prescription medication is convincing because the author provides several potential dangers of the practice.

3. Because 18% of the U.S. population speaks a native language other than English, and because industries such as technology and business require contact with people who speak other languages, Americans should put a higher priority on learning foreign languages.
4. The author's argument in favor of foreign language education is compelling because she points out the large proportion of people living in the United States who speak foreign languages, as well as the many contexts where a native English speaker would come in contact with that 18%.
   Alternatively, you might have written something like this: The author's argument in favor of foreign language education is not compelling because she does not explain the drawbacks of alternatives to foreign language education, such as enhanced English language education for those whose primary language is not English.

Lesson 4: Collect Supporting Evidence

Practice 4, page 123

These answers are samples; your answers may vary.

1. The passage states that alcohol is particularly harmful to parts of the brain that grow later in life. Another fact from the passage is that alcohol causes long-term damage to the heart and liver. In support of this position, the text further says that the United Kingdom allows younger individuals to drink and also has high rates of alcohol-related death.
2. Choose either agree or disagree.
3. You might have written something like this:

   (Agree) One personal piece of evidence I would use to support my position is that teenagers are already at higher risk of accidents when driving, and alcohol would only exacerbate this fact. (Disagree) One personal piece of evidence I would use to support my position is that 18-year-olds can enter combat in the military and can vote for the president. Claiming they are not responsible enough for alcohol is inconsistent with the responsibilities and privileges we otherwise give 18-year-olds.

Lesson 5: Plan Your Response

Practice 5, page 126

The following is a sample response. There is no objectively correct answer to the writing prompt. You may write your essay either for or against the author's position. Thus, answers to the following questions may vary.

1. **Sample thesis statement:**I think that the writer's position on owning a family pet is correct because the inconvenience and expenses cited outweigh the benefits, and because as someone allergic to cats, I agree with the writer's point that having pets can make it difficult for friends who visit.
2. **Sample outline:**
   I. The writer is correct that pets have more downsides than benefits and that families should not have pets.
   II. Monetary expenses; food, pet sitters, veterinary care, cleaning.
   III. Chores and time involved; kids may promise to help, but likely would not.
   IV. Friend can't visit; allergies, difficult with overnight guests.
   V. Pets are good friends and can be calming influence when people are stressed.
      A. Some people think this justifies any expense and difficulty in keeping animals.
         i. But, pets can keep away real friends and introduce stress as well, countering benefits.
         ii. Instead of petting a cat to relieve stress over money, it would be better to save the money you would spend on the cat's food and vet bills.
3. **Sample idea map:**
   The idea map below demonstrates how you might organize your thoughts to argue for pet ownership. Your idea map may vary.

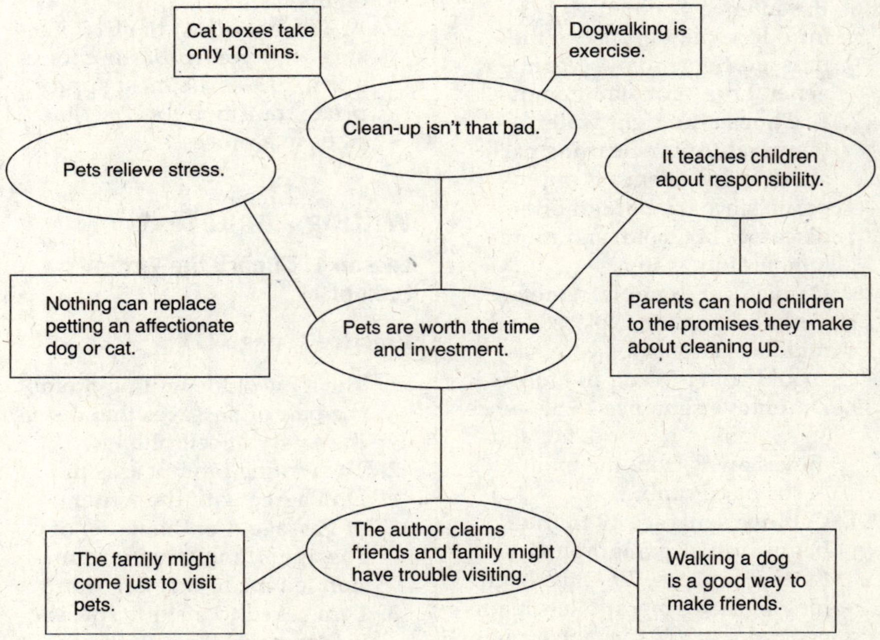

Lesson 6: Draft Your Response

Practice 6.1, page 129

Your answers may vary.

A. Sample topic sentences:
Pet ownership is a major burden, and the time and money people invest in pets could be better spent elsewhere.
The author of the passage says that keeping a pet is not worth the trouble, but he fails to consider all of the many benefits of pet ownership.

Your supporting statements may vary quite a bit, so no samples are given here. Check to make sure that your supporting statements are relevant to your topic statement.

B. Sample concluding statements:
And so, when all is taken into consideration, the conclusion is clear: the cost of a pet far outweighs the benefit.
Don't let the long list of difficulties listed by the author scare you away, because a pet can be a friend to you and your children, one whose value can't be measured against time and money.

Practice 6.2, pages 130–131

Refer to the *Reasoning Through Language Arts Extended Response Evaluation Guide* on page 225 to evaluate your response.

Practice 6.3, pages 132–133

Refer to the *Reasoning Through Language Arts Extended Response Evaluation Guide* on page 225 to evaluate your response.

Lesson 7: Revise and Edit Your Response

Practice 7.1, page 135

A, page 135

Most of us are aware *that speeding has consequences*, which range from receiving a speeding ticket to getting into an accident. *Nonetheless*, a quick survey of any highway will show that many drivers exceed the speed limit. *This raises the question:* why do people speed?

¶One common reason is that people do not think they will suffer any consequences. If they have never been stopped by the police or ~~crashed their car~~, been involved in a car crash, they don't see any reason to worry.

Another reason is that people simply need to get somewhere in a hurry. They realize that they are speeding but ~~they have such a need to arrive on time that they don't care~~ *their impatience gets the better of them.* ~~They've got ants in their pants~~.

¶A final reason is lack of respect for other drivers~~, one~~. One driver who is speeding makes road conditions less safe for everyone. Drivers who act as though they are in the Indy 500 ~~they~~ have no regard for the safety of others.

We know that people speed because ~~of impatience and they don't fear the consequences~~. they're impatient and don't fear the consequences. ~~Another reason is no respect~~. They also don't respect other drivers. Let's figure out what will make them stop speeding.

B, page 135

Refer to the *Reasoning Through Language Arts Extended Response Evaluation Guide* on page 225 to evaluate your response.

Practice 7.2, page 137

Your revised paragraphs should be similar to the following.

One common reason for speeding is that people don't think they will suffer consequences. If they have never been stopped by the police or been involved in a car crash, they've never experienced the dangers of speeding first-hand.

Another reason is that people simply need to get somewhere in a hurry. They realize that they are speeding, but their impatience gets the better of them.

A final reason is lack of respect for other drivers. One driver who is speeding makes road conditions less safe for everyone. Drivers who act as though they are in a race have no regard for the safety of other drivers.

Writing About Text Practice, pages 138-141

A. Refer to the *Reasoning Through Language Arts Extended Response Evaluation Guide* on page 225 to evaluate your response.

B. Refer to the *Reasoning Through Language Arts Extended Response Evaluation Guide* on page 225 to evaluate your response.

Polishing Your Writing

Lesson 1: Strengthen Sentences

Practice 1, page 143

A. Your revised sentences should be similar to the following. The underlined parts show where your revision marks should be:

1. First, write down what you know about your family. Then interview relatives. (Run-on sentence)
2. Videotaping or recording the interviews is a good idea. (Structure not parallel)
3. Ask relatives to provide exact names, dates, and other details. (Structure not parallel)
4. Make copies of documents such as birth certificates and marriage licenses. (Sentence fragment)
5. When older family members are interviewed, they'll often tell you stories you never heard. (Dangling modifier)
6. Carefully record all the information you get and put it in a three-ring binder. (Misplaced modifier)
7. Some people use their computers to do genealogy searches, and they get very good results. (Comma splice; coordinating conjunction needed)
8. However, one must have the time, the patience, and the know-how to use the Internet. (Structure not parallel)
9. If you do decide to learn more about your roots, don't be surprised to find yourself at a huge family reunion. (Comma needed after subordinate clause)
10. The whole process of putting together a family tree and contacting long-lost family members is rewarding. (Sentence fragment)

B. Sample revisions:
It was a beautiful day, and the blue ocean sparkled in the sunlight. It was a perfect day for going to the beach. As Renelle looked across the sand, she saw two little girls building a sandcastle and making a moat next to it. Renelle spread

out her towel, anchored it with her shoes and beach bag, and began to read a magazine. Suddenly, she heard a voice say, "Are you going to get in the water, or are you just going to lie there?" Renelle looked up and saw her friend Terry. She laughed softly and got up to greet Terry. Putting on her sandals, she walked with Terry across the burning sand to the water's edge.

Renelle loved going to the beach. It relaxed her and helped her forget about her problems. It didn't cost money like most other forms of entertainment. Most of Renelle's friends also spent a lot of time at the beach, so that was another incentive.

Lesson 2: Improve Organization

Practice 2, page 145

A. Your revised paragraphs should be similar to the following (starting after the first revision made for you):

Why do people continue to litter? One reason people litter is that they just don't care about others. It doesn't bother them to leave their trash in front of someone else's apartment building, forcing another person to deal with the problem. This inconsiderate attitude is also reflected in the refusal to recycle plastic, glass, and newspapers. People figure that they won't be around in the future when the landfills are used up, so who cares?

¶Another possible reason for littering is low self-esteem. If people don't feel good about themselves, they won't be motivated to keep their environment looking attractive. ~~Low self-esteem can cause many other problems, including depression and lack of self-confidence.~~ People who have high self-esteem believe that it's important to keep their home, the planet Earth, clean and beautiful.

B. Ask a friend or family member to evaluate your work.

Lesson 3: Word Choice

Practice 3, page 147

Sample answers:

A. **1.** nonprofit organization
2. thousands of
3. substandard
4. dollars
5. as soon as possible

B. If you ever order merchandise from a catalog, you should be aware of your rights. All companies, regardless of the state in which they are located, are required to ship your order within 30 days unless they have advertised a different shipping time. If a company is unable to meet the shipping deadline, it must send you an "Option Notice." You can choose to wait longer or get a refund.

Some consumers have complained about receiving merchandise that they did not order. Companies that engage in this practice are breaking the law. If you receive a product you haven't ordered, it is yours to keep.

If you receive a package that has been damaged, don't open it. Write "REFUSED" on the package, and return it to the seller. There's no need to add new postage as long as the package came by regular mail.

C. Have a friend or family member evaluate your work.

Polishing Your Writing Practice Questions, pages 148–151

1. **C. gardener, it's important that** Sentence 2 is a subordinate clause, not a complete sentence. Use a comma to combine it with the independent clause in sentence 3, creating a complex sentence.
2. **A. option if you live in a climate that is too extreme** The phrase *not good* is vague, since it provides no information about how a climate might be unsuitable. *Too extreme* allows the reader to anticipate the temperature and moisture requirements discussed in paragraph D.
3. **B. move sentence 8 to follow sentence 9** Sentence 9 is the topic sentence—it gives the main idea—for paragraph C. As such, it should be the first sentence of the paragraph.
4. **D. move sentence 11 to the beginning of paragraph D** The topic of paragraph C is choosing a garden spot, whereas the topic of paragraph D is choosing plants. Therefore, sentence 11, which is about choosing plants, should appear in paragraph D.
5. **C. plants to** Choice (C) best expresses the relationship between the idea of investigating plants and the reason for doing so. These clauses should instead be joined with a word or phrase that expresses the relationship between them.
6. **A. Wales and had come to** The phrase *which had come* in the incorrect answer choices implies that Wales had come to the United States, not the boy. Replace *which* with *and* to clarify.
7. **D. ocean; it** A semicolon is required to separate two independent clauses, correcting the run-on sentence.
8. **C. Could he have crossed the vast** Describing the ocean as *vast* conveys the sense of size more precisely than does the phrase *really big*.
9. **B. kidding me** All of the wrong choices employ slang, which should be avoided.
10. **B. Sentence 12** Sentence 12 does not relate directly to the story of the narrator's great-grandfather's journey from Wales to the United States. Therefore it is unnecessary and should be removed.
11. **D. and morality. She also frequently** Only choice (D) avoids a run-on sentence.
12. **B. Many consider this** All of the incorrect answer choices are unnecessarily wordy. Additionally, choice (A) uses the informal phrase *figure*, which should not be used to express the idea of thinking.
13. **C. Combine the two sentences by replacing the period with a comma.** As written, the second sentence is not a sentence at all. It should serve as an appositive describing *lupus* in the previous sentence.
14. **A. Flannery maintained many fulfilling correspondences that gave her the insight into human behavior that is evident in her writing** This construction best avoids wordiness.
15. **A. will ensure you continue** The adverb *always* is

unnecessary when paired with the verb *continue.*

16. **B. Then we will replace** The adverbs *then* and *next* are redundant when used together.
17. **C. times. You** Insert a period and remove *and* between the two independent clauses.
18. **D. However, we will adjust your bill accordingly if your service is interrupted.** Unless *However* is followed by a comma, it seems that it is being used to modify the adjustment. Insert a comma to clarify that *However* introduces the sentence.
19. **B. about the scheduled repairs, please contact our office** Choices (A) and (D) create sentence fragments, and choice (C) is missing the comma that must follow an introductory phrase.

Using Grammar Correctly

Lesson 1: Noun and Pronoun Agreement

Practice 1.1, page 153

A. 1. They
2. him
3. it
4. Her
5. she

B. 6. **D. Bonetta and I** *Bonetta and I* is a compound subject, so a subject pronoun is required.
7. **D. She always gets** The simple present tense and the subject form of the pronoun are appropriate here.
8. **B. Walter or me** The phrase *Walter or me* is an object, so an object pronoun is required.

Practice 1.2, page 155

A. 1. Sally is moving to a small town. Her mother is concerned about the health care options it offers.
2. Sally tried to reassure her mother, but it was hard for her mother to believe her.
3. Sally asked a friend who lives in the town for information about its health care facilities. OR the town's health care facilities.
4. The town has a freestanding clinic where a person can go when he or she is sick. OR where people can go when they are sick.
5. There is also a nearby hospital, and it has a very good reputation.
6. If one is concerned about health care, one should sign up for a good insurance plan. OR If you are concerned about health care, you should sign up for a good insurance plan.

B. 7. **D. will learn only that they shouldn't make their** The word *children* earlier in the sentence is the antecedent to the pronoun; *their* agrees correctly with that antecedent, while the singular *one's* does not.
8. **D. parents** Only choice (D) correctly identifies who should be clear about their expectations.
9. **C. the child to play with the group** The term *play group* is a collective noun, so the plural *them* should not be used to refer to it. In this case, repeating the word *group* is the best way to make the meaning clear.

Lesson 2: Verb Forms and Tenses

Practice 2.1, page 157

A. 1. had ceased
2. closed
3. functions
4. have visited
5. will open
6. looks
7. are thinking

B. 8. **B. is offering** The action is taking place right now, so the present progressive is the correct tense.
9. **D. If you sign up for Express Lane before April 9** The present-tense verb *sign* in the subordinate clause is appropriate, given the the future-tense verb *will receive* in the main clause.
10. **D. will amaze you** The verb *will amaze* is in the simple future tense. The future progressive tense in *will be amazing you* is incorrect and overcomplicated.

Practice 2.2, page 159

A. 1. came
2. showed
3. had spoken
4. took
5. seen

B. 6. **D. began to appear on** The action takes place in the past tense, so the verb should be in its past form, *began.*
7. **C. was broken** *Broken* is the correct past participle.
8. **B. now give viewers** The clue word *now* tells you that the action is still true, so the present-tense form of *give* is correct.

Lesson 3: Subject-Verb Agreement

Practice 3.1, page 161

A. 1. is
2. become
3. is
4. have
5. seems
6. is

B. 7. **B. have heard** In this sentence, the indefinite pronoun *most* is plural ("most of us"). The verb *have heard* agrees with the plural subject.
8. **C. That noise occurs when a plane starts to** The verb *starts* agrees with the singular subject *plane.*
9. **B. some other materials conduct sound** The verb *conduct* agrees with the plural subject *materials.*

Practice 3.2, page 163

A. 1. ~~on the market~~ carry
2. ~~carrying the seal~~ are
3. ~~an important ingredient in many toothpastes~~ strengthens, attacks
4. are
5. offer
6. ~~with fluoride and good flavor~~ is

B. 7. **C. administers its own program and has** The verb *has* agrees with the singular subject *state.*
8. **A. Wage level and length of employment** The verb *determine* agrees with the compound subject *Wage level and the length of employment.* The present tense is consistent with the rest of the passage.
9. **C. draw benefits report regularly to their** The verb *report* agrees with the plural subject *workers.*

Using Grammar Correctly Practice Questions, pages 164–167

1. **C. highly paid coaches, but it didn't happen** The past tense is required because the second clause in the sentence is discussing what happened in the past.
2. **A. they** The antecedent of the underlined pronoun is *girls*, so it should be plural. *They* is clear; repeating *the girls* (as in Choice (B)) is unecessary. Choice (D), *them*, is incorrect because the pronoun is the subject of the dependent clause *while they practiced*.
3. **B. earned** The past tense is correct here because the action happened in the past over the course of a few years.
4. **D. who live in Palm Beach Gardens, Florida, are best friends** The verb *are* agrees with the plural subject *sisters*.
5. **D. there is no trace of sibling rivalry** The main clause needs the present tense verb *is* because the introductory subordinate clause has a present-tense verb, *face*.
6. **B. people where they have received** The present perfect is correct here because the point is to find out about other people's past experiences with auto shops, not their predictions about them.
7. **D. pick a shop just because it's close** Because this sentence is a command, the simple present tense is necessary.
8. **D. these often come with restrictions attached** The verb *come* agrees with the plural subject *specials*. Choice (C) is incorrect because the past tense is not consistent with the rest of the passage.
9. **D. what's wrong, the repair job will** The pronoun *it* in the incorrect choices has no clear antecedent.
10. **C. there are** The verb *are* agrees with the plural subject *limits*. The present tense is correct.
11. **B. changes and their effect** The antecedent *changes* is plural, so the plural possessive *their* should be used.
12. **C. send photocopies of your records** *Your* is used in the rest of the paragraph, so it is appropriate here.
13. **D. our calculations, which are appended to this letter** The word *which* is the subject of a subordinate clause. It refers to the plural noun *calculations*. Therefore, the verb *are*, not *is*, is required.
14. **A. has increased** The interrupting phrase *of taxes* does not change the fact that the subject of the new independent clause is *amount*, which is singular. The verb *has increased* therefore agrees with it.
15. **B. will credit** The future tense indicates an action that will take place at a later time, which is appropriate in this sentence.
16. **B. don't** The plural indefinite pronoun *many* is the subject of the sentence; the verb *don't* (don't = do + not) agrees with it. Changing to the past tense, choice (C), would be incorrect.
17. **C. is that people with disabilities have feelings** The verb *have* agrees with the plural subject *people*.
18. **B. him or her** The pronouns are objects of the preposition *with*, so the objective forms *him* and *her* are needed. The antecedent is *a person*, so the plural *them* in choice (D) cannot be used.
19. **B. such as a wheelchair, cane, or communication board, is the person's property** The verb *is* agrees with the singular subject *equipment*, and the interrupting phrase listing examples of assistive equipment is properly punctuated.
20. **B. it** *It* is the proper pronoun to use to refer to a dog.

Using Writing Mechanics

Lesson 1: Comma Use

Practice 1.1, page 169

A. 1. Train travel is more pleasant than riding a bus, but it can be more expensive.
2. When you're on a train, you can stand up and stretch if you need to.
3. NC
4. Unlike buses, trains sometimes have seats that face each other.
5. Traveling through a scenic area, you may find that your train has a double-decker car that offers a better view.
6. NC

B. 7. **A. For starters, use cooking methods that require little or no oil or butter,** A comma is required after an introductory phrase.
8. **A. dressing, and** A comma should come before a coordinating conjunction in a compound sentence.
9. **D. low-fat version, and though not all of them may be pleasing** The words *though not all of them may be pleasing to the palate* form a subordinate clause, and no commas are necessary in that clause.

Practice 1.2, page 171

A. 1. Kwanzaa is a week-long African American holiday that celebrates culture, community, and family.
2. Kwanzaa, a wintertime holiday, is based on an ancient African harvest celebration.
3. NC
4. Kwanzaa celebrations include rituals such as singing, dancing, drumming, and poetry reading.
5. The family lights one candle every day for each of seven principles: unity, self-determination, responsibility, cooperative economics, purpose, creativity, and faith.
6. NC

B. 7. **A. home accidents are responsible for more children's injuries than all childhood diseases combined** The subject and verb of a sentence should not be separated by a comma.
8. **B. medicines, poisons, or fragile objects are stored** Commas should be placed between items in a series
9. **C. children, those ten and up,** You can mentally omit the phrase *those ten and up* and still understand the meaning of *older children*. Therefore, the appositive *those ten and up* should be set off by commas.

Lesson 2: Capitalization

Practice 2, page 173

A. 1. Last spring, I broke my arm in a car accident.
2. My internist, Doctor Claudia McNally, referred me to Waterside.
3. The center's director, Ilana Harris, assigned me a physical therapist named Ellie Royce.
4. Ellie studied physical therapy in her native London and used British methods of treat-

ment that relieved my pain quite effectively.

5. She also did therapy with me in the pool at Rainbow Health Club.
6. I finished my treatments just before Labor Day, and I feel 100 percent better, thanks to Ellie.

B. 7. **B. only emperors and nobles were** A title should be capitalized only when it comes directly before a person's name or is used in direct address.

8. **C. they were trained to hunt game and waterfowl in the mountains of Japan** A geographic feature is capitalized only when it is part of the name of a specific place, like *Rocky Mountains*.
9. **B. America by author Helen Keller** Proper nouns should be capitalized.

Lesson 3: Possessives and Contractions

Practice, page 175

A. 1. There's

2. can't, who's, it's
3. we're
4. theirs
5. ours

B. 6. **D. questions, we need your** In this phrase, the pronoun is showing ownership, so *your* is correct.

7. **B. In addition to our chain of stores, we're proud** *Were* is a verb and is incorrect in this sentence. Rather, an apostrophe should be inserted to create the contraction *we're*, the combined form of *we are*.
8. **B. parties should send their resumes** In this sentence, the pronoun is possessive, so *their* is correct.

Lesson 4: Homonyms

Practice 4, page 177

A. 1. fourth

2. know
3. whole
4. week
5. affect
6. past

B. 7. **C. have logged great achievements in the workforce, so why don't they receive fair pay** A *fare* is what you pay to get on the subway; *fair* means *just*. Choice (A) is incorrect because the correct word is *great*, meaning large, rather than *grate*, meaning a metal frame. Choice (B) uses the wrong verb number: the word *women* needs a plural verb, *have*.

8. **A. In principle, the age gap could account for the wage gap because older women still work in jobs in which attitudes and conditions of the past** A *principal* is the head of a school; *principle* means *a guiding rule*. *Passed* in choice (C) and *four* in choice (D) are also incorrect homonyms.
9. **A. The effect is that, as women get older, the gap between men's and women's salaries becomes greater.** *Affect* is a verb meaning *to influence*; *effect*, which means *result*, is required here.

Using Writing Mechanics Practice Questions, pages 178–181

1. **B. Instead, children may have tantrums, erase phone messages,** The phrase *have tantrums* is the first item in series, so it should be followed by a comma.
2. **C. understand and show** A comma should not be used between two verbs, and avoiding the comma is simpler and cleaner than adding a new subject as in incorrect choice (D).
3. **D. your kids know that you feel you're** All the possessives, contractions, and homonyms in the sentence are spelled correctly. The comma following the introductory transition *However* cannot be removed, but the comma after *know* is incorrect.
4. **C. your children aren't at home** The apostrophe in a contraction must be placed in the spot where a letter has been removed.
5. **B. down, consider** An introductory subordinate clause should be followed by a comma.
6. **B. time is to save energy** The subject (*One*) and its verb (*is*) should not be separated by a comma.
7. **B. its standard time by an hour** The sentence is about ownership: each time zone has its own standard time. The possessive form *its* is correct.
8. **B. Congress passed a law making** The name *Congress* refers to a specific body of lawmakers and should therefore be capitalized.
9. **A. For example, radio and TV stations had** An introductory phrase must be followed by a comma.
10. **C. ending dates for daylight saving time in the spring and fall** There is no need to separate the final phrase from the rest of the sentence with a comma.
11. **C. for joining Spring Valley Community Center** When a proper name consists of more than one word, all the words should be capitalized.
12. **D. Please have your membership card with you at all times when you're in the building.** The sentence is saying, "when you are in the building," so the contraction *you're* is needed.
13. **A. If you are a weak swimmer, life jackets** A *week* is seven days. *Weak*, meaning *not strong*, is appropriate for this sentence.
14. **D. children's pool unless they're supervised** The clause beginning with *unless* does not need to be set off with commas.
15. **B. register and pay** Two items joined by *and* do not require a comma unless both are independent clauses.
16. **C. than their white counterparts, often for** The word needed in the sentence is *than*, meaning *compared with*. *Then* means *after that* or *at that time*.
17. **C. from 23 states show that this policy, called racial profiling,** The phrase *called racial profiling* is an appositive but is not essential to understanding the sentence. It needs a comma before and after it.
18. **B. distinctions, for nonwhites** The conjunction *for* is connecting two independent clauses in a compound sentence, so it must be preceded by a comma.
19. **B. Illinois, yet 30 percent** Names of states should be capitalized.
20. **B. However, police superintendents, chiefs of police, and other law enforcement officials** Three items are listed in the series: *police superintendents, chiefs of police, and other law enforcement officials*. There should be commas separating them.

Practice Test

1. To practice for the actual GED® Reasoning Through Language Arts Test, you can take the following practice test. When you do, follow the same time limits you will face on the actual test.

   - **Reasoning Through Language Arts, 53 Questions and Extended Response, 2.5 Hours**
     - First Section—30 minutes: reading and language skills
     - Second Section—45 minutes: extended written response to two passages
     - Break—10 minutes
     - Third Section—65 minutes: reading and language skills

Just as on the actual test, you will work with a variety of formats:

- For the **multiple-choice questions**, you may fill in the circles next to the correct answers in this book, or you can write your answers on a separate piece of paper.
- For **other formats**, directions will indicate where you can write in boxes, on lines, or place a dot on a specific place on a graphic.
- You can write the **extended response** on a computer, or, if one is not available, on a sheet of paper.

NOTE: Writing your responses on a computer is preferable because you will be composing your responses on a computer when you take the GED® test. However, if you do not have a computer available when you take this test, write your responses on paper so that you can evaluate your writing samples.

2. **Check** your answers using the ***Practice Test Answers and Explanations*** that begin on page 221, and fill in the ***Practice Test Evaluation Charts*** on page 224. These charts will allow you to see which study areas may still need work.
3. **Confirm** your readiness to take the actual GED® Reasoning Through Language Arts Test.

Directions: Use 30 minutes to answer the following 20 questions. You may fill in the circles next to the correct answers or write your answers in boxes or on lines as indicated. Some of the questions in this section mimic the GED test's drop-down menu question format. Wherever the word "Select" appears, choose the option that best completes the passage.

Questions 1 through 6 refer to the following excerpt from an article.

Excerpted from "Sizing Up the Interviewer"

1 It is intrinsic to human nature to take the measure of the people we meet. We do it all the time, automatically. We develop an instinctive way of reading others that is sometimes the saving of us and at other times can prove to be our undoing. It is this instinct that makes us form instant, lifelong relationships with some people or causes us to give a wide berth to others because we get a "funny" feeling about them. With some careful consideration and planning, though, these "feelings" can be honed into a useful tool for gauging the personality and character of interviewers and, by extension, their expectations of potential employees. Let's examine some clues.

2 **Their e-mail.** You can tell a lot about your interviewer by his or her e-mail messages. Some interviewers are very warm, writing in a conversational style, addressing you by your first name. Others are witty, mixing little jokes and humorous remarks in with job-related questions. Still others get right down to business—no chit-chat or informality. Before you ever meet the interviewer, you begin to form certain "pictures" of the person, based on his or her approach and style. But it still remains for you to check him or her out face-to-face.

3 **Their office.** Let's begin with the physical setting of interviewers' offices. Some put a desk the size of a 747 between themselves and you. This is a clear message to you to keep your distance. A straight-backed, rigid chair for the applicant says, "O.K. Let's get down to business, and then you leave so I can get back to mine." Here, you would be advised to adopt a crisp, businesslike style, with brief, professional answers. And, for heaven's sake, **don't touch that desk!**

4 Then, there is the homey, comfortable environment—kids' pictures on the desk, executive "toys" around, soft chairs, and a sofa. There may not even be a desk between the applicant and the interviewer, but rather two chairs grouped around a coffee table. This environment invites more intimacy. It says, "Be yourself. Tell me about who you are so I can get to know you." Here, your manner, though still professional, should be relaxed and open, more personable. It would be a mistake with this employer to sit ramrod straight and give cool, truncated responses to the questions.

by Fred Jandt and Mary Nemnich, Indianapolis: JIST Works.

1. The purpose of this article is to

- A. raise awareness about incompetent interviewers
- B. describe types of interviewers and how to approach them
- C. guarantee a perfect interview with an employer
- D. explain how to email an interviewer

2. Which of the following is a generalization made in paragraph 1 but NOT supported with evidence?

- A. Your "feelings" can be honed into a useful tool for gauging the personality and character of interviewers.
- B. An interviewer's office can tell you a great deal about that interviewer.
- C. Our ability to "read" others makes us form instant, lifelong relationships with some people.
- D. There is more than one type of clue you can use to gauge the personality of your interviewer.

3. Which of the following are contrasted in this passage?

- A. interviewers who welcome questions about themselves and those who do not
- B. interviewers who frequently use email and interviewers who do not
- C. interviewers who ask difficult questions and interviewers who ask very few questions
- D. interviewers with homey, comfortable offices and interviewers whose offices seem less welcoming

4. Which of the following is an assumption the author of this passage makes?

- A. Interviewers have some influence or control over their office arrangements.
- B. Because email can be impersonal, it is a poor way to communicate with a potential employer.
- C. Managers who enjoy chatting informally with employees never have large desks in the middle of their offices.
- D. In preparing for a job interview, it is more important to "read" your interviewer than to research the company where you have applied to work.

5. Arrange the following boxes in order from first to last in the order they appear in the passage.

1st	
2nd	
3rd	
4th	

a. The author claims that an interviewer's email style tells you something about that interviewer.
b. The author claims that the arrangement of an interviewer's office tells you something about that interviewer.
c. The author makes a generalization about how your ability to "read" an interviewer can be useful.
d. The author cites specific evidence about why an interviewer's email style may be helpful to you.

6. Which of the following best summarizes the author's main point?

- A. You should never respond to an interviewer who expects crisp answers with a rambling story about yourself.
- B. You should focus on details when attempting to understand your interviewer, since details are important.
- C. You should help your interviewer get to know you during the interview and beforehand.
- D. You should try to understand your interviewer's personality and tailor your responses to him or her accordingly.

Questions 7 through 12 refer to the following excerpt from a short story.

Excerpted from *The Living Is Easy*

1 He gave them each a copper, too, though he could hardly spare it, what with four of them to feed and Mama wanting yard goods and buttons and ribbons to keep herself feeling proud of the way she kept her children. Time was, he gave them kisses for toting his bucket. But the day Cleo brazenly said, I don't want a kiss, I want a copper, the rest of them shamefacedly said it after her. Most times Pa had a struggle to dig down so deep. Four coppers a day, six days a week, was half a day's pay gone up in smoke for candy.

2 Pa couldn't bring himself to tell Mama. She would have wrung out of him that Cleo had been the one started it. And Cleo was his eldest. A man who loved his wife couldn't help loving his first-born best, the child of his fiercest passion. When that first-born was a girl, she could trample on his heart, and he would swear on a stack of Bibles that it didn't hurt.

3 The sisters put their coppers in their pinafore pockets and skipped back through the woods. Midway Cleo stopped and pointed to a towering oak. "You all want to bet me a copper I can't swing by my feet from up in that tree?"

4 Lily clapped her hands to her eyes. "I doesn't want to bet you," she implored. "I ain't fixing to see you fall."

5 Serena said severely, "You bust your neck, you see if Mama don't bust it again."

6 Charity said tremulously, "Cleo, what would us do if our sister was dead?"

7 Cleo saw herself dressed up fine as Josie Beauchamp, stretched out in a coffin with her sisters sobbing beside it, and Pa with his Sunday handkerchief holding his tears, and Mama crying, I loved you best, Cleo. I never said it when you were alive. And I'm sorry, sorry, I waited to say it after you were gone.

8 "You hold my copper, Charity. And if I die, you can have it."

9 Lily opened two of her fingers and peeped through the crack. "Cleo, I'll give you mine if you don't make me see you hanging upside down." It was one thing to hear Cleo tell about herself. It was another thing to see her fixing to kill herself.

10 "Me, too," said Serena, with a little sob, more for the copper than for Cleo, whom she briefly hated for compelling unnecessary sacrifice.

7. Which of the following would Cleo probably enjoy?

- A. jumping from a roof before an audience
- B. sewing clothes with her mother
- C. reading a good book
- D. treating her sisters to candy

8. Whose point of view is explained by this quote from paragraph 2? "A man who loved his wife couldn't help loving his first-born best, the child of his fiercest passion."

- A. Cleo's
- B. Mama's
- C. the narrator's
- D. Pa's

9. Arrange the following plot elements in order from the earliest to the latest.

1st	
2nd	
3rd	
4th	

a. Cleo envisions her own funeral.
b. Cleo's sisters offer her their coppers.
c. One day Cleo said that she did not want a kiss but wanted a copper instead.
d. Cleo asks her sisters to bet on whether she can swing from her feet in an oak tree.

10. Why did Serena offer Cleo her own copper?

- A. Serena wanted Cleo to get in trouble for taking the others' money.
- B. Serena had placed a bet that Cleo could not swing from the oak tree.
- C. Serena felt that she had no choice but to give Cleo her copper to stop Cleo from doing something unsafe.
- D. Serena wanted to show how much she loved her sister.

11. What is meant by the following quote from paragraph 1? "Most times Pa had a struggle to dig down so deep."

- A. It was difficult for Pa to find it within himself to be generous.
- B. Pa had so few coins that they were usually far down in his pockets.
- C. Pa often searched for reasons not to give coppers to Cleo and her sisters.
- D. Pa could not really afford to give Cleo and her sisters money.

12. Which of the following statements best describes the theme of the passage?

- A. Cleo is wrong to take advantage of her sisters and her father.
- B. Cleo's boldness and her family's love for her sometimes make them feel powerless to resist her.
- C. Cleo's longing to be loved makes her vulnerable.
- D. Cleo and her sisters are becoming greedy as they learn how to extract money from each other and from their parents.

Questions 13 through 16 refer to the following paragraphs.

Painting a Room

Would you like to redecorate a room in your home? Painting [Select... ▾] new look. First, remove the furniture, or move it to the center of the room and cover it with drop cloths. Prepare the room by [Select... ▾] a coat of primer if necessary.

Now you're ready to paint. Use a brush to paint a clean line along all edges where paint stops, such as where the wall meets the door frame, and in places where the ceiling meets a wall of a different color. This is called "cutting in."

The next step [Select... ▾] to paint the room in the following order: ceiling, walls, trim, doors, and windows. Put no more than 3/4 of an inch of paint in the paint pan. Run your roller through the paint, being careful not to overload the roller. Apply paint to the ceiling and walls in a "W" or "Z" zigzag pattern.

Spread the paint evenly by rolling either side to side or up and down, using gentle strokes so as not to leave roller marks. After finishing an area, look for spots you [Select... ▾] over them with your relatively dry roller.

13. Painting [Select... ▾] new look.

- A. is a fast inexpensive way to give that room a hole
- B. are a fast, and inexpensive way to give that room a whole
- C. is a fast and inexpensive way to giving that room a whole
- D. is a fast and inexpensive way to give that room a whole

14. Prepare the room by [Select... ▾] a coat of primer if line break necessary.

- A. stripping paint and excess wallpaper, fill cracks, and add
- B. strip paint and wallpaper, fill cracks, and add
- C. stripping paint and wallpaper, fill cracks, and adding
- D. stripping paint and wallpaper, filling cracks, and adding

15. The next step [Select... ▾] to paint the room in the following order: ceiling, walls, trim, doors, and windows.

- A. was
- B. being
- C. is
- D. had been

16. After finishing an area, look for spots you [Select... ▾] over them with your relatively dry roller.

- A. missed, and go
- B. missed, and going
- C. missed go
- D. missed, but go

Questions 17 through 20 refer to the following passage.

Starting a Community Garden

(A)

(1) In many cities, neighborhood groups are forming community gardens in vacant lots, in parks, or on rooftops. (2) These gardens [Select...] to work with nature while making the neighborhood more beautiful. (3) [Select...] people are truly interested in the project. (4) If they are, organize a meeting of interested people, and choose someone to be the garden coordinator.
(5) Form committees for tasks like finding money for the garden.

(B)

(6) Once your group is organized, approach a sponsor—a group or individual who can support your garden. (7) Keep in mind that contributions of seeds, tools, and land are just as important as money. (8) Schools, churches, citizen groups, and private businesses are all potential sponsors.

(C)

(9) Find out how the land has been used in the past to avoid places that may be contaminated. (10) Pick a site that gets at least six hours of direct sunlight a day, and make sure that water is available. (11) Contact the owner of the site try to get a lease that allows you to use the land for at least three years.

(D)

(12) After choosing a site, the group of gardeners needs to decide how to organize the garden. (13) What size should each plot be, and how will plots be assigned? (14) Finally, establish a procedure to follow so that the garden stays tidy and peaceful.

17. These gardens [Select...] to work with nature while making the neighborhood more beautiful.
    - A. is an ideal way for both children, and adults
    - B. are an ideal way for both children and adults
    - C. are an ideal way for both children, and adults,
    - D. ideal, since both children and adults

18. If you [Select...] people are truly interested in the project.
    - A. will like to start a community garden, first determine whether
    - B. would like to start a community garden, first determine whether
    - C. would like to start a community garden first determine whether
    - D. would like to start a community garden, first determine weather

19. Which sentence would be most effective if inserted at the beginning of paragraph C?
    - A. Next, choose a site for the garden.
    - B. Land use is a very significant factor.
    - C. We all know that you are going to need land for your garden.
    - D. Learn about the history of your site.

20. Which of the following would improve the effectiveness of paragraph A?
    - A. Start a new paragraph before sentence 2.
    - B. Start a new paragraph before sentence 3.
    - C. Combine sentences 2 and 3 into a compound sentence.
    - D. Combine paragraphs A and B.

Directions: Based on both passages on pages 206 and 207, write a response to the prompt on page 207. This task may take up to 45 minutes to complete.

Passage A: Why Physical Education Should No Longer Be a Requirement for Graduation

This is the text of Councilwoman Juanita Sanchez's speech at last week's school board meeting.

The job market is increasingly competitive. Because of this, we must ensure that our students' education fully prepares them to succeed in the future. A limited budget and limited time during the school day force us to make difficult decisions concerning what we teach. We must be willing to make these decisions with the best interests of our students at heart. With these goals in mind, I support the proposal to eliminate physical education as a core requirement for high school graduation in our district.

Time spent completing physical education requirements is time away from more productive educational pursuits. While our state's standardized test scores have continued to rise in past years, we are still seeing results that are below average in both mathematics and reading. Added instructional time is necessary to see our test scores meet the standards set for us. This additional time spent on core subjects will also better prepare students for a pursuit of higher education after high school graduation.

No one is suggesting that physical education and fitness classes be completely eliminated from our curriculum. Physical education is a worthwhile pursuit and should be provided for those students who are interested. But it should be an elective, or optional, course in the same way that music, art, and theater classes are offered as electives. Thus, this outdated requirement will no longer get in the way of more academically important pursuits.

Passage B: Physical Education Is an Important Requirement for Students

Letter from concerned parent published in the City Journal *newspaper*

No one would disagree that preparing our students for a successful future is essential. Changes need to be made in order to help our children compete for college scholarships and career advancement. But as we make these changes, we have to be careful not to cause more harm than good. The current proposal places us in danger of damaging successful programs in our efforts to make improvements.

Having a healthy lifestyle is at least as important to a happy and successful future as mathematics and reading skills are. We currently are in the middle of an epidemic of health problems caused by lack of physical fitness among the children in our community. In our state, almost 20 percent of children between the ages of 12 and 18 are classified as obese. And obesity is linked to a number of life threatening health problems including diabetes and heart disease. Thus, this is a trend that we must make every effort to reverse.

Programs to offer healthier lunch choices for students have already been introduced. It would be ridiculous to now eliminate requirements that teach our children about other aspects of healthy living. What good is longer time spent in so-called "core classes" if students aren't healthy enough to fully participate?

I understand that the School Board members have students' best interests at heart. And I agree that it is important to find ways to improve the math and reading scores of our students. Unfortunately, the current plan to eliminate physical education will do much more harm than good. There is a reason P.E. has been a part of our school curriculum for so many years!

Write an Extended Response to Both Passages

While Councilwoman Sanchez makes her case for the benefits of eliminating physical education from the required curriculum, the editorial response identifies the drawbacks of this proposal.

In your response, analyze both the speech and the editorial. Explain which position you believe is best supported by its advocate. Use relevant and specific evidence from both sources to support your response.

Type your response on a computer, if one is available. If one is not available, write your response neatly on paper. This task may require approximately 45 minutes to complete.

Use the *Reasoning Through Language Arts Extended Response Evaluation Guide* on page 225 to evaluate your response.

You may take a 10-minute break before proceeding.

Directions: Use 65 minutes to answer the following questions. You may fill in the circles next to the correct answers or write your answers in boxes or on lines as indicated.

Questions 21 through 27 refer to the following book excerpt.

Excerpt from *Small Business for Dummies*

1 The domestic automakers had a huge market share coming into the 1970s but, unfortunately, were upsetting customers left and right. The Detroit auto manufacturers were able to keep their costs low and profits high in part by producing sub-par cars. Sure, their cars looked nice on the auto dealer's lot, but after a short time in use, many of the U.S.-manufactured cars developed far more problems than their foreign equivalents. And, to add insult to injury, U.S. auto customers didn't get particularly good customer service when they brought their cars in for needed tune-ups and repairs.

2 The chief bean counters and the management of the major U.S. automakers weren't considering the bigger picture when they analyzed their companies' financial statements during the 1970s. These companies were too focused on their short-term profitability and weren't considering the after-sales service that was required as a result of their initially shoddy products.

3 Not surprisingly, the U.S. automakers lost tremendous market share at the expense of the best foreign automakers during the 1970s and 1980s. In fact, one of the big four U.S. automakers—Chrysler—nearly went bankrupt and was saved only because of a government bailout.

4 In the long run, the Detroit automakers learned the hard way that getting your product right the first time is less costly and more profitable than retrenching to play catch-up. Customers aren't stupid, and if you continually sell them shoddy merchandise (especially when better merchandise is available from other sources), they won't come back the next time they're in the market for the products and services you have to offer. What's more, they'll tell others of their lousy experience with your company.

5 Although the major U.S. automakers ultimately got their act together in the 1990s and have stopped the erosion of market share, they still feel the financial pain from the millions of customers they alienated and lost to foreign competitors in the two preceding decades.

From *Small Business for Dummies* by Eric Tyson and Jim Schell, Foster City, Calif.: IDG Books, 2000.

21. The passage states that in the 1970s and 1980s, the management of the major U.S. automakers was too focused on which of the following?

- A. Attractiveness of the cars they manufactured
- B. After-sales service
- C. Manufacturing shoddy merchandise
- D. Short-term profitability

22. According to the passage, which of the following is a lesson learned by the Detroit automakers?

- A. Getting your product right the first time is more profitable than fixing mistakes later.
- B. Servicing your product is not profitable and therefore unimportant.
- C. Bankruptcy is profitable for large companies due to government bailouts.
- D. It is easy to win back customers a company has lost to a competitor.

23. What do the authors suggest was one of the goals of foreign automakers?

Foreign automakers

- A. studied and then improved on the design of U.S. cars
- B. deliberately underpriced their cars to get a share of the U.S. market
- C. wanted to build quality cars with few repair problems
- D. put short-term profitability above all else

24. The author uses the phrase "chief bean counters" most probably in order to

- A. underscore the fact that customers will not return once they have had a poor experience with a certain company
- B. argue that foreign automakers provided better customer service than U.S. automakers
- C. emphasize U.S. automakers' preoccupation with keeping costs low and profits high in the short term, at the expense of their long-term outlook
- D. indicate that domestic automakers enjoyed tremendous market share at the beginning of the 1970s

25. Which of the following are causes, and which are effects? Place the following four causes and effects into the table below:

Causes	Effects

a. U.S. automakers manufactured cars of low quality
b. A customer chooses not to do business with a company
c. A customer has a bad experience when doing business with a company
d. U.S. automakers lost business to foreign automakers in the 1970s and 1980s

26. Which of the following best describes the authors' tone toward U.S. automakers?

- A. critical
- B. proud
- C. approving
- D. arrogant

27. Later, the authors advise: "As a small-business owner, remember that if you don't get your product right the first time, you may not have a second chance."

Based on this information and the excerpt, who did get a second chance?

- A. U.S. automakers
- B. foreign automakers
- C. small-business owners
- D. the government

Questions 28 through 34 refer to the following passage from a short story.

Excerpted from "The Twins"

1 After a while, there was a ring at the back door. The children scampered in from the garden, while Jennie answered the ring.

2 "Baker," said the man.

3 "Oh, yes," said Jennie: "wait, I'll get my purse."

4 I went on writing my letter, only half hearing the sound of Jennie's small-change as she, presumably, paid the baker's man.

5 In a moment, Marjie was by my side.

6 "Hallo," I said.

7 Marjie did not answer.

8 "Hallo, Marjie," I said. "Have you come to keep me company?"

9 "Listen," said little Marjie in a whisper, looking over her shoulder. "Listen."

10 "Yes," I said.

11 She looked over her shoulder again, as if afraid her mother might come in.

12 "Will you give me half-a-crown?" whispered Marjie, holding out her hand.

13 "Well," I said, "what do you want it for?"

14 "I want it," said Marjie, looking furtively behind her again.

15 "Would your mummy want you to have it?" I said.

16 "Give me half-a-crown," said Marjie.

17 "I'd rather not," I said. "But I'll tell you what, I'll buy you a—"

18 But Marjie had fled, out of the door, into the kitchen. "She'd rather not," I heard her say to someone.

19 Presently, Jennie came in, looking upset.

20 "Oh," she said, "I hope you didn't feel hurt. I only wanted to pay the baker, and I hadn't enough change. He hadn't any either; so just on the spur of the moment I sent Marjie for a loan of half-a-crown till tonight. But I shouldn't have done it. I never borrow anything as a rule."

21 "Well, of course!" I said. "Of course I'll lend you half-a-crown. I've got plenty of change. I didn't understand and I got the message all wrong; I thought she wanted it for herself and that you wouldn't like that."

22 Jennie looked doubtful. I funked explaining the whole of Marjie's act. It isn't easy to give evidence against a child of five.

23 "Oh, they never ask for money," said Jennie. "I would never allow them to ask for anything. They never do that."

24 "I'm sure they don't," I said, floundering a bit.

From "The Twins" by Muriel Spark, from the book *The Go-Away Bird and Other Stories*, J. B. Lippincott Company.

28. What does Marjie's looking over her shoulder suggest to the narrator?

The narrator thinks Marjie

- A. is imagining what she'll do with the money
- B. has forgotten something in the other room
- C. is shy and lacks confidence
- D. is hoping her mother won't hear her asking for money

29. Which of the following becomes evident during the discussion between Jennie and the narrator?

- A. Jennie knows the narrator wanted to lend her the money.
- B. Jennie can't believe that the narrator wouldn't lend her the money.
- C. Jennie is perplexed when the narrator blames Marjie.
- D. The narrator and Jennie eventually forget the misunderstanding.

30. If Jennie were criticized by her boss at work, what would she most likely do?

- A. resent it in silence
- B. discuss it defensively
- C. not take it seriously
- D. argue forcefully

31. The first person point of view allows the reader to know

- A. the narrator's thoughts
- B. the thoughts and actions of all characters
- C. only the actions of the narrator
- D. Marjie's opinions about the narrator

32. What kind of relationship do Jennie and the narrator have?

- A. They are cool and indifferent to each other.
- B. They frequently disagree on matters.
- C. They know each other but are not close.
- D. Jennie takes advantage of the narrator.

33. Which of the following best describes the situation presented in this excerpt?

- A. humorous
- B. sad
- C. uncomfortable
- D. sentimental

34. Match the following descriptions with the characters they best describe.

Marjie	
Jennie	
Narrator	

Obedient
Diplomatic
Proud

Questions 35 through 41 refer to the following passage and graphic.

How Should We Measure the Rate of Poverty?

1 The rate of poverty appears to be increasing. Each year, the U.S. Census Bureau estimates the rate of poverty, or how many people in the U.S. are living in poverty. According to the Census Bureau, about 15.9 percent of the U.S. population was poor in 2011. That was a 15.3 percent increase over 2010. Moreover, the rate of poverty rose each year from 2007 to 2011.

2 It has been argued that the estimated rate of poverty is too low—that, in fact, more Americans are poor. To understand this, it is important first to understand how the Census Bureau determines who is poor. The Bureau surveys people about their income and then compares that income to the official "poverty threshold" (often called the "poverty line"). This poverty threshold varies depending on age, family size, and number of children. For example, in 2011 the poverty threshold for a single individual under 65 was $11,702. For a family of four, it was $23,021.

3 Some researchers have argued that these poverty thresholds do not account for taxes, living expenses, medical costs, or differences in cost of living. For example, in a major city, higher rents may leave individuals with less money for food. If the poverty thresholds were adjusted to account for these considerations, the estimated rate of poverty might be higher.

4 A panel of experts has proposed a different measure of poverty, which they call the Supplemental Poverty Measure, or SPM. The graph below shows what percentage of people are living in poverty as measured by the official poverty threshold and compares it to the percentage of people who would be considered poor by the SPM.

5 Why does it matter how many people are considered poor by the Census Bureau? One answer is that the Bureau's estimate of the rate of poverty is used by the federal government to allot resources to states and local communities. Local governments also use the estimate to figure out how many people are eligible for anti-poverty programs.

Poverty Rates Using Two Measures for Total Population and by Age Group, 2011

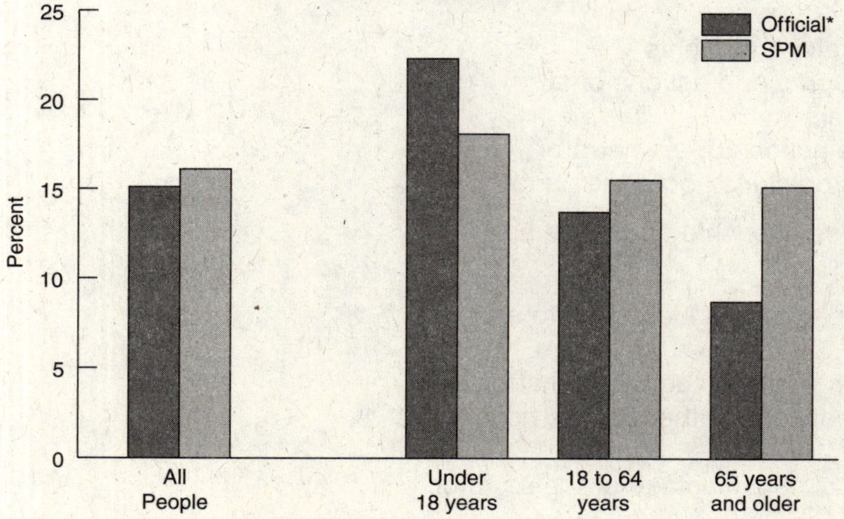

*Includes unrelated individuals under age 15.
Source: U.S. Census Bureau, Current Population Survey, 2012 Annual Social and Economic Supplement.

Adapted with permission from the U.S. Census Bureau

35. Which of the following best states the main idea of the passage and graph?

- A. The Census Bureau uses a set of poverty thresholds to determine the rate of poverty.
- B. If the Census Bureau adopted the SPM, the estimate of the rate of poverty among seniors would increase.
- C. There may be more people in poverty than the Census Bureau official estimate suggests.
- D. It is important that the government take action to combat poverty.

36. Which of the following is a supporting detail, rather than a main idea, in paragraph 1?

- A. The rate of poverty rose each year from 2007 to 2011.
- B. The rate of poverty appears to be increasing.
- C. The Census Bureau may underestimate the number of people living in poverty.
- D. Differences in cost of living should be accounted for in how the government measures poverty.

37. How does the bar graph support the information in the passage?

- A. The bar graph supports the claim that some people who do not think they are poor may actually be poor.
- B. The bar graph supports the claim that the government should do more to combat poverty.
- C. The bar graph supports the claim that a different way to measure poverty would produce a different estimate of the rate of poverty.
- D. The bar graph supports the claim that 15.9% of people in the U.S. were poor in 2011.

38. Which of the following describes a cause and effect relationship mentioned in the passage?

- A. The poverty thresholds cause individuals to have lower income.
- B. The Census Bureau's estimated rate of poverty can cause government officials to care about poverty.
- C. Higher rents can cause people to have less money for food.
- D. The SPM would cause more money to be spent on programs for senior citizens.

39. Place each of the factors below into the column that best describes it. You may or may not fill up each column.

Estimates that would be higher if the SPM were adopted	**Estimates that would be lower if the SPM were adopted**

The overall rate of poverty
The rate of poverty among people 65 and older
The rate of poverty among people under 18
The rate of poverty among people 18–64

40. A student reviewed this passage and graph and then said: "It's clear to me that if the Census Bureau adopted the SPM, then local governments would get significantly more federal money to spend on anti-poverty programs." Which of the following best describes the flaw in the student's reasoning?

- A. The student has confused the causes of poverty with the effects of poverty.
- B. The student has overlooked the fact that other factors might impact how much money local governments receive from the federal government.
- C. The student has overlooked the possibility that not all local governments work to combat poverty.
- D. The student has overlooked the fact that other countries have even higher rates of poverty.

41. This piece was most likely written by someone who ______________.

- A. worries that the government spends too much money on anti-poverty programs
- B. thinks poverty is too emotional a topic to be discussed publicly
- C. wants governmental actions to be based on an accurate estimate of the rate of poverty
- D. thinks that there is little that government can do about poverty

Directions: Questions 42 through 45 refer to the following two passages.

Glenwood Community Improvement Council Member:

As a member of the Glenwood Community Improvement Council, I fully support spending money to beautify our public parks. Over the last few years, several of our community parks have fallen into disrepair. Walking paths through the parks are not clearly marked, graffiti is visible on picnic shelters, and garden areas are overgrown with weeds. My neighbors tell me that they do not visit our parks because of the parks' condition. Some even said that they worry the parks are dangerous! We should spend money to ensure that our parks are good places to spend time with your family.

Improving and maintaining the parks would have a positive effect on crime and vandalism. If the parks are established as a source of pride for all of the community, vandals will be less likely to deface them. Well-maintained basketball and volleyball courts, picnic areas, and special events such as concerts in the parks would provide activities for the whole town and help neighbors spend time together.

Furthermore, beautiful public spaces are essential to community pride. Without community pride, Glenwood residents and others are unlikely to invest in creating and supporting small businesses. And small businesses are the heart of a thriving community. We must present Glenwood as a beautiful place to live in order to attract successful entrepreneurs from the surrounding area. If we do so, our investment in the parks will quickly pay for itself. Thus, we must improve our public parks.

Concerned Local Business Owner:

I think I speak for most of the business owners in Glenwood when I say that spending money to improve parks would be a complete waste of resources. The parks are not popular, and we do not know that they would become popular after being improved.

If we want a shining example of our town's successes to attract businesses, our growing business district is all we need! In the last four years, six new businesses have moved into vacant locations on Main Street. On top of that, several restaurants and shops downtown have survived the recent economic downturn and are now seeing more customers.

The city should do more to support these businesses. We should spend money to improve the infrastructure and appearance of the downtown business district. Improvements could be made to streetlights, signs, and building exteriors along our historic Main Street. We also currently are not able to plant public flower beds or clean and maintain the sidewalks. Investments in these areas would make downtown inviting to both customers and small business owners.

Beautifying our town is important if we want economic growth. But we should make sure that our beautification efforts are in the most important places. Clearly, beautifying downtown would help us build a healthy local economy. And once we have done so, then we can put money toward our parks.

42. The topic of both passages is

- A. the best way to enjoy public spaces
- B. what businesses should exist in Glenwood
- C. whether beautification projects create economic growth
- D. how best to spend public money

43. The writers of the passages disagree about which of the following claims about Glenwood Public Parks?

- A. They are in a state of disrepair.
- B. They are a current source of pride for the community.
- C. Improving them is a good use of funds right now.
- D. Park activities can lower the amount of crime.

44. How does the local business owner feel about projects that improve the appearance of the city?

- A. They are good when done in the best locations.
- B. They are always a waste of taxpayer money.
- C. The city parks are good enough the way they are.
- D. They have no impact on local business.

45. Which of the following would the two writers most likely agree on?

- A. Improving Glenwood Public Parks will have an immediate impact on local business.
- B. Investing in our community is important for the future of Glenwood.
- C. The parks would be used regularly if they were in better repair.
- D. Public activities are more important than encouraging new local business.

Questions 46 through 49 refer to the following paragraphs.

Sick Building Syndrome

Do you Select...? Do you experience symptoms such as coughing, sneezing, nausea, headaches and difficulty breathing? Do these Select...? If so, you may be working in a sick building.

"Sick building syndrome" is a term that refers to working in a building that makes you sick. The syndrome may be caused by improper building design. Over the past 20 years, architects have designed office buildings with an eye to saving energy. The buildings are tightly sealed so that little heat escapes, and the air inside the buildings is recirculated to avoid the cost of heating fresh air. Although this design reduces energy costs, the lack of ventilation causes a buildup of toxins in the air. On the other hand, Select... the syndrome. Even if Select... originally opened to let in fresh air, adding insulation, caulking, and weather stripping at a later date may have made the windows airtight.

Toxins in the air come from a variety of sources. Biological agents, including bacteria, viruses, fungi, and pollen, may be found in poorly maintained air circulation systems and dirty washrooms. The deadly gas carbon monoxide can seep into a building's air through an improperly ventilated garage or a leaky duct. Formaldehyde is frequently found in furniture, paneling, draperies, glues, and upholstery.

It is possible to "cure" a sick building. Steps to take include eliminating tobacco smoke, providing good ventilation, keeping the ventilation system in good repair, and removing all sources of pollution.

46. Do you [Select...] ?

- A. often feel sick when at you're workplace?
- B. often feel sickly when at your workplace?
- C. often feel sick when at your workplace?
- D. often feeling sick when at your workplace?

47. Do these [Select...] ?

- A. symptoms seem to disappear magically once you leave work?
- B. symptoms seem to disappear once you leave work magically?
- C. symptoms seems to disappear once you leave work magically?
- D. symptoms seem to disappear once magically you leave work?

48. On the other hand, [Select...] the syndrome.

- A. an older building isn't necessarily immune to
- B. an older isn't necessarily immune to
- C. an older isn't necessarily immune too
- D. an older building isn't necessarily immune, to

49. Even if [Select...] originally opened to let in fresh air, adding insulation, caulking, and weather stripping at a later date may have made the windows airtight.

- A. them
- B. it
- C. the building
- D. the windows

Questions 50 through 53 refer to the following flyer.

Save Compton Point!

(A)

(1) Compton Point, home to many animal species that are threatened with extinction, now faces a threat of its own. (2) Developers are attempting to change the zoning in order to build a hotel, a tourist center, and an observation tower. (3) If they succeed in getting the rights to build, construction will begin next August.

(B)

(4) Sam Wanamaker, director of the Society for the Protection of Nature, warns that construction of the development is likely to drive out more than 30 animal species that live on the point. (5) Select... .

(C)

(6) The Compton Point area is zoned as natural parkland. (7) There are several other areas in the county that are zoned as natural parkland. (8) However, because this project is potentially so lucrative for the city, the zoning board seems to be bending to the will of the developers.

(D)

(9) Developers argue that the new jobs Select... . (11) Certainly, everyone in the community agrees that the economy around here could use a lift, but this is not the way to do it.

(E)

(12) Register your opposition to the development of Compton Point! (13) Come to a demonstration at 10 A.M. on Select... . (14) Bring signs with slogans that tell how you feel. (15) A strong turnout at this demonstration will send a message to developers.

50. [Select...]

- A. Tourism increases both air pollution and litter, which will further reduce the animals' chances for survival.
- B. Air pollution from tourist traffic will further reduce the animals' chances for survival, not to mention litter left behind by floods of tourists.
- C. Air pollution from tourist traffic and also litter from tourists flooding through the area will further reduce the animals' chances for survival.
- D. Tourism will further reduce animals' chances for survival because of air pollution from tourist traffic and floods of litter from tourists.

51. Which revision would improve the effectiveness of paragraph C?

- A. remove sentence 6
- B. move sentence 6 to follow sentence 7
- C. remove sentence 7
- D. move sentence 7 to follow sentence 8

52. Developers argue that the new jobs [Select...].

- A. resulting from their development would boost the region's sagging economy, and the influx of tourism would too.
- B. and influx of tourism resulting from their development would boost the region's sagging economy.
- C. resulting from their development would help along the economy of the region. The influx of tourism would too.
- D. and also the influx of tourism, that would result from their development, would cause the region's economy to boost.

53. Come to a demonstration at 10 A.M. on [Select...].

- A. Saturday, May 7, in front of the mayor's office 34 wilton road.
- B. saturday, May 7, in front of the mayor's office, 34 Wilton road.
- C. Saturday, may 7, in front of the mayor's office, 34 Wilton road.
- D. Saturday, May 7, in front of the mayor's office, 34 Wilton Road.

Answers and explanations begin on page 221.

STOP

Congratulations! You have completed the GED® Reasoning Through Language Arts Practice Test.

Reminder: your next step is to check your answers with the Practice Test Answers and Explanations and fill in the evaluation charts that follow those explanations.

Practice Test Answers and Explanations

Pages 199–219

1. **B. describe types of interviewers and how to approach them** The author is chiefly concerned with explaining that different interviewers have different personalities and that you should approach those interviewers differently.
2. **C. Our ability to "read" others makes us form instant, lifelong relationships with some people.** The author makes this general claim in the first paragraph but does not support it with evidence. Choices (A) and (D) are stated or implied in the first paragraph and then supported with evidence in paragraphs 2–4. Choice (B) is a generalization made in paragraph 3, not paragraph 1.
3. **D. interviewers with homey, comfortable offices and interviewers whose offices seem less welcoming** The author contrasts these two types of interviewers in the third and fourth paragraphs of the passage.
4. **A. Interviewers have some influence or control over their office arrangements.** In paragraphs 3 and 4, the author explains that you can learn a great deal about an interviewer's personality from the type and arrangements of furniture in the interviewer's office. However, in order for this to make sense, the author must be assuming that interviewers have some say about their office arrangements. If an interviewer had no influence over her office, then the office would not provide reliable information about the interviewer's personality. The passage does not discuss the virtues of email (choice (B)) or the relative importance of different aspects of preparing for an interview (choice (D)). Choice (C) is out of scope. This passage is about prospective hires, not employees.
5. Arrange the elements of the author's argument in the order in which they appear:

   1st c. The author makes a generalization about how your ability to "read" an interviewer can be useful.

   2nd a. The author claims that an interviewer's email style tells you something about that interviewer.

   3rd d. The author cites specific evidence about why an interviewer's email style may be helpful to you.

   4th b. The author claims that the arrangement of an interviewer's office tells you something about that interviewer.
6. **D. You should try to understand your interviewer's personality and tailor your responses to him or her accordingly.** Only choice (D) summarizes the author's overall argument. The other choices are either details (choice (A)) or not mentioned in the passage (choice (C)).
7. **A. jumping from a roof before an audience** Cleo loves attention. Her bet that she can swing upside down from an oak tree would have resulted in her either winning her sisters' money or gaining attention because she got hurt. Jumping from a rooftop would provide Cleo with attention whether it went well or poorly.
8. **D. Pa's** In this paragraph, the author describes Pa's love for Cleo and why she has so much influence over him.
9. Arrange the plot elements in chronological order:

   1st c. One day Cleo said that she did not want a kiss but wanted a copper instead.

   2nd d. Cleo asks her sisters to bet on whether she can swing from her feet in an oak tree.

   3rd a. Cleo envisions her own funeral.

   4th b. Cleo's sisters offer her their coppers.
10. **C. Serena felt that she had no choice but to give Cleo her copper to stop Cleo from doing something unsafe.** Serena does not want to give Cleo her copper; rather, Cleo is "compelling unnecessary sacrifice." Cleo does so by threatening to do something dangerous.
11. **D. Pa could not really afford to give Cleo and her sisters money.** The quote explains that Pa did not really have enough money to give some to Cleo and her sisters for doing chores. The phrase "dig deep" suggests that it was a sacrifice for him to do without that money, although he wanted to be generous. The language in the quote is figurative rather than literal, so choice (B) is incorrect.
12. **B. Cleo's boldness and her family's love for her sometimes make them feel powerless to resist her.** This passage is chiefly concerned with Cleo's character, which is bold and daring, and with the fact that her family members clearly love her. Both in the case of Pa giving the girls coppers and in the case of the sisters giving theirs to Cleo, Cleo's family members sometimes feel that they cannot refuse her.
13. **D. is a fast and inexpensive way to give that room a whole** A hole is a place that is dug out of the ground; whole means "entire."
14. **D. stripping paint and wallpaper, filling cracks, and adding** The verb "add" should end with -ing to match "stripping" and "filling." All the verbs in a series should be in the same form.
15. **C. is** The sentence should be in the present tense because the rest of the paragraph is in the present tense.
16. **A. missed, and go** Choice (A) uses the correct conjunction and correct verb form.
17. **B. are an ideal way for both children and adults** The verb "are" agrees with the plural subject "gardens."
18. **B. would like to start a community garden, first determine whether** In a complex sentence, a comma should follow the dependent clause at the beginning of the sentence.

19. **A. Next, choose a site for the garden.** Choice (A) is specific enough to be clear and general enough to cover all the details in the paragraph. It also includes a transition from the preceding paragraph.

20. **B. Start a new paragraph before sentence 3.** The first two sentences are about the benefits of community gardens. Sentence 3 begins a discussion of the steps involved in forming a community garden. Thus, a new paragraph is warranted.

Extended Response Evaluation Guide: Use the *Reasoning Through Language Arts Extended Response Evaluation Guide* on page 225 to give your response a score between 0 and 6. Enter your score on the *Evaluation Chart* on page 224.

21. **D. Short-term profitability** The last sentence of paragraph 2 states that "these companies were too focused on their short-term profitability."

22. **A. Getting your product right the first time is more profitable than fixing mistakes later.** The correct answer comes from the first sentence of paragraph 4: "In the long run, the Detroit automakers learned the hard way that getting your product right the first time is less costly and more profitable than retrenching to play catch-up."

23. **C. wanted to build quality cars with few repair problems** The U.S. automakers produced cars with "far more problems than their foreign equivalents." This suggests that quality was a priority for the foreign automakers but not for domestic automakers looking to "keep their costs low and profits high."

24. **C. emphasize U.S. automakers' preoccupation with keeping costs low and profits high in the short term, at the expense of their long-term outlook** "Bean counter" is a derogatory term for an accountant or manager who is excessively concerned with keeping expenses low. The author uses this term to underscore the idea that the U.S. automakers failed to consider the "bigger picture"—that is, failed to consider their long-term outlook.

25.

Causes	Effects
a. U.S. automakers manufactured cars of low quality	d. U.S. automakers lost business to foreign automakers in the 1970s and 1980s
c. A customer has a bad experience when doing business with a company	b. A customer chooses not to do business with a company

26. **A. critical** The authors speak negatively of the cars produced by U.S. automakers in the 1970s and 1980s and include comments such as "to add insult to injury" and "weren't considering the bigger picture."

27. **A. U.S. automakers** The last paragraph states that U.S. automakers eventually "got their act together in the 1990s and have stopped the erosion of market share."

28. **D. is hoping her mother won't hear her asking for money** The narrator misinterprets Marjie's actions. She thinks Marjie is asking for money for herself, not her mother. She therefore interprets Marjie's actions as trying to hide her request from her mother.

29. **C. Jennie is perplexed when the narrator blames Marjie.** When the narrator explains that she thought Marjie wanted the money for herself, "Jennie looked doubtful."

30. **B. discuss it defensively** Jennie meets with the narrator directly to try to explain what happened and express concern. However, she misunderstands the narrator's explanation, apologizes for trying to borrow money, and reacts defensively when it is suggested that her daughter would ask for money on her own. Jennie would likely have this same defensive reaction if criticized by a boss.

31. **A. the narrator's thoughts** The passage is written with a first person point of view from the narrator's perspective. This allows the reader access to the thoughts of the narrator as well as a description of the action that the narrator sees.

32. **C. They know each other but are not close.** The narrator is visiting Jennie and her family and obviously knows them, yet there is a formal tone to Jennie's explanation about borrowing money, and the narrator is unable to explain how she misunderstood Marjie and is left "floundering." Those aspects of their relationship help you infer they are not on close, intimate terms.

33. **C. uncomfortable** Jennie feels she has to explain why she was going to borrow money from the narrator, and the narrator not only misinterprets Marjie's actions but has a difficult time explaining to Jennie "the whole of Marjie's act." Jennie appears to doubt her and states her children would never ask for money, leaving the narrator "floundering a bit." The entire situation ends with the narrator (and perhaps even the reader) feeling uncomfortable over the situation.

34.

Marjie	Obedient
Jennie	Proud
Narrator	Diplomatic

Marjie follows the instructions of the older characters. Jennie is defensive and quick to explain that she normally wouldn't ask for money or allow Marjie to. The narrator attempts to smooth over the misunderstanding.

35. **C. There may be more people in poverty than the Census Bureau official estimate suggests.** Overall, the passage conveys this main point. Choices (A) and (B) are details rather than main ideas, and choice (D) is not supported by the passage.

36. **A. The rate of poverty rose during each year from 2007 to 2011.** The main idea of paragraph 1 is that the rate of poverty is increasing. This detail supports that main idea. Choice (B) is the main idea of paragraph 1. Choices (C) and (D) are suggested in later paragraphs.

37. **C. The bar graph supports the claim that a different way to measure poverty would produce a different estimate of the rate of poverty.** The bar graph shows that the SPM would produce different estimates of how many people are poor, a claim that the author makes in paragraph 4.

38. **C. Higher rents can cause people to have less money for food.** Paragraph 3 explains that "higher rents may leave individuals with less money for food": higher rents are the cause, and less money for food is the effect. Choices (B) and (D) are too extreme. Choice (A) distorts the passage: the poverty thresholds measure who is poor—they don't cause people to be poor.

39.

Estimates that would be higher if the SPM were adopted	Estimates that would be lower if the SPM were adopted
The overall rate of poverty	The rate of poverty among people under 18
The rate of poverty among people 18–64	
The rate of poverty among people 65 and older	

Only the estimated rate of poverty among people under 18 would be lower if the SPM were adopted. (In your answer, the items in the left-hand column do not have to be in the order presented here.)

40. **B. The student has overlooked the fact that other factors might impact how much money local governments receive from the federal government.** The student has read in the passage that government spending on poverty is affected by the estimated rate of poverty. But even if the estimated rate of poverty were higher, that does not necessarily mean that government (at any level) would automatically spend more on poverty. After all, many factors go into governmental decision-making.

41. **C. wants governmental actions to be based on an accurate estimate of the rate of poverty** The author's chief concern is with the estimated rate of poverty and whether or not it is accurate. Moreover, the author states in paragraph 5 that this matters because government spending is involved. None of the other choices here are supported by the passage.

42. **D. how best to spend public money** Both writers discuss their thoughts about the best way to use funds to improve Glenwood.

43. **C. Improving them is a good use of funds right now.** While both writers agree that the parks are not in good repair, they disagree over whether improving them is the best way to use resources at the present time.

44. **A. They are good when done in the best locations.** The local business owner doesn't feel that improving the public parks is the best use of funds right now, but he does feel that using those resources to improve the appearance of the business district would contribute to economic growth.

45. **B. Investing in our community is important for the future of Glenwood.** Both writers are arguing that public resources should be invested in improving the community to help ensure its prosperity in the long term.

46. **C. often feel sick when at your workplace?** Because the workplace belongs to you, the possessive pronoun *your* is correct.

47. **A. symptoms seem to disappear magically once you leave work?** What happens magically is that the symptoms disappear, not that you leave work. Magically should be placed close to the part of the sentence that it modifies—symptoms disappearing.

48. **A. an older building isn't necessarily immune to** A sentence needs both a subject and a verb. Choices (B) and (C) are missing a noun to serve as the subject. Choice (D) is incorrect because it adds an unnecessary comma.

49. **D. the windows** Using a pronoun instead of the word *windows* would make it unclear what it was that originally opened.

50. **A. Tourism increases both air pollution and litter, which will further reduce the animals' chances for survival.** Choice (A) avoids wordiness while making it that tourists cause both pollution and litter.

51. **C. remove sentence 7** The flyer focuses on the land on Compton Point. This sentence about other areas in the county is irrelevant and should be deleted.

52. **B. and influx of tourism resulting from their development would boost the region's sagging economy** Choice B smoothly combines the two ideas into a single sentence with a compound subject.

53. **D. Saturday, May 7, in front of the mayor's office, 34 Wilton Road.** All parts of a proper noun must be capitalized.

PRACTICE TEST EVALUATION CHARTS

Questions 1–53

Circle the numbers of the questions that you got correct and then total them in the last column of each row.

Content Area	Question Numbers	Number Correct/Total
Interpreting Nonfiction and Informational Text Pages 30–53	2, 3, 5, 21, 22, 23, 24, 25, 26, 27, 36, 38, 39, 41, 44	____/15
Analyzing Nonfiction and Informational Text Pages 54–69	1, 4, 6, 35, 37, 40, 42, 43, 45	____/9
Interpreting Fiction Pages 70–85	7, 8, 9, 10, 11, 12, 28, 29, 30, 31, 32, 33, 34	____/13
Writing Effective Sentences Pages 86–103	14, 16, 47, 48, 50, 52	____/6
Connecting Ideas Pages 104–115	19, 20, 51	____/3
Using Grammar Correctly Pages 152–167	15, 17, 49	____/3
Using Writing Mechanics Pages 168–181	13, 18, 46, 53	____/4
SUBTOTAL		____/53

Extended Response

Use the evaluation guide on page 225 and assign each category a number 0–2. Add to find the subtotal. On the GED® Test, your Extended Response score subtotal will be doubled. Multiply by 2 as shown in the table below.

Writing About Text Pages 116–141	**Creation of Arguments and Use of Evidence**	____/2
Connecting Ideas/Polishing Your Writing Pages 104–115, 142–151	**Development of Ideas and Organizational Structure**	____/2
Using Grammar Correctly / Using Writing Mechanics Pages 152–167, 168–181	**Clarity and Command of Standard English Conventions**	____/2
SUBTOTAL		**____/6. Then multiply your subtotal by 2: ____/12.**

Composite Score

Add both Subtotals to get the total number of points you earned on *Reasoning Through Language Arts.*

Questions 1–53	____/53
Extended Response	____/12
TOTAL	____/65

If you do not have time to review the entire *Reasoning Through Language Arts* unit, you may want to review the sections that need the most work. You can use your total above (____/65) to figure out your percentage correct for the entire *RLA* test. Divide the numerator by the denominator and multiply by 100.

GED® REASONING THROUGH LANGUAGE ARTS RESOURCES

Extended Response Evaluation Guide

You can use this guide to evaluate your own writing. You can also provide the guide to another person whom you ask to read your paper. Read a paper three times—once for each trait. Circle a score for each trait in the chart at the bottom of this page. Add to find your total score and then analyze your results.

Trait 1 – Creation of Arguments and Use of Evidence

Rate the response as 2, 1, or 0 based on these criteria:

2 – makes **text-based argument** with **clear thesis;** uses **relevant and specific evidence** from the text; **analyzes the validity** of the **claims** and **reasoning** in the source text(s)

1 – makes **argument** with **some connection to text;** cites **some relevant evidence;** makes **limited analysis** of the **claims** and **reasoning** in the source text(s)

0 – makes **little or no argument** with **minimal or irrelevant evidence** from the text; makes **little or no analysis** of the **claims** and **reasoning** in the source text(s)

Trait 2 – Development of Ideas and Organizational Structure

Rate the response as 2, 1, or 0 based on these criteria:

2 – demonstrates **logical organization;** uses a **clear progression of ideas** with well-chosen **transitions;** uses **adequate supporting details** and connects them to the main idea; utilizes **appropriate style, tone,** and **word choice**

1 – demonstrates **inconsistent organization** with **vague reasoning;** uses **disjointed ideas** with few **transitions;** contains **some supporting details** but may not explain their connection to the main idea; utilizes **inappropriate style or tone** and **vague and misused word choice**

0 – demonstrates **insufficient or illogical development** with **unclear progression** of ideas; uses **few, no, or irrelevant supporting details;** utilizes **incorrect** or **inappropriate style, tone, and word choice**

Trait 3 – Clarity and Command of Standard English Conventions

Rate the response as 2, 1, or 0 based on these criteria:

2 – exhibits **mainly correct and varied sentence structure; avoids awkward or overly wordy constructions;** uses **transitional words and phrases** to connect ideas; **competent application of grammar, capitalization, punctuation,** and **spelling** - with some mistakes allowed

1 – exhibits **inconsistent control** of **sentence structure;** may display **some awkward or wordy constructions;** inconsistent use of **transitional words and phrases; frequent errors** in **grammar, capitalization, punctuation,** and **spelling**

0 – exhibits **flawed or highly repetitive sentence structure;** may use **overly wordy, awkward, or confusing constructions; lacks transitional words and phrases; little or no control** of **grammar, capitalization, punctuation,** and **spelling**

Trait	Circle Score
1	0 1 2
2	0 1 2
3	0 1 2
Added Total	

Analysis of Score Total

0 to 3	Weak – needs improvement with all three traits
4 to 5	Fair – needs work with traits with a score of 0 or 1
6	Strong – mastery of all three traits

NOTE: This guide is Kaplan's simplified interpretation of the official GED® *Reasoning Through Language Arts Extended Response* rubric. It has been developed for ease of use in evaluating extended written responses to one passage or paired passages.

INDEX

A

Adjectives, 96, 172
Agreement
  interrupting words, 162
  nouns and pronouns, 152, 154
  Reasoning Through Language Arts, 25
  subject and verb, 25, 29, 160, 162
Analyzing nonfiction text
  argument, 56, 58, 62
  graphic information, 64
  paired passages, 60, 61
  purpose of text, 54
Answers. See also Checking answers
  unanswered questions, 72, 80
Antecedents, 152, 154
Apostrophe, 174
Appositives, 170
Argument
  definition, 56, 118
  development of, 25, 29
  effectiveness of, 56
  Extended Responses, 116–117, 225
  identifying, 118
  opposing, 62
  thesis statement, 128
  validity of, 58
Assumptions, 56, 62, 118

B

Bars on computer screen
  Question bar, 27
  Time Remaining, 27

C

Capitalization of words
  Extended Responses, 29, 225
  guidelines for, 172
  Reasoning Through Language Arts, 25
Cause and effect
  conjunctions for, 88, 90
  interpreting nonfiction, 36
Characters in fiction, 74
Choppy sentences, 94
Chronological order, 48
Citing evidence, 121, 128. *See also* Evidence
Clarity in writing
  effective paragraphs, 104, 105
  evaluation of writing, 225
  modifiers, 96
  parallel structure, 98
  pronouns and antecedents, 154
  revising sentences, 142
  word choice, 146
Collective nouns, 154, 160
Comma
  appositives, 170
  comma splices, 92
  compound sentences, 88, 92, 94, 168
  coordinating conjunctions, 88, 168
  interrupting words, 162
  lists and series, 98, 170
  modifying phrases, 96
  run-on sentences, 92
  subordinate clauses, 90
  transitions, 110
  use of, 168, 170
Common nouns, 152
Comparisons
  compare and contrast, 38
  figurative speech, 44
  transition words for, 110
Complex sentences, 90, 91, 94
Compound sentences
  commas in, 88, 92, 93, 168
  definition, 168
  for flowing sentences, 94
  run-ons fixed, 92
Compound subjects, 162
Computer-based test format
  editing features, 134, 145
  grammar check, 136
  highlighter tool, 28, 122, 124
  Question bar, 27
  Reasoning Through Language Arts, 25–27
  spell check, 136
  text box, 28
  Time Remaining bar, 27, 124
Conclusions
  arguments, 56, 118
  Extended Response, 128
  interpreting nonfiction, 40
  jumping to, 40
  paired passages, 60, 61
  transition words for, 110
Conflict in plot, 70
Conjunctions
  comma use, 170
  complex sentences, 90
  compound sentences, 88
  compound subjects, 162

coordinating conjunctions, 88, 168
run-on sentences, 92
Connecting ideas
effective paragraphs, 104, 105
logical order, 108
paragraph flow, 110
relevant ideas, 108
Connotations, 44
Contractions of words, 174
Contrast
compare and contrast, 38
coordinating conjunction for, 89
transition words for, 110
Coordinating conjunctions, 88, 168. *See also* Conjunctions
Critical thinking, 56, 58, 72

D

Dangling modifiers, 96
Days of week capitalization, 172
Details, 96. *See also* Supporting details
Dialogue in fiction, 70
Drafting response
in text box, 28
read aloud, 134
time management, 124, 128
wide margins, 144
Drag-and-drop questions, 27
Drop-down questions, 26

E

Editing and revising responses
computer tools, 134, 144
organization of text, 144
questions to ask, 135, 136, 142, 144
read draft aloud, 134
revision marks, 142, 145
time management, 124, 133
word choice, 146
Elaboration text structure, 48
Emotional appeals, 58
Essay main idea statement, 106
Evaluation of writing, 225–226
Evidence. *See also* Evidence-based writing
arguments, 56, 58, 62, 118
citing, 121, 128, 225–226
collecting, 122, 124
conclusions from, 40
evidence statements, 122
generalizations from, 42
paragraph logical order, 108
thesis statement vs. opinion, 120
wipe-off board, 122
Evidence-based writing
Extended Response, 25, 27, 28–29, 225
prewriting strategies, 125
purpose of, 116
successful answers, 225
Examples
text structure, 48
transition words for, 110
Exclamation point, 86
Extended Responses
arguments and assumptions, 118
evaluation of, 225–226
highlighter tool for, 28, 122, 124
practice for, 142
pretests, 1
Reasoning Through Language Arts, 25, 116–141, 225
strategy for, 124
successful answer qualities, 29, 225
thesis statements, 121
wipe-off board, 28, 122, 124
writing prompt then passages, 116, 122, 124
writing prompt unpacked, 116–117, 124

F

Faulty generalizations, 42
Fiction texts
dialogue, 70
interpreting, 70–85
Reasoning Through Language Arts, 25
Figurative language, 44, 80
Fill-in-the-blank questions
Reasoning Through Language Arts, 25
Formal language
assessed, 25
as writing style, 46, 78
contractions, 174
slang versus, 29, 146

G

Generalizations, 42
General nonfiction. *See* Nonfiction texts
Grammar
computer grammar check, 136
correct usage, 152–167, 225
Graphic information
analyzing nonfiction, 64

H

Helping verbs, 156
Highlighter tool
  Extended Responses, 28, 122, 124
Holiday capitalization, 172
Homonyms, 25, 29, 176

I

Ideas
  application of, 34
  connecting, 104–115
  idea map, 125
  main idea vs. details, 29. *See also* Main idea
  modifiers of, 96
  relevant, 108
  restating, 32
  subordinate ideas, 94. *See also* Supporting details
  support of. *See* Evidence
  transition words for, 110
Illustrations. *See* Graphic information
Indefinite pronouns, 160
Independent clauses, 88, 90, 92, 168
Inferences, 72
Informational texts
  interpreting, 30–53
  Reasoning Through Language Arts, 25
Interpreting fiction texts
  characters, 70, 74
  figurative language, 44, 80
  inferences, 72
  plot elements, 70
  style and point of view, 78
  theme, 76
Interpreting nonfiction texts
  application of ideas, 34
  cause and effect, 36, 88, 90
  compare and contrast, 38
  conclusions, 41. *See also* Conclusions
  generalizations, 42
  main idea vs. details, 29. *See also* Main idea; Supporting details
  restatement, 32
  structure of text, 48
  summary, 32
  tone and point of view, 46
  word choice, 44
Interrupting words, 162
Introductory elements
  introductory phrases, 168
  thesis statement, 128
Inverted sentence structure, 162
Irregular verbs, 158
Irrelevant details, 108

L

Language Arts. *See* Reasoning Through Language Arts
Legal matters. *See* Law
Lists
  commas in series, 98, 170
  parallel structure, 98

M

Main idea
  details versus, 30
  effective paragraphs, 104, 105
  essay main idea statement, 106
  idea map, 125
  topic sentences, 106
Manufacturing. *See* Industrialization
Mapping as prewriting, 124
Metaphors, 44, 80
Modifiers, 96, 172
Month name capitalization, 172
Multiple-choice questions
  pretests, 1
  Reasoning Through Language Arts, 25

N

Narrative, 54, 74, 78
Nonfiction texts
  analyzing, 54–69
  interpreting, 30–53
  Reasoning Through Language Arts, 25
Notation in math. *See also* Symbols in math
Nouns
  collective, 154, 160
  possessive, 174
  pronouns and, 152, 154
  proper vs. common, 152, 172

O

Object pronouns, 152
Opinion
  thesis statement versus, 120
Organizational structure, 29, 144, 225
Outlining as prewriting, 125

P

Paired passages, 60, 61
Paper-based test format. *See also* Wipe-off board
Paragraphs
  drafting response, 128
  effective paragraphs, 104, 105
  flow of, 110
  paragraph breaks, 144
  topic sentences, 106
Passing scores. *See* Scores needed to pass
Period (punctuation), 86. *See also* Decimal point
Personifications, 44, 80
Photographs. *See* Graphic information
Plot elements, 70
Point of view
  fiction, 78
  nonfiction, 46
  theme of story, 76
Possessives
  apostrophe use, 174
  pronouns, 152, 174
  Reasoning Through Language Arts, 25, 29
  singular vs. plural, 174
Predicates. See also Verbs
  compound predicates, 168
Premises of arguments, 56, 118
Pretests
  Answers and Explanations, 19–24
  next step after taking, 18, 220
  purpose, 18, 220
  Study Planners, 22–24
Prewriting strategies, 125
Process text structure, 48, 110
Prompt. *See* Writing prompt
Pronouns
  indefinite pronouns, 160
  nouns and, 152, 154
  object pronouns, 152
  one vs. you, 154
  possessive pronouns, 152, 174
  subject pronouns, 152
Proper nouns, 152, 172
Pros and cons text structure, 48, 110
Punctuation. *See also* Comma
  exclamation point, 86
  Extended Responses, 29, 225
  period, 86. *See also* Decimal point
  question mark, 86
  Reasoning Through Language Arts, 25
  semicolon, 92, 110
  writing effective sentences, 86, 88
Purpose of text, 54

Q

Question bar, 27
Question mark, 86
Questions. See also Extended Responses; Multiple-choice questions
  drag-and-drop, 27
  drop-down, 26
  fill-in-the-blank, 26
  Question bar, 27
  question mark, 86
  to edit work, 136, 142, 144
  to improve organization, 144
  to revise work, 134, 142, 144
  to strengthen sentences, 142
  unanswered, 72, 80

R

Reasoning Through Language Arts (RLA). See also Extended Responses
  analyzing nonfiction texts, 54–69
  computer-based format, 26–28
  connecting ideas, 104–115
  grammar, 136, 152–167, 225
  interpreting fiction texts, 70–85
  interpreting nonfiction texts, 30–53
  score needed to pass, 25
  writing about text, 116–141
  writing effective sentences, 86–103, 142
  writing mechanics, 168–181
  writing revision, 142–151
Regular verbs, 156
Resources for GED. *See also* Natural resources
Restating ideas, 32
Revising and editing responses
  computer tools, 134, 144
  organization of text, 144
  questions to ask, 135, 136, 142, 144
  read draft aloud, 134
  revision marks, 142, 145
  time management, 124, 133
  word choice, 146
Run-on sentences, 92

S

Scores needed to pass
  Reasoning Through Language Arts, 25
Season capitalization, 172
Semicolon, 92, 110

Sentences
assessed, 25
comma splices, 92
complex, 90, 92, 94
compound, 88, 92, 94
effective paragraphs, 104, 105
effective sentences, 86–103, 141
flow of, 94, 110
fragments, 87, 90
independent clauses, 88
inverted structure, 162
logical order, 108
parallel structure, 98
run-ons, 92
simple, 86, 88, 92, 94
topic sentences, 106
Serial comma, 98, 170
Short-Answer questions
pretest, 1
Short sentences, 94
Similes, 44, 80
Slang
as writing style, 46, 78
avoiding, 29, 146
Spelling
assessed, 176
computer spell check, 136
Extended Responses, 29, 225
homonyms, 176
Reasoning Through Language Arts, 29
Statement sentences, 86
Structure of text. *See* Organizational structure; Text structures
Study planners, 22–24
Style of writing, 78
Subject of sentence
compound subject, 162, 168
simple sentences, 86, 88
simple subjects, 160
subordinate ideas, 94
verb agreement, 25, 29, 160, 162
Subject of story vs. theme, 76
Subject pronouns, 152
Subordinate clauses
comma use, 90, 96, 168
complex sentences, 90, 94
dangling modifier fix, 96
Subordinate ideas, 94
Subordinating conjunctions, 90
Summarizing
Extended Response, 124, 128
interpreting nonfiction, 32
Supporting details
effective paragraphs, 105
idea map, 125
irrelevant, 108
main idea versus, 30, 106
modifiers, 96
subordinate ideas, 94
Supporting evidence. *See* Evidence
Synthesis of information, 60

T

Tenses of verbs, 156, 157
Test questions. *See* Questions
Text box
Extended Responses, 28
Text structures
interpreting nonfiction, 48
inverted structure, 162
parallel structure, 98
style of writing, 78
Theme
interpreting fiction, 76
paired passages, 60
subject versus, 76
Thesis statement
developing, 120, 123, 124
drafting response, 128
opinion versus, 120
Time management
drafting response, 124, 128
editing response, 124, 134
Extended Responses, 27, 28, 124
Time Remaining bar, 27, 124
Time order text structure, 47, 110
Time Remaining bar, 27, 124
Tone of writing, 46
Topic, 60, 106
Transition words, 29, 48, 110

U

Unanswered test questions, 72, 80

V

Validity, 42, 58
Verbs
compound predicates, 168
helping verbs, 156
irregular verbs, 158
parallel structure, 98

regular verbs, 156
simple sentences, 86, 88
subject-verb agreement, 25, 29, 160, 162
subordinate ideas, 94
tenses of verbs, 156, 157

W

Wipe-off board
evidence gathering, 122
Extended Responses, 28, 124
Word choice
figurative language, 44, 80
polishing writing, 146
Reasoning Through Language Arts, 25, 29, 44
restating ideas, 32
Workers. *See* Labor
Write-on board. *See* Wipe-off board
Writing prompt
read before passages, 116, 122, 124
unpacking, 116–117, 124
Writing skills. See also Clarity in writing; Word choice
effective paragraphs, 104, 105
effective sentences, 86–103, 141
evaluation of, 225–226
flow of writing, 94, 110
mechanics of writing, 168–181
polishing your writing, 142–151
prewriting strategies, 125
Reasoning Through Language Arts, 25, 27–29
tone of writing, 46
writing about text, 116–141